AN INCONVE

Fiona Forde

An Inconvenient Youth

Julius Malema and the 'new' ANC

Portobello
BOOKS

A previous edition of this book was published in 2011 by Picador Africa, an imprint of Pan Macmillan South Africa

This fully revised and updated edition first published by Portobello Books 2012

Portobello Books
12 Addison Avenue
London
W11 4QR

A CIP catalogue record is available from the British Library

9 8 7 6 5 4 3 2 1

ISBN 978 1 84627 456 5

www.portobellobooks.com

Typeset by Avon DataSet Ltd, Bidford on Avon, Warwickshire
Printed and bound by CPI Group (UK) Ltd, Croydon, CR0 4YY

For Mum

Contents

Abbreviations & Acronyms

ANC	African National Congress, initially founded as the South African National Native Congress
ANCWL	African National Congress Womens League
ANCYL	African National Congress Youth League
AAC	All-Africa Convention
AZAPO	Azanian People's Organisation
CCP	Chinese Communist Party
CODESA	Convention for a Democratic South Africa
COSAS	Congress of South African Students
COSATU	Congress of South African Trade Unions
CPSA	Communist Party of South Africa (later renamed the South African Communist Party)
DA	Democratic Alliance, South Africa's main opposition party, founded with components of the National Party from the apartheid era
ICU	Industrial and Commercial Workers' Union
ISL	International Socialist League
MDC	Movement for Democratic Change
MK	Umkhonto we Sizwe, or Spear of the Nation (the former armed wing of the ANC)
NDR	National Democratic Revolution
NEC	National Executive Committee
NPA	National Prosecuting Authority
SACP	South African Communist Party (previously Communist Party of South Africa)
SANNC	South African National Native Congress (later renamed the African National Congress)

SASCO	South African Students Congress
SRCs	Student Representative Councils
TRC	Truth and Reconciliation Commission
YCL	Young Communist League
ZANU-PF	Zimbabwe African National Union – Patriotic Front
UNISA	University of South Africa

Foreword

This unusually bold and astutely written book retraces the multiple paths of Julius Malema's rise as one of the most controversial political figures of post-apartheid South Africa.

Rich in its insights and original in its perspectives, it is a major contribution to our understanding of the multi-layered lives and intricate workings of the African National Congress (ANC) as the former national liberation movement, now the ruling party, struggles with power, with itself, and with the idea of South Africa.

Fiona Forde shows how the oldest modern political organisation in Africa has mutated into a patchwork of unstable, segmented and shifting networks of interests less and less united by principle or ideology and more and more bound by ruthless expediency.

Born and raised in poverty, Julius Malema is at once atypical and symptomatic of his times. He embodies both the passions and contradictions of post-struggle politics and the dark and troubling undercurrents of a long South African tradition of lumpen radicalism.

Lumpen radicalism is a political tradition of unruliness – and at times resistance – in which fantasies of male power, control and desire have always been deeply entangled with 'war envy' and an almost insatiable appetite for money, luxuries and women.

It is a direct product of the influx-control system, the mass

1

forced removals and relocations and the relentless and all-pervading social and economic insecurity that became the hallmarks of black urban experience under apartheid.

A hybrid cultural and political style the ANC did not hesitate to instrumentalise during the struggle, but which it safely kept at the margins of the liberation movement's core ethos, it is also a tradition in which acts of pseudo-revolutionary rage are mixed with various forms of care.

Within this tradition, power is first conquered on the street before it is translated into the domain of home and formal institutions. A life of shame, social humiliation and dishonour is thought to be retrieved from abjection through conspicuous display and consumption of wealth.

Politics is less about the patient and disciplined building of a civic ethos than the performance of mob power while cohorts, cliques, gangs or, eventually, the crowd stand for 'the people' or 'the masses'.

A distinctive feature of lumpen radicalism in South African politics since the formation of the ANC in 1912 has been the cyclical re-emergence of the youth as a force across the social and cultural landscape.

The ascendancy of the youth, its attempt to wrestle power from the older generation and to take charge of the adults, has usually coincided with periods of intense fracture of the black life experience and the concomitant crisis of imagination within the liberation movement.

During the twentieth century, three such notable episodes stand out. The first happened in the early 1950s when, under pressure from the Youth League, the ANC adopted increasingly radical positions that ultimately led to the assumption of armed struggle.

The second was the Soweto uprising in 1976, when black students led a revolt against a policy that was forcing them to be instructed in Afrikaans, the language of the apartheid regime.

The third was the phenomenon of the 'comrades' in the 1980s when the apartheid state's hold over the township was weakened. Vast urban zones were declared 'ungovernable'. In many townships, state power was replaced by popular civic structures and, in a dramatic reversal of apartheid urban planning, informal settlements and shacks sprawled out in all directions.

Today, a similar crisis of imagination is at work in the party, in society and in culture. One of the main tensions within South African politics today is the realisation that there is something unresolved in the constitutional democratic settlement that suspended the 'revolution' in 1994 but did not erase apartheid once and for all from the social, economic and mental landscape.

For each of the historical protagonists in the South African drama, this settlement resulted in no final victory and no crippling defeat. Seventeen years later, the country is still caught between an intractable present and an irrecoverable past; things that are no longer and things that are not yet.

This is ironically the stalemate many hailed as 'the South African miracle'. It is the stalemate Malema would like to puncture. It is in the failure of South African government and society to build creatively on the extraordinary rupture, or promise, of 1994 and radically confront black poverty that Malema sees his political opportunity.

His ascendancy highlights the current dangers South Africa faces: a gradual closing of life chances for many; an increasing polarisation of the racial structure; a structure of indecision at the heart of politics itself; and a re-balkanisation of culture and society. These trends clearly undermine the fragile forms of mutuality that have been painstakingly built in South Africa over a decade and a half and further weaken the prospects of true non-racialism.

The signs of entropy are there for all to see. They are particularly dramatised by the dilemmas of unemployment and the expansion of spaces of vulnerability in all arenas of everyday life. Despite the emergence of a solid black middle class, a rising superfluous population is becoming a permanent fixture of the South African social fabric with little possibility of ever being exploited by capital.

Most young black youth are barely holding on to the ledge. They are likely never to get full-time formal employment or to enter the proletarian economy. Stuck in a field of blighted possibilities, they scavenge to live or simply to get through the day – so many bad jobs available to so few in one of the most racially unequal countries on Earth; so much rage and almost no future.

For those in survival mode – and who know all too well what it means to experience social humiliation first hand – Julius Malema fills the gaps of disappointment and failure at a time when the promise of liberation has become privatised and the ideals of reciprocity and mutuality enshrined in the Constitution are struggling to find the political and cultural platforms they deserve.

His stock is rising in a landscape of ruins: the ideological bankruptcy of the official left; the racial and class narcissism of the main opposition party; and an ANC consumed by corruption and greed, brutal internecine battles for power and a deadly combination of predatory instincts and intellectual vacuity.

To stem the rising tide, technocratic sermons on 'service delivery' and 'decent jobs' will not suffice.

Techno-managerial reason will have to be supplemented by the rehabilitation of the political itself, that is, the conscious engagement with the fundamental choices that will determine the nature of the South African experiment in democracy: questions of how to right historical wrongs; the relationship between personal or collective injury and larger problems of equality and dignity; private ownership and the right to a fair share of the nation's wealth; freedom from race and racism.

It is the widespread failure to confront these fundamental

dilemmas that has created the moral void in which Julius Malema is swimming. The shock troops he is assembling before the final push are replete with those imprisoned in shack life, vulnerable subjects our unequal social order keeps ejecting, who are condemned to undertake the labour of social mourning amid crushing poverty.

To all of them, he promises an unworkable mirage: nationalisation of mines, land expropriation without compensation, economic emancipation and control over resources they do not own.

For the democratic project to have any future at all in South Africa, politics should break with the depressive realism that has characterised post-apartheid life.

It should not simply attend to the feeling many have of having been defeated. It should be about re-opening the future for all. More radically, it should take the form of a conscious attempt to retrieve life and the human from a long history of waste.

Achille Mbembe
Cape Town, July 2011

Preface

The offices of the African National Congress were under construction the day I first visited them and I had to watch my step as I made my way through the entrance and down the corridor that wound its way along the ground floor of the building. Cables were scattered across my path, loose wiring hung from the ceiling and dust rose from the floor with every step I took.

It was the last Tuesday in October of 2007, less than seven weeks before the landmark ANC conference would take place in Polokwane, the capital of the northern province of Limpopo, and the ruling party was about to undergo an overhaul as radical as the one the building was getting that day. The party's membership had collapsed either side of a nasty cleavage that had wedged its way through the former liberation movement as Thabo Mbeki and Jacob Zuma slugged it out for the party presidency. Change was afoot and the man I was about to meet would turn out to be one of the biggest drivers of that change.

Julius Malema was dressed in casual attire, a red T-shirt and dark denims, and his manner was as understated as his dress that day. I had not met him before and had not intended to meet him then either. I worked with the Independent Newspapers group at the time and had been sent to Limpopo on a week-long assignment to write a piece about the province that was about to provide a backdrop to the party conference, the likes of which takes place every five years. But while there, the political editor asked me to track down Malema, who was then the provincial secretary of the ANC Youth League (ANCYL) as well as one of Zuma's loyal henchmen, and talk to him about the state of play in the party's provincial branches that were beginning to finalise their nominations for the leadership race.

Malema was 26 at the time. He was a tad less robust than he is today and a tad more reticent to talk, initially at least. When he did talk, he was guarded and some years later he would tell me that he thought I was a spy. I wasn't the first white female journalist to visit the province asking questions about the race for the presidency, but I was a foreigner and his knee-jerk reaction was telling: the woman in his midst could only be an agent, because he had been taught that the foreign element should naturally rouse suspicion. But in fairness to him, he was also polite and helpful.

About six months after this, Malema was elected president of the ANCYL, having emerged from that twist in the South African transition that eventually brought Zuma to power during that Polokwane conference, and the deft young politician was quick to manipulate his new ranking. In an able manner he began to stretch his power base beyond the youth and pitch himself as a budding strongman in the mother body, the ANC. He traded as a populist typically full of empty promises and before either he or South Africa knew what was happening, he became the talking point of the country.

In many ways, Malema was the latest thing out of South Africa but there was no real understanding of who he was or what he stood for and it gave me good cause to ask my editor if I could shadow the youngster for a week to try and capture a clearer picture of the man who was lurking behind the headlines. That was in October 2009 and the short time I spent with him gave me enough of an insight to know that I wanted to know more. It led me to write this book, the research for which began in March 2010.

But as luck would have it, Malema's life began to fill with more drama than a comic book in the couple of years that I had access to him and his unfolding story kept my nib frantically busy. His lifestyle began to raise the suspicions of the revenue collector the year I began my research. His businesses fell under the spotlight of the serious crimes office a year later. The office of the Public Protector was called in to check him out. Not once but twice was he hauled over the coals by the ANC for his outlandish political behaviour and finally, in the early months of 2012, and as I was putting the finishing touches to the international edition of this book, the luckless youth leader was finally expelled from the party.

But going back to 2009, it was also then that the Nigerian writer Chimamanda Ngozi Adichie addressed a gathering in Oxford. She talked about the 'single story' and the dangers of interpreting life or people through a narrow lens. To make her point, she went back to her childhood.

She grew up in Nsukka, the town that is home to the University of Nigeria, where her father was a professor and her mother a university registrar. As a young girl she was an avid reader, but her middle-class upbringing exposed her to American rather than African children's books. So when she started dabbling with her own short stories, as young girls do, she found she was mentally locked into the characters and tales she had read about. She wouldn't understand why until many years later.

Her opening words would always be followed by characters 'who were white and blue-eyed. They played in the snow. They ate apples. And they talked a lot about the weather, how lovely it was that the sun came up,' she remembered. All this despite the fact that she had never set foot outside Nigeria.

'We didn't have snow. We ate mangoes. And we never talked about the weather because there was no need.

'I did not know that people like me could exist in literature,' she continued. 'I had become convinced that books, by their very nature, had to have foreigners in them. And had to be about things with which I could not personally identify.'

All that changed when she began to read Chinua Achebe, her fellow countryman, as well as other African writers. That was when she realised that 'people like me, girls with skin the colour of chocolate, with kinky hair that could not form ponytails, could also exist in literature'. That was when her 'single story' began to take on a new dimension.

But the 'single story' went beyond books and coloured Chimamanda's upbringing in other ways. She gave the example of Fide, her family's 'houseboy' as she referred to him.

He came from a very poor background and when, as a child, Chimamanda would not finish the food on her plate, her mother would remind her that 'people like Fide don't have food at all'. Chimamanda heard it so often that she began to attach a single identity to Fide: poverty.

A few years later she accompanied Fide to the villages to visit his family. To her shock, she found his brother weaving a beautiful basket. She could not connect what Fide's brother was doing with the mental image she had crafted of Fide's world, because the lens through which she viewed him was so narrow and singular that she couldn't imagine his family as anything other than poor. Creativity didn't fit with the box into which she had placed Fide.

'Poverty was my single story of them.'

Years later she found herself at the other end of the narrow lens when she went to the United States. Her university roommate was surprised to find that Chimamanda could speak English fluently, ignorant of the fact that it is the official language in Nigeria. She was also disappointed when Chimamanda whipped out her Mariah Carey CD after she had asked to listen to her 'tribal music'.

'She had a single story of Africa.'

Julius Malema was also viewed through a very narrow lens, his life and times recorded by way of a 'single story'.

His followers cast him as a victim, a freedom fighter whose bravery was becoming his biggest bane, a man whose ideas were unsettling the status quo. They didn't see his wealth as conspicuous. They regarded him instead as a young African who had 'landed', much to the fury of the whites. It was a harmless hero that was captured through their lens.

A different single story was crafted by his detractors who placed him into a box that varied from politically dangerous to radical, racist, bigoted, stupid, corrupt, ignorant, and so on, each of the attributes woven into a damning, dark tale.

Like Fide, a single identity was always attached to Malema. But it was neither comprehensive nor complete.

Perhaps it was as Adichie had said: some people couldn't personally identify with him so they misplaced him instead.

Yet in the time I spent with Julius Malema in the course of researching this book, I encountered a character that I liked, irrespective of the politician. In the man I found someone who was sensitive, witty, humorous and thoughtful, in the strictest sense of the word. He never gave me the impression that his words were meaningless or throwaway. He was a calculating person. He was also open-minded enough to engage in conversations of all sorts. Malema was good company.

I also found him to be what I call 'a woman's man', emotionally open and never shy to bare his heart. He would talk about relationships, hurts and disappointments with brutal honesty. With the same strength of emotion, he would recall the happier chapters in his life. At many levels I could not find a trace of the macho man who pounded the boards of the political stage in his very narrow-minded way.

But there was a side to him that was extraordinarily wily and cunning and it was there that the overlap between the man and the politician began to emerge.

As a politician, Malema disturbed me. In his public appearances I couldn't see the person I had come to know in private. It didn't surprise me that he was razor sharp as a political strategist – I had always found him to be extremely clever. But it was the sulphurous relationship he developed with much of society that unsettled me. White South Africans were always placed in the firing line of his political messages, his weapons of mass destruction. The negotiations that paved the way for a peaceful end to apartheid in the mid-1990s were intended to lay such retaliation to rest, but then all these years later along came this raffish youth from a township called Seshego, a place many of them had never heard of, a place in South Africa that is so far from their cosy worlds that it could well be situated in some far-off, distant place.

Perhaps it was arrogance that had allowed a large portion of white South Africa to assume they would never have to give the Seshegos a second careful thought. Township and suburban life are poles apart in this African country that is nestled at the tip of the so-called 'dark continent' and the comfortable suburban dweller would not last half a day on the other side of life. Townships are uncomfortable places. They are crowded and densely populated. They reek of poverty and general desperation and ghastly social ills. Unemployment is rife and the young and old who saunter the streets each day are walking reminders of that. Of course some draw a living wage and some more make it to a modest existence. But the vast majority of the township's people live the kind of lives that the urban folk cannot even begin to contemplate. And now Malema, the *beaux ideal* of the country's so-called masses, was all but telling the better off that their game was over as he spearheaded a populist juggernaut that seemed to be routing the ANC's old guard as he and his faceless backers made their bid for supreme power.

But he too was guilty of looking at life through that narrow lens. The whites were not the problem, they were merely the epitome of it, or partly so. The problem was far greater. The country – with its raw and worrying socio-economic divide – was fundamentally unworkable. Whether it was whites or blacks or a mix of the two that sat either side of that taut divide was almost irrelevant. Structurally the country was in a mess.

Malema chose to overlook that as he developed a unilateral politics and policy that was worrying and bore no resemblance to the open-minded side of him I had seen, and which I believed, and still believe, was very real and exists. The heavy-handed manner in which he dealt with dissent depicted a political demon far removed from a likeable person. When his business dealings came to light I started to follow them and what I unearthed in the course of researching this book was astounding.

I had a dilemma on my hands and didn't know what to do with it. I would tell the full story – and from the material scattered across my desk I knew it couldn't be a 'single story' – but I was struggling to capture the right story when it came to depicting Malema in a fair light. After all that had been said and done, and after all I had come to know about him, there were parts of his person – though not the politician – that I still liked.

'But how can you?' I used to ask myself.

'Because he is a complex character,' Cameroonian philosopher and historian Achille Mbembe suggested to me.

Mbembe watched over my shoulder as a structural editor in the final stages of this book and helped me commit to paper what was lurking in my head when he put it to me the following way:

'The register of our humanity extends from cruelty to mercy to love to thuggery, and all of that. The more an individual has all these facets, the more interesting he is as a character.'

Mbembe was not encouraging me to portray what did not exist, but instead to find a way to represent Malema's reality without overstating or understating who he is.

Julius Malema ticks many of the boxes on the 'register of

humanity' as Mbembe so aptly puts it, and irrespective of the politics that are now playing out in the ANC, Malema is still influential in South African contemporary life. The part he plays in dictating the course of the country is no small role, hence it was critical that I paint the full spectrum of who he really was.

The challenge, then, was to take him out of the box into which he had been placed and away from the light in which he had been cast and tell his story anew, if I was to really get under his story at all.

And so I told it, but in a way that neither robs him of his dignity nor glorifies him wrongly. I simply told it as I saw it, with the good, the bad and the ugly.

I feared that many South Africans would have reservations about the book. I am, after all, a foreigner who didn't live South Africa's past and therefore could never have a real sense of its present. Like my subject, Julius Malema, I have no 'credentials' that date back to the time of bitter struggle against apartheid. I'm an outsider.

But then that's what got me into this in the first place. Being an outsider enabled me sometimes to see things that were invisible to South Africans, and to ask questions that might not have occurred to some.

You might not like all the answers, but what can I do? I spotted a good story and chased it.

Fiona Forde
Cape Town, May 2012

When Julius Malema became a regular feature of South African life, the local press hounded him, placing him on their news pages just about every single day.

The depiction rarely changed: a young man with a lot of pluck and a big Breitling watch.

He used to wear a gold, diamond-studded ring on his left pinkie. And he wore flashy clothes and designer baseball caps. He drove big cars and he mingled with almightiful people. And he wore a Breitling watch. Always a Breitling.

So when it came to choosing a title for this book, it came naturally: 'The man with the Breitling watch'.

It stood for Malema as a new kind of ANC politician. And it stood for all the other modern-day cadres who, like him, wear their wealth, like their politics, on their sleeves. These are new times in South African politics that will always be remembered for the unstable stability that has come to define the country, the fast-lane lifestyle of our politicians and their easy-come-by money.

But the Swiss watchmaker was reluctant to attach its brand to Malema and turned down my request to use it in the title, even though he had chosen the brand to associate with his wealth.

So I chose an alternative title, 'An Inconvenient Youth', because like the preferred title, it fits the man like a glove.

He is inconvenient on a number of fronts: for his party, for putting the spotlight on the underbelly of ANC politics; for society, for unsettling the hard-won gains of the democracy; and for South Africa, because through his radical (though empty) utterances Malema has ironically become a walking reminder for many people of the unfulfilled promises of 1994. And in an even more bizarre twist of irony, it is those same unfulfilled promises that have created the kind of socio-economic inequalities that have allowed the likes of him to emerge.

So that's the story behind the front cover. And what follows is the story behind the man.

1

The devil wears Breitling

24 April 2010
Caracas, Venezuela

It's Saturday morning, shortly after 09h30, and for the past half hour or so I've been watching the young delegates make their way down the stairs, out of the hotel and onto the single-decker bus parked out front at the foot of the sloping, lush lawns. But there's still no sign of Julius Malema. So I settle into my armchair and wait as the foyer slowly empties.

The steady hum of the tens of thousands of cars that clog the streets of Caracas on Venezuela's dirt-cheap petrol can still be heard high up in the suburb of San Bernardino on the flanks of Mount Avila, but it's a dim noise that doesn't intrude. The air is hot and humid, but not unbearably so. And it is a comfortable lull that settles over Hotel Avila, a serene spot to while away some time.

The ease is only broken when the pert-breasted woman behind the reception desk begins to dole out the day's duties to her colleagues as her shift comes to an end, her stiletto-sharp voice carrying right across the foyer as she struts between the front office and the back. Minutes later she slings her black handbag over her shoulder and skips down the front steps and into a waiting taxi.

'*Hasta mañana*,' she shouts, raising her hand in a casual wave to the young man who has taken over for the morning.

'*Hasta mañana,*' he shouts back.

The hotel settles into an easy silence for a second time, with only the occasional guest strolling through its front doors. But the big brass clock hanging on the wood-panelled wall is ticking towards 10h00 and still there's no sign of Malema.

The waiter fills my cup with another black coffee as I flick through yesterday's copy of *El Universal*, which blatantly hacks away at the thin shred of credibility that remains of Hugo Chávez's so-called Socialism of the Twenty-First Century.

Splashed across its front page is the news that Venezuela has agreed to repay its US$20 billion loan from China with 100,000 barrels of oil a day for the next 10 years. There's talk elsewhere in the paper about how the public sector wage bill is ballooning. And how the bolivar, the local currency, is on a serious slide against the greenback, the next best thing to official tender now. Inflation is soaring. Rolling power cuts are on the rise. Venezuelans now account for the second-largest number of Latin American exiles in the United States.

And little wonder, says Jorge Urosa Savino, the cardinal of the Catholic Church in Venezuela. On an inside page, the clergyman reminds his followers that 18 April 1810 was the date that marked the beginning of independence from Spain. But what was fought for has been forsaken for Marxist Socialism, which does no one any good he says, and he appeals to the Virgin of Coromoto to protect his country from 'dictatorships, totalitarianism and violence'.

But *el Comandante* appears to be taking it all in his stride. He is in the Bolivian city of Cochabamba, where he's attending a conference on climate change, and it seems he went off on a tangent yesterday to remind his followers that 22 April was the day when Vladimir Lenin was born, way back in 1870. A man forever to be remembered, he tells his audience. *Viva la revolución!*

There are a few short articles about the upcoming FIFA

World Cup in South Africa. Venezuela hasn't qualified, but they beat Honduras, which has, in an impressive friendly game on Thursday night. The paper dubs it a 'win at World Cup level'. There's some talk about Bafana Bafana, the national South African soccer team and their draw against North Korea. But no mention of the South African renegade youth leader's visit to the country.

Malema only arrived in Venezuela on Thursday morning but he is already bailing out tonight, ahead of time. He has decided to cut short the week-long trip in an all-out effort to put a stop to the disciplinary charges that are hanging over his head back home in South Africa.

The executive of the ANC will meet on Monday to discuss the political fate of Malema, whose public behaviour has gone from woeful to wicked ever since he became president of the ANCYL in April 2008. In all that time, and for reasons known only to themselves, the leaders of the mother body have tended to turn a blind eye and deaf ear to the young man's controversial style of politics. Even the prominent men and women in the ranks of the party, people who were once fearless in the face of the brutal apartheid regime during the struggle era, opted for silence when Malema was at his worst; when he was inviting shame on the party and the country, trousering his fair share of public tenders, and instilling confusion and fear in many ordinary South Africans, most of whom had arrived at the dismaying conclusion that Malema was untouchable.

But the patience of the senior ANC leadership finally snapped a couple of weeks back when the 29-year-old began to lose the run of himself on a number of fronts. Within a few weeks of his trotting out the old struggle song 'Shoot the Boer,' the country's most notorious Boer, Eugene Terre'Blanche, was murdered on his farm in North West province. The day he was killed, Easter Saturday, Malema was singing high praises for President Robert

Mugabe in Harare at a time when South Africa was supposedly acting as a neutral broker, trying to keep the fragile peace put in place by Zimbabwe's year-old unity government. Then, a few days later, Malema made a fine international spectacle of himself when he hurled some extraordinary verbal abuse at a journalist during a televised press conference as the whole world looked on. That was the day he earned himself the nickname Kidi Amin. And to top it all off, he then compared President Jacob Zuma to his predecessor Thabo Mbeki. Benign though the comparison was, it touched a very raw nerve in the incumbent.

And that's when the ANC finally began to move towards disciplinary measures in a desperate attempt to deal with the youth, something which is not customary practice for the party and which it has done only a handful of times in its 100-year history. Monday will decide just how far the leadership is intending to go this time.

'And if I'm not there, I don't exist,' Malema says.

His only option is to take the overnight flight from Caracas to São Paolo tonight, spend the day in the sprawling Brazilian city tomorrow and take the overnight connection to Johannesburg on Sunday, touching down at O.R. Tambo airport on Monday morning about an hour ahead of the scheduled start of the meeting.

The only reason I'm here is to gather information for this book, and I've changed my tickets so that I can travel back with him. And there's little point in my leaving the hotel until I know what his movements are for the day.

The lift is out of order and I see him shuffling down the stairs a short while later, his bodyguard trotting two steps behind him. Malema's face is like thunder and though he is no towering giant in any physical sense – standing tall at just shy of 1.65 metres – his negative energy appears to sap the sunlit room of its gaiety.

I tell him that the bus has left without him, though I suspect he already knows that.

'I'm not going to that thing,' he says in a low growl, flicking his hand dismissively as he lowers himself into the armchair next to mine.

That 'thing' is the conference of the World Federation of Democratic Youth taking place in downtown Caracas this week. Malema has led a delegation of more than a dozen South Africans to the meeting, among them young men and women from the ANCYL, the Young Communist League, the Pan Africanist Congress, the South African Students' Congress and the Congress of South African Students. South Africa is scheduled to host the World Festival of Youth and Students in Soweto, outside Johannesburg, at the end of this year, 2010, and the delegation has travelled here to pick up the baton. Malema did that yesterday at the City Hall.

The conference will wrap up today, but it seems he won't be there when it does. But it's not a big deal. He has already fulfilled his official duties. And besides, Chávez is not here to meet him anyway, contrary to what Malema was led to believe.

So he has decided to bow out and focus his mind instead on his political future back home on the far side of the Atlantic, more than 10,000 kilometres away. Small talk is not coming easily this morning.

President Zuma had a meeting last night with Fikile Mbalula about the disciplinary move. Mbalula was the president of the ANCYL before Malema took over the post and he then went on to become a cabinet minister in Zuma's government and a new power player in the ANC. Throughout it all, he has remained a close friend and tight political ally of Malema's. On the eve of the departure to Venezuela, Zuma had requested a private meeting with Malema himself and as much as Malema wanted and needed that man-to-man talk, he simply could not agree to it with one foot already on the transatlantic jet. So he sent his right-hand man along instead to try to talk the president down.

He gives me the thumbs up when I ask how it went, though he

refuses to utter a word. His gesture would suggest the outcome was positive, or relatively so, yet he's looking awfully bothered.

In his mind, I guess, it is Monday morning, not Saturday morning. And already he is in the ANC headquarters in downtown Johannesburg, not here in Hotel Avila in the Venezuelan capital.

In fairness to him, it's hard to read the situation. His enemies have been crawling out of the woodwork this past week or so, gathering behind the pending disciplinary charges, and he's still not sure who is with him and who is against him in that 86-member national executive committee (NEC) of the mother body. Even in the ranks of the Youth League, he can no longer count on the support of some of his own.

Last Monday, the League's top leaders met their seniors in the ANC to plead their case and argue why Malema shouldn't be taken to task. On Tuesday, some of the country's main newspapers carried front-page splashes announcing that the charges had been dropped. But later that morning the ANC called a press conference and told the media otherwise. The charges hadn't been dropped at all. So some of the juniors had misread their seniors or, if not, one of them was playing a very dirty game.

'Why did you tell me the charges were dropped when they weren't?' one journalist asked what he thought was his ANCYL source over the phone just minutes after the press conference ended that morning.

But the journalist had unwittingly dialled the wrong number. Not only that, but he had identified himself by name at the top of the conversation and also revealed the identity of his source to the listener on the other end of the line when he uttered his name in a greeting. He only realised his mistake when the listener identified himself, a man who bears the same first name as the source the journalist thought he was calling.

To make matters worse, he was speaking to someone who immediately picked up the phone to Malema and relayed the story in full. And that was when Malema knew he had a snitch in his midst peddling all sorts of information to the press.

Malema has no idea how many more are busy plotting against him while he's here in South America. And this is also virgin territory for him. He has been getting away with blue murder for so long but it looks as if it could all come crashing down at any time now. So I opt to keep the conversation light.

'Where's the Breitling?' I ask, when I notice that the wrist-watch he's wearing is not the expensive, flashy-looking one that is forever featured in photos of him in the press.

'It's broken,' he tells me, again waving his hand in that characteristic dismissive gesture of his, his face still set in a firm frown.

I ask what happened to it and he blithely launches into the sorry tale.

The watch, which was from the exclusive Breitling for Bentley range, met its demise late in 2009, roughly around the same time as the Malema brand began to fray. It happened one afternoon when he was spending some time with his son Ratanang, his only child, at his home in Polokwane.

Ratanang was a big fan of *Ben 10*, the American animation series about young Ben Tennyson and his watch-like device with its supernatural powers that allow the young boy to transform into alien characters. And to three-year-old Ratanang, Dad's flashy Breitling looked just like Ben's extraordinary watch.

'Can I play with it?' he asked.

'You can,' his father answered as he unstrapped the wristwatch and handed it to the child.

Ratanang began to fiddle with the dials of the watch, just like Ben does. He imagined himself programming it with the DNA of the alien he was about to transform into, just as Ben would have done. Then, as he had seen Ben do a thousand times, he swiftly raised his chubby little arm upwards, as if he were getting ready for take-off into some other world. And that's when the big Breitling slid off his small wrist and soared into the air before falling flat on the floor seconds later.

With the thud, the Breitling signature gold wings became detached from the top of the face of the watch and were left swivelling at the bottom beneath the glass.

The child could still hear the tick-tock of the watch and he could see that the second hand was still in motion, but the gold wings were out of place. And one look at his father told him he had done something terribly wrong.

He continued to look at him, but he had no words to match his father's stare. So the pair just looked at one another in silence.

The watch was not beyond repair, but in one small innocent act the young boy had damaged one of his father's most distinguished symbols of status and wealth. And that was the end of the Breitling Bentley.

I can picture it all so vividly. I can see that look of rage on Malema's face, that thunderous growl we have all seen a thousand times. I can imagine the child rightfully wilting in front of his father and I can't speak for laughter as the story comes to an end.

'It's OK,' Malema says as he attempts to dismiss my laughter, suggesting the watch was no big deal. It was nothing that money couldn't put right anyway, which he duly did in the weeks that followed, adding to his impressive watch collection, which by now is worth a fair penny.

'I bought another one,' he says as he unstraps the watch he is wearing and hands it to me.

It's a very nice watch and I tell him so. But it's not a Breitling and I wonder why he didn't replace it with one from the same brand.

'No, I did. This is just another one,' he says. 'I have many watches. Many, many watches, to match my shoes.'

'Why to match your shoes?' I want to know.

'Fiona,' he goads, looking at me with an expression that is heaped with scorn, pity and dismay, all rolled into one.

'The leather in your shoes is supposed to match the leather in your belt and your watch. So if you wear brown leather shoes,' he tells me, as he points to his soft, brown leather Yves Saint Laurent slip-ons, 'you must wear a brown leather belt,' he says as he tugs at the waist of his trousers, 'and a brown leather watch,' tapping on his left wrist with his right forefinger in a confident gesture, happy now that he has the upper hand in the conversation again.

The heavy mood of a few minutes ago is well and truly behind him.

This is the young South African who preaches on behalf of the poor and to the poor, the man who promises to bring on a socialist revolution in South Africa; and here he is in Hugo Chávez's Venezuela lecturing on the finer points of fashion.

'Far from co-ordinated leather you were reared,' I remind him.

'That's the way it is,' he replies.

'Who taught you all of this?' I want to know. And why would he care to abide by it all, he who shows scant respect for any kind of rule or reason at the best of times.

'You don't know what you are talking about,' he responds. 'Look at you.'

Venezuela has never seen so many designer labels as it has these past 48 hours since the arrival of the South African young ones. They descended on the city with their expensive suitcases and travel bags, top-of-the-range baseball caps, flashy T-shirts, snazzy shoes and sneakers, sleek manbags and a string of other expensive accessories hanging out of them – and a bodyguard in tow – all dressed up for a socialist youth conference.

I have been wondering how they must appear in the eyes of the other youth who have flown in from all over the world, and who are also staying at the Avila. The three-star hotel is swarming with casually-dressed young delegates and among them, to my mind at least, the South Africans seem to stand out a mile. They are misfits in this mix. They look as if they don't belong. Some of them look more like mafia than young militant activists. But the look on Malema's face suggests that it is I who has been conspicuous all this while, among the South Africans at least, and I appear to have let the side down badly.

I'm not wearing a belt or a watch, but the problem seems to be with my red patent, open sandals and black-and-brown leather bag.

'What's wrong with me?' I ask.

By now curiosity has crept up on the receptionist as he fixes his look in our direction. I'm not sure that he speaks English well enough to understand fully what is being said, but he seems to be getting the gist of Malema's body language.

'Your shoes are not the right colour for your bag,' Malema tells me, pointing to my feet. 'They should be matching. They should be the same.'

'Who said?' I ask again.

Malema's hometown friend, Patti Nkobe, tells me she suspects that his friend Fana Hlongwane, who is embroiled in the 1999 multi-billion-rand arms deal scandal, advises Malema on his style (as she claims he does on everything else). But if he does, Malema is not letting on.

'That's fashion, man,' he tells me. 'I know.'

The conversation is just getting into a steady swing when a young American man brings it to a halt.

'Are you Julius Malema?' he asks in a broad North American twang.

'No,' Malema answers with brazen mendacity, as he swiftly looks the other way.

'Are you sure you are not Julius Malema from the African National Congress in South Africa?' the man asks for a second time, before explaining that he is a locally-based journalist who has been asked by one of South Africa's Sunday newspapers to try to track Malema down to find out what he is up to.

'No, no. Sotho. Sotho,' Malema says, suggesting he can only

speak in his mother tongue as he tries to confuse and discourage the journalist.

'Oh, I'm sorry,' he says as he takes a few steps back, the look on his face suggesting he is not entirely convinced that this is not his subject. But he's not about to challenge the sullen-looking character either.

'Yes,' Malema grunts.

The journalist turns on his heel and begins to walk slowly towards the front doors but within seconds he is marching back towards Malema, his hand outstretched as he holds up the mirror image of the Youth League leader that he has cleverly sourced on his cellphone. The young man sitting in front of him, decked out in designer regalia from head to toe, could not be anyone but the South African youth whose tail he is supposed to be tracking.

'Are you sure you are not Julius Malema?' he ventures again with a broad smile on his face as he holds up the phone for Malema to see.

Malema breaks into his mother tongue for a second time and he rants on for a minute or two, gesticulating with his hands and flicking his wrists as he does when he gets hot under the collar. He then stands up and hails a taxi and stomps out of the hotel, leaving the journalist looking bewildered in his wake.

2010 is turning out to be a black year for Malema and the world is closing in on him. Not even here, on the other side of the world, can he escape the pressures that are weighing on him back home.

'I am the ANC.
I will lead this ANC.
You must put it in your archives.
I will lead the African National Congress.
It doesn't matter what time it takes.'

The luckless but hopeful Julius Malema shortly after he was expelled from the former liberation movement on 24 April 2012.

2

The man with nine lives

If anything, 2010 turned out to be Julius Malema's *annus horribilis*, the year when he was forced to face the sobering truth that his popularity within the party had waned and that his leash would never be so long again. Henceforth, he would have to fight for his political survival and secure his clout by other means, neither of which was beyond him.

It was a frustrating how-do-you-do for the young man who had inhabited a piece of paradise ever since he took over the presidency of the ANCYL a couple of years earlier, by which time the ANC was well and truly ripe for the picking for a man of Malema's calibre and ambition. Outwardly, the ANC was a giant force resting on the overwhelming majority of support from the country's 20-million strong electorate, but it was the internecine rivalry within its ranks that was tearing it apart. The tensions pre-dated the Malema era and went as far back as 1990 when the party was unbanned, and that was the great irony: during its 30 years as an underground movement, with its leadership in exile and its members scattered throughout South Africa and all over the world, the former liberation movement held together better than it ever did after that period. Of course, that had everything to do with the common enemy it had in the apartheid regime and which it eventually brought down. Yet though the ANC could dote on its past achievements as a liberation movement, it struggled to define itself as a ruling party and instead of the revolutionary tradition giving way to the people-centred democracy that they talked of, the ANC became a self-serving organisation.

Naturally the competing factions were quick to surface, even long before Nelson Mandela stepped down in 1999, but they became more aggressive under Thabo Mbeki's stewardship that followed. There was a time when Mbeki was South Africa's great hope. A well-educated man, he had a good grasp of the intricacies of a country that was still socially defined by half a century of white exclusivity, and he had a vision of what he wanted South Africa to become. But Mbeki was also an aloof man with a healthy authoritarian streak running through his veins, and the distance he manifested between himself and 'his people' eventually brought him down.

Zuma had been Mbeki's deputy president, both at the party and state level, but he had been fired from government in 2005 when he became implicated in a massive corruption scandal. The move backfired in a dramatic way when the members of the ANC saw Zuma's demise as an opportunity to put Mbeki in his place; they decided they would unseat him at the party's national conference in 2007 and replace him with Zuma, who they presented as 'a man of the people'. In his comeback campaign Zuma promised to unite the ANC, but it began to fracture even further under his leadership and only a fool would have been blind to the opportunities the new milieu presented.

Though Malema was only in his mid-twenties at the time and, based in Limpopo, a budding leader in the party's youth wing, he was one of the key people who pushed for Zuma's comeback and he made a name for himself as one of the new power guys. His pickings were rich, to begin with at least, and doors swung open for him in all directions. His lap was laden with largesse, he was cut into big business deals and he was drawn close to the party's decision-making table. Within a few months of the ANC party conference, he was elected president of the Youth League. For Malema, it was like a windfall.

He and Zuma were as thick as thieves in those early months and they would have defended one another to the death, despite their 40-year age gap. They were also quite similar in character. There was something brutish and crude, if not mean, about them both and their louche behaviour. Neither man was lacking in guile nor did they care a whit for the good of the country. Their sole concern was power, something that Zuma would eventually struggle to maintain.

During his first year as party leader, Zuma was insecure and weighed down by the corruption scandals he was fighting in the courts. His apprehension was understandable as the charges were damning enough to have him locked up for a few years. Yet even when they were mysteriously dropped on the eve of the general elections in 2009 that made him state president, Zuma still never managed to find a steady footing in the years that followed. His first year in office was rocked by the scandal of a love child that he fathered with a friend's daughter, adding to the twenty-plus children he already has from his polygamous marriages. Allegations of corruption and fraud continued to hound him, his family and his close friends. He packed his cabinet with cronies and they too began to pluck from the public purse. The Zuma era also marked a fairly radical shift in government planning, yet he didn't seem to grasp the complexity of it all. He was inarticulate on his own policy and it was hard to understand what the toneless leader really stood for or where his legacy would eventually lie. Of course he had his strengths and there were moments of greatness, but there were more times when he appeared to be an apology away from a presidential demise. From the day he was sworn into office, his mind was focused on one thing and one thing only: staying there and away from the glare of the judiciary that still wanted to pore over his corruption charges.

On the whole, Zuma was unfit for the purpose of leading South Africa, and I suspect he knew as much. Like any feeble leader would in such circumstances, he developed a deep sense of paranoia. During the struggle against apartheid, he had been a spy chief for the ANC and that began to show in his early years as state president. Adamant to control the climate and keep the various forces at bay, he manipulated state security structures to keep an eye on those around him. He dared not appoint any degree of excellence to his cabinet, lest they outshine him. It wasn't too long before he began to amass an army of enemies both at government and party level. Malema became one of them.

Despite the similarities between the two of them, there was one crucial thing that set them apart: Malema had the kind of political skill that Zuma could only dream about. He was one of what cartoonist Zapiro called the 'Pirates of Polokwane' and he was fast becoming the most vocal of this new breed. The sun had not long set over the Polokwane conference when it became apparent that he was arguably one of the more astute among them as well. In his early days as president of the ANCYL, he began to cash in on one of Zuma's biggest failings: the neglected masses, the tens of millions of poor South Africans who are the biggest and most important constituency in the country by a very long way. Zuma had lobbied them aggressively in his comeback campaign, but he was quick to turn his back on them as soon as he got into office and became one of the new elite. And though Malema had also found firm footing among the elite, he knew better than to turn his back on the core of South African society and in a clever move he began to play a cunning double game. He promised them all sorts of everything that they wanted to hear, starting with the spreading of the country's wealth and the nationalisation of the mines. He then turned to the thorny issue of the land, and threatened to imitate Mugabe's style of 'land grabbing' if need be. Whatever it was they wanted, he told them he could make it happen.

Only very few among them questioned Malema's sincerity. It was common knowledge that he was a young man of conspicuous wealth, yet they seemed to allow him the contradiction. And so with remarkable ease and little effort, his national profile began to grow as he became a locomotive force among the masses.

He was a young political genius, but it was an adage that few were willing to grant him then. In the minds of many he was also a notorious populist, the kind of figure who bodes no good. A malicious genius was the more fitting title.

For just as the past was beginning to recede into history, Malema was bringing it back to life again as he began to cast the minds of millions of South Africans back to the struggle era, reminding them of what they had fought for, who they had fought against and why the battle is still far from over. He situated his argument and his outlook in the 1940s and 1950s and particularly in the 1955 Freedom Charter, a collection of demands for a free South Africa that was best summed up by its opening demand, 'The people shall govern'. And from there Malema began to march, armed with the notion that upping the ante on the so-called National Democratic Revolution (NDR), which the ANC still regards as its driving force for a social and democratic post-apartheid society, was the only means for him to truly transform South Africa on behalf of those he felt he had come to represent.

The meaning of Malema was truly beginning to emerge. He became the epitome of millions of South Africans, young and old, who battle to lay to rest the ghosts of the past as the country struggles to forge a lasting identity eighteen years into the new democracy. He was articulating the racial and social anger that continues to bubble beneath the surface of society and the tensions that cast a long and lasting shadow over life. He was feeding that very common South African desire for people to define themselves by their awful past rather than what they might like to become. He was saying what many felt but dared not put words to. He was hitting on society's raw nerves and for that he earned kudos in many quarters. And so he soldiered on.

In many respects, Julius Malema assumed the role that Winnie Madikizela-Mandela had played many years before him while her then husband, Nelson, was serving life imprisonment. In pretty much the same manner as Malema does today, Madikizela-Mandela fanned the flames in townships across South Africa for many years during the apartheid era. She was a wild revolutionary figure who preached to the masses with her rafter-raising words. Like him, she was fearless and radical and pushed too close to the edge.

Like her, he was a political entrepreneur, and though he was operating in an environment of ample opportunity, he tapped into the same constituencies and appealed to the same mentality that she had once done. With carefree abandon he spurned the project of non-racialism, rubbished the notion of a rainbow nation and challenged the goals of the transition. He started a social tug of war, one that is still playing out in the interregnum that South Africans now inhabit.

That ancient Roman term – *interregnum* – was used to define the period of time between the death of a royal sovereign and the enthronement of a successor. It allowed for a break with the past and it harboured expectations of change that would eventually unfold during the ensuing *justitium,* or transition.

In the 1930s, the Italian philosopher Antonio Gramsci took the concept of the interregnum into socio-political thinking and used it to define extraordinary periods of social and political change during which 'new frames' that are being introduced to make the 'old frames' useless are still in the stage of design[1]. It is a period of limbo, a time when there is little clarity and hardly any knowing, and when nothing is as yet complete.

'The old is dying, and the new cannot be born; in this inter-regnum there arises a great diversity of morbid symptoms,' in Gramsci's own words.

In 1982, the South African Nobel laureate Nadine Gordimer addressed the New York Institute for the Humanities and talked about 'living in the interregnum' in South Africa at a time when apartheid was drawing to an end.

'Historical co-ordinates don't fit life any longer; new ones, where they exist, have couplings not to the rulers, but to the ruled,' she contemplated.

Neither she nor any other South African knew then that apartheid would not end until 1994, though it was clear that the white-led regime was losing its footing and that some kind of change was afoot.

Thirty years on, and South Africans are again 'living in the interregnum,' though it is different to the one that Gordimer talked of. It is a period that is often referred to as the second transition, only, unlike the first, this one affords less clarity about what the future might hold. Twenty years ago, the vast majority of South Africans willingly threw their weight behind the ANC to guide them into the democratic dispensation. But as the country entered its teen years, the rules began to change as greed, bigotry and corruption created an ethical black hole that started to weaken the democratic plan. The concerns of many South Africans were quite real: was South Africa headed down the same route as other African nations that had failed to sink the roots of democracy into their new countries?; was Malema really going to revive the revolutionary tradition he preached about?; would he define the 'new frame' that has yet to come?

Malema thrived on the chaos he was creating because it was awakening a new kind of militancy among millions of South Africans, many of whom were falling into step behind him. He had become an extraordinary phenomenon and was wiping the floor with his party peers and seniors. But while as a political strategist he showed brilliance, he lacked discretion where it mattered most. He enjoyed a lavish lifestyle that drew understandable scrutiny. At the beginning of 2010 he was netting a monthly salary in the region of R42,000 from the ruling party, an income that should have placed him firmly in the bracket of middle-income earners, yet he lived a life that befitted a man of far greater wealth. He had developed an approach to business through politics that linked his name to a string of shady deals done on the back of public tenders that began to raise questions around what was beginning to look like a lack of muscular integrity on his part. Amid allegations of corruption and fears that his business interests might not withstand the scrutiny of the taxman, a number of public investigations were started into his financial and business affairs.

It was all too much for the ruling party. Malema was drawing too much attention to the dark side of their politics. He was not the first to become conspicuously wealthy in their name, and he wouldn't be the last to feed off the fiscus, but a focus on his excesses would surely extend to other party members and the system of patronage that had become commonplace.

Malema was also rising too fast in the eyes of many of his party seniors. The ANC's planning in terms of succession was clearly lacking – the Polokwane conference had exposed that much. But if Malema were to continue rising at the pace he was going, he could easily wipe out a generation of cadres who had been patiently and diligently working their way up through the ranks. He would have to be nipped in the bud. And the only way to do it would be through a disciplinary process. That was the thinking in the early months of 2010.

In hindsight, it was an ill-considered notion that reflected more negatively on the ANC than on Malema himself. In an ideal world, he should have been challenged in a thorough internal political debate or taught that a party puts policy in place for good reason. But this 'new' ANC lacked the leadership to see that through. It had become an organisation of factions, as mentioned earlier – one of which Malema belonged to. And the contours of each faction had blurred, making the task of challenging him all the more difficult. Talking him down would not work. The only means to deal with him would be to unseat him through a harsh disciplinary hearing.

'We needed to see who was behind Malema,' one member of the mother body's executive team told me around that time. 'We knew that a lot of the senior comrades were with him, but we didn't know for sure. And the only way to find out would be to discipline him and see who would come to his defence. And it worked. We saw it clearly.'

It had come to that. The ruling ANC had fractured to the extent that the left hand didn't know what the right hand was doing at the executive level. The interregnum had not just become a feature of society, but a hallmark of the ANC.

Malema was eventually disciplined in the South African autumn of that year and he was dealt a severe blow. His party tried to disown him. Zuma said as much when he suggested his behaviour was 'alien' in the thick of the first round of disciplinary charges. They slapped him with a suspended sentence, like a parent would treat a child. One step in the wrong direction, the finger wagged, and he would be out.

That May Malema was a political outcast who seemed set to become a man of the past. The media rushed to write his obituary. His time had come and the game was over. But it was a statement of political death that was written in haste because a year to the day after I had sat with him in that hotel foyer in Caracas, Malema was revelling in his new-found status. He had become a political hero as the villain in a hate speech trial brought by the white civil rights group Afriforum over his singing of the struggle song *'Dubula iBhunu'*, or 'Shoot the Boer'. And it was a court case that played right into his lap.

Like his political forebears, Malema finally had his day in court. It was an important moment for him and one that would give him the political legitimacy he was begging, because the court plays a pivotal role in ANC struggle and contemporary history. Until then he had no struggle 'credentials,' as ANC types are wont to say. He was born in the latter years of the apartheid regime and was therefore too young to have served his time in exile, or in the ANC trenches within the country, or behind bars in South Africa or in some other place. He traded instead on the fact that his mother was a domestic worker, a fact commonly flagged by many black South Africans to exemplify their wrongful place of servitude to the whites. And now Malema was about to earn his stripes within the confines of a Johannesburg courtroom.

Nelson Mandela, Walter Sisulu, Govan Mbeki and a number of other 'greats' of the struggle era had come to prominence during the Rivonia Trial in the early 1960s when they were tried, though not convicted, for treason (though they were given life sentences for sabotage) in what became one of the most high-profile cases of the apartheid era. In taking on the white judiciary they had become martyrs in the eyes of the masses.

Zuma also had his day in court during a controversial rape trial that ironically made him a man of the people while he was still deputy president.

Then came Malema. As a prominent young blade he strode into the courtroom each day of that week-long trial with Madikizela-Mandela on his arm, the pair of them flanked by a small army of security guards carrying large machine guns, no less, so that he could comfortably defend his militancy in peacetime South Africa.

He took the stand and he handled himself impeccably. His tone was calm and his argument coherent; not once did he allow his cage to be rattled, though he was afforded ample opportunity to vent some rage.

'I belong to a militant and very radical organisation and if you are not militant, you run the risk of being irrelevant,' Malema told the Johannesburg High Court. 'We are heroes. Yes, we are warriors because we have won war battles.'

He was bent on becoming a powerhouse politician and he was showing few signs of defeat that week. The only chink in his armour was a physical one. Malema was suffering from gout and it hit him 'always after we have been drinking a lot and eating a lot of meat,' he had once told me. But it hit him hard at the courthouse during one particularly long and drawn-out cross-examination. He was on the stand, though he was seated, and he forced himself to his feet to try and relieve the pain in his legs. He was mid-spiel at the time, talking up the revolution, but he didn't flinch. And it was an unforgettable portrait: the 30-year-old commander in chief of economic freedom, defending the ANC's war songs while fighting off the self-inflicted rich man's disease.

But in defending himself in that very high-profile trial, Malema not only became the custodian of ANC struggle songs, but a hero in the eyes of millions. He was back in the saddle (though he would later lose that case).

It gave him an extraordinary boost and it came at an extraordinary time. He was facing a re-election for the presidency of the ANCYL two months later, and despite the popular image portrayed of him during that trial, Malema had his fair share of detractors within the ranks of the Youth League by then. During his first term as president he had developed an intolerant and dictatorial style of rule. Like George W. Bush, he believed he was burdened by a strange axis of evil. Those who were not with him were against him and he was quick to oust them from the party's ranks. So by the time the ANCYL elective conference was pencilled in for June 2011, there was an army of opponents who were preparing to take him on, rallying behind Lebogang Maile, the chairman of the League in Gauteng, who would challenge Malema for the position of president.

Malema's court days made Maile's challenge all the more difficult. For many, Malema had become much more than a leader of the youth. He was a man of the people now, the 'boy brave' of the country's suffering classes. He was finally ranked among his forebears.

It all coincided with the campaign for the local government elections of May 2011 and Malema hit the campaign trail early on, knowing it would provide him with the platform he was looking for. He had a profile to build and the publicity he was about to earn himself would go a long way. He wasn't thinking about the Youth League conference that would follow a month later. The hate speech trial had unwittingly sewn that one up for him. He was thinking ahead to the end of 2012 when his party peers would descend on the city of Mangaung, and where he hopes to unseat the leadership he helped put in place in 2007, so that he can continue his march towards greater power. Malema will not be in the running for a place in the party's structures, but if he can lobby for his allies to be installed, then it will pave the way for a place for him somewhere down the line. That's where Malema's mind was focused halfway through 2011 when he started out on the campaign trail.

Those local elections marked a shift in the thinking of the regular voters who for years had voted with their hearts, based on the emotional attachment that so many had had to the ANC, the party that had freed them from the brutal shackles of apartheid, the liberation movement that actually gave them the vote. But all these years on, the electorate was now looking for results and if the ANC could not provide them, then they would have to think twice. So Malema appealed to them with extraordinary charm and talked to the masses in a way that no other politician did on that campaign trail. Not even Zuma.

Malema stole the show and he, more than Zuma, became the face of the ANC – the 'new' ANC – during that month-long campaign. He even had many of the media on his side. They clapped him warmly on the back for a job well done, and there was not a whisper of the controversies they had been peddling not too long before then. A month later he secured himself a second term as ANCYL president, by which time his chest was well and truly protruding with pride.

It was a remarkable turn of events in the space of twelve or so months. Malema had come back against all the odds and despite enormous hostility. And he seemed unstoppable now. He had Malema-ised South African politics to the extent that it appeared no one could bring him down and he was still only 30 years of age.

But there was an even darker side to the Malema coin. Beneath that very brash veneer lurked a host of dark secrets about the wheeling and the dealing that had become his way of life. They were talked about and scorned upon but never trotted out as fact until one day in July when one of the country's newspapers broke a story about what it called his 'secret slush fund'. In the days and weeks that followed, details of Malema's money-making rackets occupied inches of the country's newspaper columns. The authorities were quick to jump in and as this book went to print, four of the law enforcement agencies were busy wading through stacks of damning evidence.

Malema was floored for a second time and that's when his party decided to kick him very hard. Within weeks of the alleged corruption scandals, the ANC slapped him with a second round of disciplinary charges. Not because he may have been embroiled in corruption, mind you. The ANC still tends to turn a blind eye to fraud and graft and all sorts of other illegal activities at the best of times. Malema was instead charged with 'sowing division in the ranks of the party', shorthand for posing a threat to Jacob Zuma's chances at a second term as ANC leader.

When the ANC had disciplined him a year earlier, Malema pleaded guilty and got off with a pathetically light sentence: he was forced to apologise to the ANC, which he did; he was asked to pay a R10,000 donation to a charity of his choice, which he didn't; and he was ordered to enrol in anger management classes, which he scoffed at.

But he knew he would not be so lucky a second time round and in the dying months of 2011 Malema was fighting for his political life. The New Year brought no reprieve: the five-year suspension he was handed in November turned to a full expulsion on the leap day of 2012 on appeal. He challenged that verdict too, but lost, and was eventually kicked out of the party at the end of April.

Though Malema was out of party politics, there was nothing craven about his following. He could still fill a soccer field with supporters for a political rally and Twitter would go into overdrive with each appearance he made. His words were carried as widely by the media as they had been while he was at his peak and the TV cameras tailed him with the same kind of intensity as they had always done.

There was still plenty of political life left in Malema, and throughout his fightback I was often reminded of the sense he had of himself, as he had once relayed it to me.

'They can't get me,' he had laughed heartily a couple of years earlier when he had managed to escape the wrath of his party. 'I'm the one with the nine lives. They can't bring me down.'

That much was true where his political profile was concerned, but it is unlikely he will be able to shake off the corruption charges with the same ease when they are brought.

Even so, Malema's story is far from over. He may be 'a scratch on the mind' of many South Africans, to borrow Harold Isaacs' term. But in essence, Julius Malema reflects something more profound about the country, about its failings and about the failings of the ruling party.

Sarah Malema is sitting in the living room of her Seshego home, relaying her family's history to me, when her cell phone begins to purr. But before the 81-year-old can reach into the front pocket of her patterned dress to retrieve the handset, the voice of Jacob Zuma begins to reverberate around the small room.

Umshini wami mshini wami
khawuleth'umshini wami
Umshini wami mshini wami,
. . .

And on it goes, one bar after another, as the ANC president belts out the Zulu struggle song he has claimed as his own and which the old woman, one of his ardent supporters at that time, had saved as her ringtone.

She answers the cell phone and chats briefly to the caller. Then, with a gentle nod in my direction, she picks up where she left off and tells me about the Malema family, in Pedi, one of the Northern Sotho languages which she speaks, but which I don't, and which her daughter, Maropeng, and grandson, Tshepo, translate into English.

3

Do you know who I am?

In the late 1940s, a man named Mohanwa Johannes Malema
met Mathebu Sarah Thobakgale in what was then called the
northern region of the Transvaal. She was born in the town
of Louis Trichardt and he was from the Batlokwa region. She
was also much younger than him, some sixteen years his junior.
But he was a widower and he was not about to throw away
his second chance at happiness because of his new lady friend's
age. So, shortly after their paths crossed, he took her hand in
marriage and they settled down and worked as farmhands not
far from the village of Ga-Ramokgopa, where he came from.

Ga-Ramokgopa is a low-lying settlement located about 500
metres off the N1, the highway that cuts through South Africa
in a diagonal direction, from the Western Cape in the south-west
through to Limpopo's border crossing with Zimbabwe in the
north-east, forming the first leg of the Cape-to-Cairo highway.

But it is also a desolate part of the world that throws up few
opportunities for a man to make a go of his life, and if Johannes
Malema was to father a new family and fend for them as well,
he knew he would have to try his luck at finding a job in the
city of Polokwane, formerly known as Pietersburg, some 60-odd
kilometres south.

He did as most other men had done before him and went
ahead of his new wife in search of work. He headed straight
for New Pietersburg, the industrial stretch to the west of the

city, and within a few weeks he found a job at the local cement factory and a place to lay his head at night in nearby Disteneng.

Disteneng had originally been developed on a large swathe of land that was cleared for the workers who serviced New Pietersburg, or for men who were travelling from far afield and for whom transport was a problem. But it instantly became an area attractive to squatters and in an all-out bid to put a halt to that, the earlier settlers were given the opportunity to buy out the small plots of land on which they then built their homes, hence the name Disteneng, the Pedi word for 'stand owners'. Over the years, it developed into a densely populated, multi-racial settlement that was home to Africans, Indians and coloureds (that awful apartheid racial categorisation that has carried into the new South Africa).

On each stand stood a small house with a tin shack, if not two or three, in its back yard, and it was into one of those tumbledown dwellings that the Malemas moved when Johannes sent for Sarah and their first-born, Maropeng.

But they were a pitiful lot. Though they had a wage coming in, it was hardly worth talking about. And the family was ballooning. After Maropeng was born, five other children followed in quick succession: Philemon, Florah, Nurse, Annie and Francina, and with so many mouths to feed, it was often the case that they didn't have two pennies to rub together at the end of each week.

In the 1960s the white government decided to break up the multi-racial block in Disteneng and forcibly removed the dwellers to three different areas. The Africans were relocated further out to the north-west of the city to the new township of Seshego. The Indians were moved closer to the city to the suburb of Nirvana, while the coloureds were relocated to Westenberg, to the west of the city centre.

The shack dwellers of Disteneng were the first targets of forced removal, on the assumption that they would put up least resistance with the offer of a house that they could call home.

And that is how the Malema family got their first permanent roof over their heads when, in 1964, they were allocated house number 1103 in what was called Zone 1. Seven other zones followed to make up Seshego, but Zone 1 was where the first cluster of houses was erected and house 1103 was on the street where the first strip of bungalows was unveiled.

Zone 1 was a large area made up of hundreds and hundreds of homes and it was subsequently broken down into five sub-sections by the people who lived there. They gave each sub-area an informal name which had resonance for them and which has stuck to this day.

For example, Groovy took its name from the first soccer club that was formed in that area. A big marula tree in a nearby section gave Moruleng its name. Each house had at least four numbers that determined its address, and those that began with the digits 12 fell into what became known as the Di 12 section. And by the same logic, those that began with the numbers 15 fell into a cluster known as Di 15.

The section where the Malemas lived was called Masakaneng, the Pedi word for 'sacks', because that was all the residents had to cover the windows of their new homes. Curtains were a luxury then. For people who had known nothing other than shack life, so too were the windows, if not the houses as well, in some respects. And the best they had to drape over the apertures were the sacks from mealie meal, or maize, the staple food of the South African diet then and now.

'Masakaneng was a name that was taken from Disteneng,' says Thabo Makunyane, the former executive mayor of Polokwane and a prominent ANC member. 'The sacks were made from hemp. And we used to use the sacks and cardboard and anything else we could get our hands on to make *mukhukhu* [shacks],' he remembers. 'And when we moved to Seshego, that name came with us.'

'The people of Masakaneng had nothing, nothing,' says Matlala

Maremane, a man who was born in the 1960s in that stretch of the township. 'It was the poorest of the poor who lived there. And it was the worst part of Seshego, with every bad element to be expected of a run-down area like that. I know. I grew up there.'

'I remember there were no street lights', says Freddie Rama-phakela, who was also reared in Zone 1. 'And it was dangerous to go out at night. Even by day, the area wasn't safe.'

It was in Masakaneng that the Malemas spent the rest of their days. Theirs was a four-roomed house, comprising two bedrooms, a living room-cum-dining room, and a kitchen. In the yard outside stood the toilet that fed into a sub-standard sewage system. House 1103 had running water, but no electricity. But that was their lot for which they paid little more than R2 a month in rent.

As a family they struggled. Sarah found it hard to make ends meet on Johannes's income, which was not always regular and her family was still growing. After they moved to Seshego, she had three more children: Maria, Anna and Martha.

Then the grandchildren began to appear and the household numbers began to swell. With the exception of Maropeng who left home when she got married in 1971, and Annie who left home in 1986, the rest of the Malema daughters as well as Philemon stayed at home. Anna and Martha did not have children. Philemon did, but the child was reared by the mother elsewhere. Altogether, Florah, Francina, Nurse and Maria had nine children out of wedlock, all of whom were reared in house 1103 (though two of Florah's children died in infancy).

One day in the early 1970s, Johannes upped and left when he met another woman, leaving Sarah to rear the largely female family on her own.

'But we were no different to many others,' Sarah says.

She was a traditional healer, or a *sangoma* as it is referred to locally, and a firm believer who put her faith in the gods and her ancestors to help see her and her family through, but the best years of her life were marred by one form of hardship after another.

Philemon, who became the main breadwinner after Johannes left, had a nervous breakdown and was forced to give up work. Florah, Sarah's third child and Julius's mother, was in Standard 6 when she was diagnosed with epilepsy. She was in her late teens when the doctors explained her condition to her and she was forced to abandon her schooling.

By then Sarah was really struggling with the single-headed household, holding down a full-time job in a local mill trying to keep the roof over their heads. Seeing the strain it was taking on her mother, Florah decided to go out and find a job to help pay her way. Like the vast majority of black women then, and even now to some extent, Florah, who was known to all around her as Sesi Mahlodi, worked as a domestic helper for a family in the largely Indian suburb of Nirvana, but she continued to live at her Seshego home and covered the distance to and from her workplace each day by mini-bus taxi.

She wasn't long in the job when an epileptic attack crept up on her one day, leaving her maimed for the rest of her life. She was standing over the gas stove in her employers' kitchen, cooking them a meal, when her body went into convulsions. The young woman fainted and as she collapsed she brought down on top of her a pot of boiling water, which instantly licked at the skin on her neck and chest, scorching it into a fine layer.

After a brief stint in hospital, and on the doctor's orders, she was forced to give up her job and never worked another day. She returned home to her mother's house where she lived until 2006 when a severe epileptic seizure overcame her early one morning and she died. It was 14 August and she was 50 years old.

Complicating Florah's life was the fact that she was apparently mentally unstable. Friends and neighbours recall a frail person whom they describe as emotionally challenged, a grown woman who maintained the innocence of a child until the day she died.

The Malema house sits on a T-junction and opposite it stands the Corner Store, a busy hub and hangout and a magnet for the children of Masakaneng. Florah would spend her days stretched out under the mango tree outside her family's house, watching out for her son who rarely left the streets. She would doze in the shade of the tree for hours on end and when she wasn't taking a nap, she would say little and simply sit and watch the street life unfolding around her. All the children who grew up in Masakaneng knew Florah Malema well.

But her son insists that mentally his mother was as normal as the next woman and that any suggestion of emotional instability stems from the social mores that come with epilepsy. Though it is not caused by mental illness and does not result in mental impairment, the condition often carries with it a social stigma because of the unsightly bodily behaviour a seizure can bring on. The medical books describe it as an abnormal electrical discharge from the brain cells. There is no advance warning. The muscles often go into spasm and the body can become rigid before going into convulsions. The person will lose consciousness and wail and moan as the body goes into fits. Breathing becomes laboured and to see a person in the throes of an epileptic fit is not pleasant by any standards, but in many African cultures it is often regarded as watching a person possessed or truly deranged.

Seeing Florah come out of a seizure, half-dazed and incoherent, was not nice, her son says. It could have been misleading.

Even with the full appreciation of her condition, there is no one who will say a bad word about Florah. She was just another woman who was unlucky in life, through no doing of her own.

Florah was 23 when she gave birth to Aida, but the young girl died as a toddler. A couple of years later she fell pregnant again and Julius Sello Malema was born on 3 March 1981, sharing the same birthday as his mother. Julius was two years old when Florah gave birth to her third child, Sarah, who was named after her grandmother. But like Aida, she too did not live to see her third birthday.

There are not many photos of Julius's early childhood or of his siblings. There is one of him and one of his sisters, posing with their grandmother. He was too young to remember it being taken, but it is one of his dearest possessions. There are a couple of others of him, and some more of his mother, but none of him and her together, no enduring visual proof of his immediate family.

That doesn't hinder his memory of his mother or his feelings for her in any way. Julius speaks very fondly of her, and openly so.

'She was always there. Always. And I never had to compete for her affection. It was just me and her,' he says, one small unit in the larger Malema lot.

Florah had a very fiery character, which she got from her father and clearly passed on to her son. And though Julius was the apple of his mother's eye, she was never shy to reprimand him whenever he gave her occasion.

'She could raise the roof, that one,' says her sister, Maropeng. And whenever she did, Sarah would come to the young boy's rescue.

And so it was that he developed a deep love for the two women who watched out for him in life. His grandmother understood him in ways his mother never could and she would always stand by him, through thick and thin, both as a young boy and in later life. And while he and his mother didn't always see eye to eye, least of all on his hot-headed outlook on life, she was his number one and he hers.

Julius Malema is well defined by his tough and bullish personality, yet his eyes brim with emotion when he talks about the morning his mother died and how he fell apart when the paramedics told him they were unable to resuscitate her. He remembers how he had to pull himself together as the man of the house and organise her funeral. And how late one night, many weeks later, the full weight of his mother's death came to bear when it finally dawned on him that she was never coming back. He cried his fair share of tears that night as that prospect sank in.

He was driving through Polokwane at the time, towards his house in the suburb of Flora Park which he had bought earlier that year, when it hit him like a bolt out of the blue. He began to weep uncontrollably.

'I couldn't stop. I was screaming. I had to stop the car and pull over,' he remembers.

He had never known his father. His mother was now dead. And though he knew he could always count on his grandmother, he was on his own in life.

His then girlfriend – Maropeng – was heavily pregnant at the time and she gave birth to their son, Ratanang, two months after Florah died. But in that brief period after his mother died and before his son was born, Julius felt empty for the first time in his life.

'I had never known emotional pain. Real pain,' he remembers. 'I had never known death so close.'

But he still had Sarah, a woman he looks up to and, perhaps oddly, appears to obey.

It was she who took him to task when he insulted Naledi Pandor, one of the ANC's senior comrades and then minister of education, during a dispute over student fees at Pretoria University in 2009. Pandor is well spoken and her accent could easily be mistaken for that of a member of England's upper crust. But in trying to take Pandor down a peg, Malema made more of a fool of himself when he said:

'We've got a minister who's using too much time using an American accent without assisting our people. That is the main problem. Let the minister use that fake accent to address our problems and not to behave like a spoilt minister.'

Within a few hours of his unfortunate utterance hitting the

headlines, Sarah was confronted twice in Seshego by fellow senior citizens who told her it was not right for her grandson to speak to a senior member of society in such a manner. She was quick to pick up the phone to her grandson to remind him that he had been reared to respect his elders.

'You will apologise,' she told him.

And he did. Though the ANC had called on him to do likewise, it was Sarah's words that echoed loudest in his mind. It was not often she would call him to order and when she did, he knew it would have to be with good reason. He apologised to Pandor within hours of putting down the phone to Sarah.

'When she talks like that, I listen,' he says.

Yet there is not a whisper of his father. Little is known about the man and his identity is a secret the Malema family appears determined to keep. Whether this is because he never paid the so-called damage money required in African culture when a woman falls pregnant out of wedlock, or whether it is because neither she nor her family ever wanted to establish a relationship with him, or he with them, is hard to know.

Sarah says she never met him and that only Julius's mother, who is now dead, would have been the appropriate person to talk about him. Julius also claims never to have met his father. Yet his aunt, Maropeng, says he died a few years back, while neighbours and friends insist the man is well known to all of the Malemas and still lives in Seshego in a shack on the far side of the busy Nelson Mandela Drive that cuts through the township.

But regardless of who he is, he never did and still does not feature in Julius Malema's life; nor does Malema harbour any hopes that he ever will.

'I never had a father in my life,' he says. 'I had my mother and my granny. I didn't know anything else. Why do I need a father? I am a father myself now.'

So it was that he was reared as an only child, though he was born into a crowded four-roomed house that was home to his mother, his grandmother, his grandfather for a while, his aunts, an uncle and several cousins.

There was a time when the household numbers would swell to a dozen and more, forcing the Malemas to build two tin shacks in the backyard to help house them all. But what once was a small and run-down house is now an impressive double-storey home tucked into the confines of that original plot in Zone 1, towering over every other house in the immediate vicinity.

Around 2005 and 2006, as Julius began to make his money, he renovated the family home. He had wanted to demolish the existing structure and build a bigger and better house in its place, but his grandmother wouldn't hear of it. When Johannes abandoned the family years earlier, Sarah had come close to losing the house in which she had reared her children and grandchildren. The house was registered in her husband's name and he wanted to sell it. But Sarah dug in her heels. Johannes could do what he wanted, but she was not going to move an inch and she was forced into a bitter and protracted battle to keep that roof over their heads. She was understandably loathe to entertain her grandson's plans years later when he told her he wanted to raze it to the ground.

'This one is mine,' she told him. 'I fought for it and I'm keeping it.' She would not budge.

Julius modernised the small house instead. In the back yard he built a two-storey structure, which was just at roofing level when his mother died. And around both houses he had high walls erected and tall gates put in place at the front to give the family some privacy.

But early in 2011 Malema finally got his way and he demolished the single-storey house. He wanted more for his grandmother as she entered the evening of her life and he set out to build something better. The new house bears no resemblance to the old in any manner at all, double as it is in size and grandeur, yet it somehow continues to bear the hallmark of that bygone era, perched on that grit-strewn street in one of the poorest stretches of Seshego, a corner of the world still reminiscent of the 'old' South Africa.

The township lies about 10 kilometres west of Polokwane, according to the traditional measure that covers the distance between one post office and another. It sits at the end of Nelson Mandela Drive that connects it to the city centre and beyond. Many of the houses have been spruced up in the last few years and row after row of neat and well-kept homes now line many of Seshego's streets. Yet Masakaneng still remains the poor cousin of the sprawl.

The houses there are run down and dilapidated, and without fail they all hark back to the 1960s when the separation of whites from blacks not only meant sub-standard housing for the latter, but the creation of a monotonous feature on the social landscape of urban South Africa.

The pokey-looking units feature side by side on streets that zigzag through the area. All of the dwellings sit just a few metres back from the street, some behind hedges, high walls or low-lying partial fences, while others sit behind nothing at all and gape out vacantly onto the dusty roads. By and large they vary little and are devoid of character. Pride of ownership in many instances is non-existent and looking at those houses today, it is not difficult to imagine the environment that Julius Malema grew up in.

As a child he shared the back bedroom with his mother, an aunt and some of his cousins. On a quiet night as many as six of them would tuck down to sleep in that confined space.

'I slept with my mother until my cousins started laughing at me,' he remembers. After that he found his place on the floor along with the rest of the young ones.

His grandmother, his grandfather while he still lived there, and some other family members slept in the second bedroom, and the floor space of the kitchen was put to good use to cater for the rest.

'It was a good time,' recalls Sarah, a woman with a hardened but optimistic outlook on life. 'We had nothing, but we shared everything we had with one another. Everything we had belonged to all of us. It wasn't ideal. But that's how it was.'

As she sketches the early days of Julius's life, she paints a picture of a young boy who had an upbringing that was no different from that of thousands of other African youth from that era. He knew nothing but poverty. He was a second-rate citizen in his country of birth. He was reared among his extended family, in his case the majority of whom were women, and he learned to raise his voice at a young age if he wanted to be heard.

He attended local schools and was brought up speaking Pedi. He was a ruffian, a young hustler who scraped through life and who lived for his time on the streets.

The Malema home was not a political one, nor was it an ANC house, not because the family did not have an appetite for the struggle or what it stood for, but because its members were trying to eke out an existence and were mindful of the repressive apartheid legislation that made most forms of black-led political activity a crime. People like the Malemas could ill afford to find themselves on the wrong side of the law.

Nor was it a house of books or lofty teaching. And it wasn't a particularly religious home. The Malemas were simply a very ordinary and poor family. And though Sarah cut her cloth accordingly, it was often the case that she simply didn't have enough money to feed her family and Julius would be forced to find his own way.

He went from street to street collecting old tin cans and bottles and any other items that could possibly be recycled and then he would haggle with the right men for the best price. And when the going got very tough, he would invariably end up knocking at the doors of neighbours and future comrades at meal times.

Daisy Sebate, then a well-known political activist in the township, remembers how Julius would put his head round her door just as the food was being dished out onto the plates, his impeccable timing an indirect plea for a place at the table.

'But at least he asked, even if he did it in his own way,' Ramaphakela points out. 'He didn't steal. He didn't snatch. That's what most of them did. But he didn't.'

If Julius hadn't had the cunning to know which door to knock on and at what time, he would have had little choice but to beg for food, and that he refused to do.

'Never,' he says in a tone of fierce pride. 'I would never allow myself to do that.'

But begging is what most of the young boys of Masakaneng resorted to. They would go to Polokwane and find a street corner to work and when begging didn't yield the returns that they wanted, they would turn to petty crime. As young *tsotsis*, or criminals, dark habits came naturally. And from glue sniffing many of them sank into a larger underworld and went on to become big gangsters.

'But Malema was streetwise,' Sebate remembers. 'He was a survivor and he knew how to get by.'

Julius Malema was thirteen when apartheid came to an end and he lived the rest of his formative years in the democratic dispensation. But for him and many others, 1994 did not bring transformation overnight. His teen years were very tough and the Malema family still struggled to get by. The poverty that hung over that household in some ways became even more endemic because it was one of the millions of families that 1994 left behind.

Though Malema is often criticised for trading on his past and the fact that his mother was a domestic worker cleaning up the mess of people more privileged than herself, it is a fact that he was reared in miserable hardship.

He might have little to complain about today, but the early years of his life, his most important years, were cruel. He was also reared in a city over which the stench of racism still hangs.

Modern-day Polokwane still has a strong Afrikaner feel to it. In 1884 the Zuid-Afrikaanse Republiek bought the eastern half of a large farm called Sterkloop and two years later it was proclaimed the site of a new town called Pietersburg, which was named after Commandant-General Petrus Jacobus Joubert. But during the Second (Great) Boer War that followed in 1899, the town became home to one of the country's 31 concentration camps set up by the British: the Pietersburg camp housed more than 4,000 Afrikaner women and children. Not surprisingly, the town developed a strong Afrikaner identity in the post-war years. It was also the centre of an agricultural heartland and after apartheid was introduced in 1948, it became a service point for many of the surrounding bantustans, the territories that were established by the apartheid regime to house the various ethnic African groups when the project of racial separation became entrenched.

By the time Julius began to get his head around the ANC and the struggle, the Afrikaners were about to face loss for a second time and they began to cling to their Afrikaner identity. A 'them' and 'us' mentality settled in to the town, perhaps made even more stark by its size. Pietersburg was not a large urban centre and was only proclaimed a city in 1992. But when it became the seat of the provincial government two years later, it attracted tens of thousands of Africans from all over what was then called the Northern Province, until it was later demarcated and renamed Limpopo in 2002. Afrikaners found themselves at the wrong end of the pecking order. They felt threatened and they closed in on themselves. And it was within that social divide that Malema grew up, on one side of the society of Pietersburg.

All told, his early years made him fearless as well as defiant, and it was a period in his life that turned him into an angry hothead.

That anger stayed with him as he got to know the struggle, because it was inevitable that a young man of Malema's fiery character would seek out the mischief that came with the heady days immediately before and after the end of apartheid in 1994.

If there was anyone Julius Malema wanted to be like, it was the late Peter Mokaba, who led the ANCYL after it was unbanned in 1990.

As he stood at the gates of history, Mokaba seemed to dislike much of what lay ahead, not least a peaceful transition, and whenever the opportunity presented itself he challenged the status quo. It was what he was most remembered for after he passed away in 2001, apparently a victim of the HIV/AIDS epidemic that had begun to sweep across the country.

It was his defiance that Malema loved him for. It was Mokaba who turned the struggle song 'Shoot the Boer' on its head when he changed its words to chants of 'Kill the Boer, Kill the farmer' at the same time as his party leadership was trying to negotiate an end to apartheid with the white regime. When Mokaba sang it, millions sang with him, and when Malema trotted it out in its less radical form twenty years later, it was a curtain raiser all over again.

I was with Malema in Zimbabwe when he gave a talk to the youth wing of Mugabe's Zanu-PF party on the Easter weekend of 2010, evoking the spirit of Mokaba for his neighbours' benefit.

'Peter was a very charismatic leader of the youth. He had an Afro perm. Nice clothes,' he said, describing the man he calls his mentor.

Initially 'we thought Peter was a sell-out, because of how he dressed.' But what Mokaba was teaching them was how to be relevant to the people around them.

You must be hip for the youth. You must be cool. You must be amongst them to be one of them. And you must fight for your place amongst the people.

'Because of the type of work we do, we can drive whatever car we drive. We can wear whatever watch we wear. And stay in nice houses, but when it comes to a fight [for the support of the people], we put all the luxuries aside and get to the ground.' And they fight to win 'because we know that without the African National Congress, we are hobos. We are nothing.'

Those last few words came back to me over and over again a couple of years later when Malema was fighting for his political life. He was powerful by then, but he saw his political identity as meaningless if he didn't have a place in the ANC that governed the country and its purse strings.

4

Rising through the ranks

Julius Malema, in retrospect. That was the tricky part about documenting his early years in politics while he was still at his peak in the ruling party: his story was relayed so far after the fact that a thick haze of fancy had begun to obscure the early Malema years, particularly in his hometown of Polokwane. Though he was based in Johannesburg around the time that I was charting that chapter of his life, he was, without any doubt, the most powerful person in Polokwane and throughout the province of Limpopo. Weeding out the cheerleaders was hellishly difficult.

Then along came Freddie Ramaphakela and he began to piece together that era for me. It is he who lays claim to 'discovering' Malema, a badge he wears with great pride, though with Malema's blessing, it has to be noted. To be sure, his recall of that time had also acquired a favourable construction of its own. But here's how he tells it.

In 1989, just three days before the anniversary of 16 June, the day in 1976 when black students led a revolt against a policy that was forcing them to be instructed in Afrikaans, the language of the apartheid regime, Ramaphakela found himself on the wrong side of the white police force. The 24-year-old was a member of Umkhonto we Sizwe, or Spear of the Nation, the armed wing of the ANC that is commonly referred to as the MK, and he was attached to an underground cell at the blacks-only University of the North, located 40 or so kilometres east of Polokwane.

Throughout the apartheid era, the university had been a hotbed of resistance, and though Ramaphakela was not a high-profile target of the security forces by any stretch, his movements were nonetheless monitored, particularly in his home township of Seshego, or so he says.

On that day, 13 June, Ramaphakela was holding court on the veranda of the Corner Store, the general grocer in front of the Malema family home in Masakaneng, with six young boys who were quizzing him about the struggle.

'What is June 16th all about?' they wanted to know; 'What are you really fighting for?'; 'Are the whites our only enemy?'; 'Are we going to win?'; 'When?'

Malema was one of the six and he was eight years old at the time.

Ramaphakela wanted them to understand the basics of why black South Africans were fighting against white domination, but he knew he would have to simplify his message. These boys were young, the oldest among them no more than ten or eleven years old, so he gave it to them in general terms.

Had their mothers ever told them how they suffered at work under their white bosses? Had they ever seen a white person work in a kitchen? How often did they see a mini-bus taxi packed with white people going to work in the morning? Did they know of any whites who worked for blacks?

'That is how unfair and how wrong the system is,' he told them. 'It is set up to work against us. Whites don't give blacks a chance in our own country. And we are trying to change that.'

'*De boy ga a na verstaan,*' Malema said in local slang. He was suggesting the boys wouldn't be able to grasp what Ramaphakela was saying. It is possible that the eight-year-old didn't have a mental grip on it either, but his pride wouldn't allow him to admit that.

So Ramaphakela trotted out one or two more examples, and while he was in full spiel, a police van pulled up in front of

him and two officers got out. The young boys skedaddled, but
Malema stayed put. He backed away towards the wall of the
shop, but he didn't run.

'What are you doing?' the officers demanded of Ramaphakela
as they began to approach him.

He was bluffing his way through a response when he saw the
knuckles of one of the officers' fists was within a whisker of his
right eye, and as he tried to duck the blow, the second officer
kicked him in the stomach and sent him reeling to the ground.

Ramaphakela's instinct was to run.

'But then I thought, how could I? I had just been telling these
young boys about the importance of fighting the fight. Julius
was still standing there. And as I tried to defend myself, I heard
Julius shout out, *"Hey wena. O ska betha dai man."'*

The officers didn't heed the young boy's plea not to hit his
older friend, but Ramaphakela remembers thinking afterwards,
'Now there's someone who's fearless and not afraid to fight.'

When in the months that followed Ramaphakela decided to
start an underground MK cell for a few juniors to train them
in guerrilla tactics, Malema was one of a handful of youths he
decided to bring under his wing.

'I knew they were young and I wasn't about to tell them to
get out onto the streets and fight. No. But we knew we needed
a back-up in case 1994 never happened and it was obvious to
me that we needed to begin to train up young boys, just in case.

'But I had to be careful. If their families knew my plans, they
would expose me to the police and that would have been the
end of me. People were very afraid then.'

Child fighters were not uncommon in struggles on the African
continent or elsewhere, and around that time in South Africa
the MK was rounding up teenagers in many townships and
sending them off to Uganda for military training. But Ramaphakela was recruiting much younger boys, children who were
hardly old enough to spell their own names, and he was taking

them underground in their own country. It was an outrageous plan. Ramaphakela was also a very small player in a much larger scheme and he was initiating a move that carried infinite potential for disaster.

'That's why I knew I had to do it right,' he explained. 'I would start with paramilitary activities. And then, bit by bit, I would make them feel like they are part of the core of the MK, and then the ANC, and then the bigger picture. We didn't know what was ahead of us at that time. Nobody did. Not even the ANC (which was still outlawed). We could have been headed for a bloodbath. And if we were, we needed resistance.'

It had all the trimmings of a tall story and when I ran it by a few veterans of the MK, they each scratched their heads in bewilderment, adamant that the armed wing did not recruit children at any time during the struggle. There was also uncertainty around Ramaphakela's credentials: no one could vouch for his membership of the armed wing while it was still underground in the pre–1990 period.

'Ask him who his commander was,' one of them suggested. 'And then we will know if this is not just another distortion of our history.'

Ramaphakela claimed his commander was Jacob Rapholo, a well-known MK fighter from that era. But according to Rapholo, Ramaphakela only joined the MK after the ban had been lifted on all political parties and their armed wings in 1990 'and he was never part of anything underground or anything secret. Never.'

But Ramaphakela stands by his story. He formed a cell and Malema was one of his recruits. Malema also stands by this version of his early life. That's how it was, or at least that's how they wanted it to be remembered.

What is true, though, is that it was Ramaphakela who placed the first gun in Malema's hands and taught him how to pull a trigger, be it for the purposes of the formal military training he says it was, or for some kind of street plan he concocted off his own bat.

Ramaphakela had known Malema ever since the young boy was in nappies. He knew the Malema family who, like his own, came from Masakaneng, and as Malema was growing up he became a familiar face to him in that neck of the township, one of the more wayward children in his midst.

'He lived on the streets and he was caught up in everything he shouldn't have been. He was a loudmouth and he was cheeky,' Ramaphakela remembers.

'But he could always sustain an argument until he won it. And he was a fighter – in a physical sense – and to this day I firmly believe that if I hadn't led him into the ANC, I would have put him into boxing.'

As tough as he was, Malema also had the innocence of a child of his age and he laughs today as he thinks back on his outlook then.

'You know, I thought victory would be so easy. If the problem was the whites being in charge, then all we had to do was put the blacks in charge and the problem would be solved.'

It was simply a matter of raising the right flag. They may have to put up a fight, but it was nothing Malema's young mind could not contemplate, and he was ready for battle when Ramaphakela began to rope the young boys in very, very slowly in the first few months of 1990. There were only four of them and they were carefully hand-picked, their new master told them. What was critical was that they keep their activities under tight wraps. It was their secret, and theirs alone. One false move, one whisper to family or friends in Masakaneng, and they would be out.

'I told nobody,' Malema says. 'Nobody.'

During their first few months, Ramaphakela talked to them about the basics of the struggle and the importance of armed resistance and why the ANC was resorting to heavier means. He used to take them to a dry riverbed in a stretch of wasteland at the back of the township and teach them what he felt they needed to know.

He got them to stockpile tyres, from old cars and trucks, for barricading roads. He talked to them about combat activities. He gave them some physical training. And he eventually taught them how to use a Makarov 9mm pistol.

First he taught them how to focus their aim, and then one day a year or so later he loaded the gun with live ammunition and got each of them to pull the trigger.

'And he taught us how to dismantle it and clean it and put it back together,' Malema remembers.

'I was teaching them to be brave,' Ramaphakela says. 'And even if they were never going to be used in combat activities, I knew I would use their fearlessness to penetrate and gather information and infiltrate other organisations in the township. At some point we wanted to make sure AZAPO [Azanian People's Organisation, another black anti-apartheid movement] never existed in our township. But we didn't want confrontation with them. We wanted to outmanoeuvre them on political strategy. And that's where I knew I could count on the likes of Malema to help with gathering information.'

By this time the mood in South Africa had begun to change. The troubled 1980s had ebbed into 1990 and Nelson Mandela was released from prison after 27 years of incarceration. Though Malema had heard mention of the famous prisoner, it was only when Madiba walked free on 11 February that Malema began to fully understand his importance.

The ANC, which had been outlawed by the racist regime 30 years earlier, had been unbanned 10 days before Mandela's release and with it the veil of secrecy was beginning to lift from black politics and – there was talk of little else on the streets of Seshego. Beyond the northern township, South Africa was dizzy with expectation, and Julius Malema found himself caught up in the thick of it. He was very young at the time, but he remembers loving every minute. The world around him was taking on a very different hue.

When Malema relays his story to me or to anyone else, his starting point is always 1990, when he was nine and the ANC became the ruling party in waiting and his political career began.

'But I don't remember Malema being with us in 1990,' says Thabo Makunyane who had been released a year earlier from Robben Island, the former blacks-only prison island located 12 kilometres off the coast of Cape Town and where hundreds of anti-apartheid activists were holed up during the struggle years. The decision to legalise the ANC that February had taken the party leadership by surprise. Its membership had grown during its three decades underground and was aligned to a leadership exiled in Tanzania, but in the absence of any formal network of branches in South Africa they now had the hurried task of establishing the necessary structures and offices to accommodate its domestic members as well as the thousands who were beginning to return from exile. Convenors were quickly appointed around the country to do just that, and Makunyane was named the point man for Malema's home province. He was naturally familiar with all of the cadres, old and new, but he does not remember Malema.

'Definitely not,' says Makunyane. 'But then again, I spent a lot of time travelling throughout the province at that time ...'

But Malema talks about how, shortly after he celebrated his ninth birthday, he was drafted into the Masupatsela, the children's social wing of the ANC, when he donned his marshal's uniform for the first time. Polokwane was organising a rally for Elias Motsoaledi, a local man (and uncle of current national health minister Aaron Motsoaledi) who had been sentenced to life for sabotage along with Mandela and seven others at the Rivonia Trial in 1964. Racial segregation was so entrenched in the country by then that it existed even in prisons. Seven of the eight were sent to Robben Island, while the only white man among them was imprisoned at the whites-only jail in Pretoria. Mandela, the most high-profile of the eight, was held in isolation on the island and later removed to Pollsmoor prison on the mainland, but the rest of the black so-called Rivonia Trialists remained on Robben Island until their release in late 1989. When South Africa turned the corner in 1990, homecoming celebrations were laid on for all of the Trialists, and in the case of Motsoaledi it took place in the stadium in Seshego, within walking distance of Malema's house.

By then the young boy had also captured the attention of Lawrence Mapoulo, today a provincial power man on the back of Malema's influence. At the time he was a taxi driver and had joined the Seshego branch of the ANC shortly after the liberation movement was unbanned, like many more who flocked to the organisation at that time. Attaching oneself to the ANC during the struggle era came with enormous sacrifice and little or no advantage, but the latecomers were plentiful when the outlook began to change. But more of that later.

The branch operated out of a small unit over a shop at the Mabenkeleng shopping complex in Zone 1, and Malema made sure that he made himself known to Mapoulo. The youngster was like his shadow, constantly nipping at his heels. Every event he organised, every cat-fight that took place, the young boy was there.

Mapoulo was one of many who helped organise Motsoaledi's homecoming. They were expecting a record turnout at the Seshego stadium and he needed all the help he could get, so he roped Malema in as one of the marshals. He told him he was to be there at the crack of dawn and was to be decked out in full regalia.

Malema wore his old school clothes: a short-sleeved khaki shirt and matching full-length khaki trousers. Pinned to the epaulettes was an ANC badge and pulled down over his unkempt Afro hairstyle was a black beret, the signature cap of resistance.

It didn't matter to him that the clothes were hand-me-downs, nor did he think twice about the fact that the soles of his shoes had already worn thin. The ANC had called him to duty. In his young mind he was a comrade now, a big man in the making.

'And there's nothing that you can tell me about the ANC that I don't already know,' he now says.

Nobody in his family – not his grandmother, his mother, his aunts or his cousins – was aware of what the junior member of the family was up to. It was surely just innocent mischief, they thought, the stuff of young boys.

According to Sarah, his grandmother, it was not until Malema was twelve and had hopped onto a bus to Johannesburg for the funeral of Chris Hani (a former leader of the South African Communist Party (SACP) who was assassinated in 1993, while he was at the prime of his political life and certain to play a leading role in the imminent democratic dispensation) that they realised he was kicking up dust on the fringes of the struggle, a fact she likes to share with a certain degree of pride now.

Throughout that day in April when Hani was being laid to rest, Malema was nowhere to be found in Seshego. Not even his friends knew that he had planned to sneak onto one of the buses taking the comrades to Gauteng.

'Every time I tried to get rid of them, I would turn a corner and they would be there,' Malema remembers. When he finally managed to shake them off, he found his moment and, faster than a March hare, darted for the nearest ANC bus.

He would later tell the Johannesburg High Court during the hate speech trial in 2011 that he was carrying a pistol when he boarded that bus, which he claimed the leadership of the ANC had given him, and that he brandished it with confidence when he and his party seniors ventured into the suburbs of Johannesburg that evening, taunting the local white residents (though in all the hours I spent talking to him about this event, not once did he mention the gun or the evening adventures).

Makunyane was co-ordinating the buses that day and he doesn't remember Malema being armed, though Ramaphakela insists he gave the pistol to him.

'It was a Makarov. It belonged to the MK. I was using it and I gave it to him,' are his exact words.

For the second, if not the third or fourth time during our conversation, Makunyane raises his eyes in mock surprise at what he is hearing.

Whether Julius was armed or not was the farthest thing from Sarah's mind. That was not her concern. She just didn't know where her grandson was that day.

'We knew nothing about what he was up to until he came home,' she says.

It was not something she or the other family members found easy to come to terms with at the time. Though the ANC was no longer an illegal organisation, fear of political involvement was still widespread, but they could do nothing to stop him. Every spare moment the youth had he gave to his new-found comrades, particularly in the run-up to the 1994 elections.

'By then we all knew him,' says Makunyane. 'He was every-where. And he was a popular youth.'

In the period before the first democratic elections of 1994, Malema did whatever odd job was asked of him. He hung posters. He helped with registrations. He did the legwork in organising events.

'Not long after that, I even bought him his first cell phone,' Makunyane remembers. He was a ready foot soldier for the cause, and the comrades helped him as much as he helped them.

'He would come looking for taxi money,' recalls Sam Rampedi, another local politician. 'And I would give it to him. He was just a young activist and his heart and mind was in his work. He was the kind of youth you wouldn't hesitate to help. He was determined. And it was all in the name of the ANC.'

That's the tragedy of Malema during his 20s: he started out

with his head in the right place, but his moral compass weakened as his political strength grew. It only took a few years in formal positions in the ANC to corrupt him.

While he insists he joined the ANC in 1990, it is unlikely that he had any substantial grasp of formal politics at that time. He was lured more by the mischief and excitement of the period than by any real understanding of what South Africa was about to witness, or the complexities that had brought the country to that point, or indeed what lay ahead.

It is also possible that his upbringing, fragmented and difficult as it was, played an even bigger part in his decision to throw himself wholeheartedly into the embrace of the ANC, a political party of adults.

Malema never knew what it was to be shouldered by an older male figure. As mentioned, he had never known his father. His grandfather had left the house before he was born. The only older male in his life was an uncle who lived with him, but he eventually buckled under the strain of a nervous breakdown.

Then at the age of eight or nine, Malema found himself among people who were old enough to be his parents: men and women who regaled him with great stories about the struggle and exciting yarns about exile, or what life was like behind bars for those who had chosen to stay behind, and their gallant efforts to put an end to white rule.

'There was only one person that I was older than and that was [Jacob] Lebogo. But the rest of them, each of these people could have been my father,' he says. And they each had an enormous influence over his young mind.

Malema was deep in his element, as any child of his age would have been. In his mind, these people were heroes. He was in awe of them and could hardly believe his luck. From a fairly hellish life and a humdrum township upbringing, Julius Malema woke up one morning to find himself in the thick of a liberation movement that was no longer outlawed, a political party that was the talk of the country and which was on a steady march towards victory in the elections of 1994. It couldn't get much better than this in the young boy's mind. And there was no going back. From then on, he began to live and breathe the liberation movement in whose structures he was becoming embedded, starting out in the youth and student movements that were being established in schools all over the country.

Malema attended schools in the township, starting out at Mponegele Lower Primary before moving to Kgobokanang Senior Primary, a school that he left because it used corporal punisment. He then spent a few years at Letlotlo Senior Primary before attending Mohlakaneng High School.

It was during his years at Letlotlo and Mohlakaneng, in the years immediately after 1994, that Malema truly began to cut his teeth as a political activist. He had joined the Congress of South African Students (COSAS), the ANC-aligned student movement that exists at the high school level. As soon as he turned fourteen he joined the ANCYL, which had been formally re-established in 1991. He kept his ties with older comrades in the ANC all the while, attending rallies and meetings whenever he could, growing more and more confident in himself and his new place in the world as he shed the schoolboy carapace.

It was a time of great change in South Africa, and it was no different for school students. They were speaking out about their rights, demanding better learning conditions, and politicising playgrounds with the establishment of Student Representative Councils (SRCs).

For the black teachers, who had spent their entire professional lives compromised in the inferior system of black education, what they were witnessing worried them. In the early days of apartheid, the racist regime enforced an inferior form of education exclusively for blacks, known as Bantu Education. The thinking of Hendrik Verwoerd, the chief architect of that awful plan of social segregation, was that the quality of education blacks had received until then from the missionary-run schools was 'misleading' for the natives as 'there is no space for him . . . above certain forms of labor' in the white-only communities 'where he is not allowed to graze'. The Bantu (a collective term for languages spoken in central and southern Africa) system was introduced in 1953 and black teachers were paid by the white government to impart this sub-standard form of learning. They were often regarded with a degree of suspicion, if not disappointment, by their own communities, a sentiment that hardened during the post-1994 transition because the institution of apartheid did not end overnight with the fall of the white government. The teachers sensed this new unease, particularly from their own students, who were questioning their authority. The new black government was promising to bring change, but the teaching community was not sure what kind of change or what it would mean for them, and their initial reaction was to resist it.

Jeff Legodi was the principal of Mohlakaneng when Malema was a student there, and he tried to prevent the students from establishing an SRC. Malema claims he was expelled because of it, though Legodi and other teachers say Malema was never forced to leave the school.

Malema also takes credit for leading a campaign to dislodge Legodi, who was part of the management structure of the old set-up and regarded as an obstacle to reform by the new authorities. But Legodi insists he resigned of his own accord in 1999.

'I had more influence over Malema than he could ever have had over me,' he claims all these years later.

While the former principal is set on downplaying Malema's role as the school ringleader, there are a few truths that point to the raffish and fearless nature of the budding youth leader.

Onismas Letlalo was a teacher of history, fond of laying down his own rules and whipping his students into line. One day he went too far and gave some young girls a severe beating that sent them limping to Malema for help. He called Joyce Mashamba, who was then a provincial minister of education in the Limpopo government, to relay to her what had happened. Within minutes, she and her team were marching through the school gates demanding answers.

Journalists who reported on that area and era and who covered the student protests remember Malema well and how he would inevitably creep into their stories. A ringleader then as now, he was usually a part of the township student protests, if not the one behind them, and always on the frontline with something to say.

'That's true,' claims Thomas Namathe, who was a teacher at the school and went on to become deputy principal in Malema's time. 'Malema would never allow anyone else to speak in his name or in the name of the students. If the media came to cover a story and we, as the staff, tried to give our point of view, he would be the first to speak up on the side of the learners.'

'I was enjoying student politics,' Malema says as he thinks back to that era. 'It was clear to me what our rights were as students and what we should fight for. It was well defined. I could see the path of student politics clearly.'

Legodi suggests this should come as no surprise because Malema's school fees were paid by ANC members and the youth was a willing handler of their dirty work in return.

Although the former principal refuses to say who it was within the party who paid the youth's fees, if there's truth in it at all, it did not stop Malema from speaking out against the ANC. In 1997 he was elected provincial chairperson of COSAS in Limpopo, a position that allowed him to cast his net further afield than the township of Seshego. Not long after that, he decided to take on Joe Phaahla who had replaced Mashamba. Malema was of the view that Phaahla was also dragging his heels on some reform issues.

You are 'a contraception to transformation,' Malema told him in a comic public statement that he circulated on every media platform that would care to carry it at the time. The ANC tried to rein in Malema, telling him that as if the gaffe in his choice of words was not in itself bad enough, it was not right to turn on one of his own in such a manner.

'Phaahla asked me to have a word with him,' Makunyane remembers. 'But, hey . . .' he says, shaking his head slowly from side to side.

Phaahla then threatened to sue Malema if he didn't lay the matter to rest. But the words fell on deaf ears. Malema had no fear.

Those in the ANC who express surprise at Malema's behaviour today ought to think back to his teens. This man has been a long time coming.

As much as Malema lacked fear, he also lacked focus at school. He was distracted by his political activism and his schoolwork hardly got a look-in. His teachers say they couldn't get through to him, that his mind was elsewhere, but that this didn't make him the school dunce either. He was a good listener when he cared to listen, and he had a remarkable ability for recall. They just couldn't get him to settle down to books.

Nor did he give a hoot about his appearance and would file into the classroom most mornings looking the worse for wear. He was scrawny and skinny at the time and wore a large Afro. Yet despite his waif-like frame, he struggled to get a school uniform to fit him, so he invariably wore his long school pants flying at half-mast throughout his high school years.

The ill-fitting trousers were not exclusive to Malema. In township South Africa they were called 'Don't touch my shoes' and his peers remember that he wore them day in, day out. Outside school hours his wardrobe varied little. He was a carefree youth who wore open sandals and short pants, always topped with an ANC T-shirt.

Not today. When he was his late 20s, Malema became a slave to top-end designer labels and all sorts of gimmickry associated with his new money and his puffed-up image of himself. But as a teenager, he had no interest whatsoever in fashion and that he didn't look too stylish bothered him little at the time. He found his kudos in his activism instead.

In June 2000 he decided to run for national president of COSAS, a position that was ironically held at the time by Lebogang Maile, the young man who would later try to unseat him as ANCYL president in 2011. As a provincial chairperson of COSAS, Malema sat on the national executive body of the student organisation and enjoyed the support of many of his peers in that group in his bid for the presidency, Maile included.

'It wasn't difficult to support him because he was very courageous. He was militant, when we needed militancy. And he was a leader. That much went without saying,' says Maile today of the Malema of yesterday.

However, at the branch level it was a different matter. The vast majority of branches favoured Kenny Morolong, who was the provincial chairperson of COSAS in North West province. A month ahead of the June conference, when all the branches had spoken and nominated their preferred candidate, it was clear that Morolong would win the race. He had the backing of six of South Africa's nine provinces, while Malema had only Limpopo, Gauteng and Northern Cape behind him.

'But just a few days before the conference, rape charges mysteriously surfaced out of nowhere,' Morolong remembers. 'I was accused of raping Mosa Molale,' a woman Morolong was intimately involved with at the time.

'There were no criminal charges preferred against me. There was no criminal investigation to determine whether such allegations existed. I was simply told that I had raped a member of COSAS, a woman who was a member of the provincial executive committee in my province. And the NEC suspended me,' on the grounds that it couldn't field a candidate with such allegations against him.

Morolong was innocent, he hadn't raped Molale or any other woman, but he knew he was a threat to Malema's ambitions so he decided to defy the suspension and attend the conference, which took place in Johannesburg. But security denied him entry. And when he was turned away, the delegates, whose support he still enjoyed, went wild.

Fikile Mbalula, who was then the secretary-general of the ANCYL, was also attending the COSAS conference. As a senior to the COSAS delegates, he appealed to them to negotiate their way out of the crisis and try to settle on a consensus leadership. He proposed that Morolong would become president and Malema would be his deputy, but the delegates refused to accept it. They wanted to elect their president and deputy president by a vote only. They wouldn't have it any other way. Then, as the conference was about to resume, all hell broke loose and the delegates started fighting.

'I started receiving death threats. I was told I wouldn't live. I even remember having to go to the bathroom with two well-built men escorting me,' says Morolong.

The havoc continued and the violence worsened.

Eventually Molale spoke up and denied that she had been raped or that she had laid charges, but her words came too late. Some senior ANC people were brought in to try to break the deadlock, but to no avail. Winnie Madikizela-Mandela, who had been divorced from Nelson Mandela since 1996 but still played an active role in politics, was then called in and briefed about what was going on. She quickly assessed the matter for herself and a short while later disbanded the conference. It resumed a year later, but Morolong was no longer a contender.

'Every time I tried to attend a COSAS meeting after that, I was threatened or bullied. And I eventually resigned. It was one of the most painful periods of my life. Even though it was only student politics, and it might not sound like much to you, it meant everything to me. Coming from my background, I knew what it meant to fight for our rights. And back then, I really thought this would be my life. But I just couldn't take it any more. And I left.'

A short while later Morolong started to drink heavily and his fondness for the bottle eventually got the better of him, reaching an all-time low at the end of 2002 when one of the ANC's provincial leaders had him checked into rehab. He celebrated his 21st birthday in the clinic and was discharged only in May 2003.

'And I have never drunk alcohol since, though I will always be a recovering alcoholic,' he says.

Today he's a member of the provincial executive committee of the ANC in the North West. Youth politics passed him by entirely. Malema, meanwhile, pushed on to greater heights: a year after the shambolic election, he ran again for the presidency of COSAS.

But in the run-up to that conference he found himself in a bind. He had a physical temper to match his vicious tongue and he pummelled a peer's face so badly with his fists that his opponent's mother wouldn't allow him to leave the house for weeks because his face was such a mess. She threatened to bring charges against Malema.

The COSAS election was only a few months away and Malema knew that if the boy laid a charge, there was a good chance he wouldn't make it, so he asked Ramaphakela to talk to the boy's family instead. Ramaphakela obliged and it turned out to be nothing that a small 'donation' couldn't put right. When I reminded Malema of this all these years later, he threw his head back and laughed heartily.

Malema won the election comfortably. That was in 2001 and he was 20, though still in high school, which would not have been at all uncommon at that time, or even now. He moved to

Johannesburg to be close to the national offices of the student movement, which were housed in the ANC's headquarters.

Malema headed straight for Hillbrow in the inner city, an area that is often referred to as the Bronx of the South African metropolis, and he rented a small flat with two of his friends in the Fontana block of flats. A brief stint in the notorious high-rise Ponte Towers followed until he finally settled down in a flat opposite Oriental Plaza in Fordsburg, on the edge of the city centre.

By then the school books were well and truly forgotten, though Malema was still enrolled at Mohlakaneng and registered to sit his Matric – the national end-of-school exam – a year later. But Seshego was more than four or more hours away from Johannesburg by car, and given the physical distance that separated him from his classroom, he decided to attend some classes at a high school in Soweto instead, though he mostly stayed away from school altogether, setting a fine example to the millions of young South Africans he was leading as head of the high school student movement.

The least he could do was sit his exams, though he fared badly and failed most of his subjects. He got a C in English, a D in History and an E in his mother tongue, Pedi, as well as in Afrikaans. There was an F in Geography and a G in Woodwork, both of them at standard grade.

Years later, his Matric results started popping up in email inboxes all over the country when one of his many adversaries tried to shame him. Maropeng, the mother of his child, contacted him to warn him what was happening, but there was little he could do about it. Before long a copy of his results certificate landed in the lap of the media who were quick to splash it across the front pages of the country's main newspapers. It was the G in Woodwork that tickled most people.

'At least we know he'll never make a cabinet maker,' quipped one wit at the time.

In his own defence, Malema says he never actually wrote the Woodwork exam. Rather than not show up, 'I just went in and wrote my name at the top of the exam and walked out' without writing another word, he says.

Did he feel shame or embarrassment about his results, particularly when they became public knowledge?

'That's what it was,' he says. 'I was an activist first. I still am. I always will be.'

Despite what he says, I do believe the exposure of those results bruised Malema in a big way. By nature, he's a very proud person. He is also extremely clever, despite the public opinion of him as a young buffoon, but he had failed the one exam against which so many South Africans benchmark an individual's intellectual ability. That was the key point about Malema, which was always overlooked: he didn't have a formal education or training worth speaking of, but that did not make him stupid. His ability to manipulate information – one of the key definitions of intelligence – is as acute as his ability to recall it, which is what makes him the cunning and wily character that he is.

His other big failing in the eyes of the public was his poor grasp of English, which is not his first language but his fourth (after Pedi, Sotho and Afrikaans). When he began to introduce himself, his iron nerve and revolutionary posture, to South Africa in those early months of 2008, he spoke a vulgar kind of English that was made all the more crass by the content of his political message. The chattering classes had a belly-full of laughs when his desultory Matric results started doing the rounds, which was in poor taste.

Malema didn't make much of it publicly at the time, but what was telling was a short text message he forwarded to me at the end of 2010. He had received it from the University of South Africa (UNISA), the country's distance learning institution, where he was studying for a two-year diploma in Youth Development. In a few words the SMS conveyed to him that he had completed the course and passed it. By forwarding it to me, it somehow seemed important to him to have it known. One small detail weighted with sentiment.

A few months later he enrolled for a Bachelor of Arts degree at UNISA. Though his major has still to be decided, he has started out with two subjects: Communications and African Languages. Neither is a subject one would associate with Malema, least of all Communications: his track record for meaningful dialogue is often wanting. But he insists it's a stepping stone and that his major is more likely to reflect his chosen career of politics, which he feels will be enhanced by a university degree.

Again, it's not something he talks much about in public, though he seems to take his studies seriously. In May 2011, when the local government elections took place, he went home to Polokwane to cast his vote, with the national TV crews on his tail as he walked to the polling station with his grandmother by his side. But a few minutes later he was at his desk preparing for an exam the following day, while the vote count got underway. After such a strong performance on the campaign trail, his absence during the count was noticeable, but he made up for it a day or so later when he turned up at the Pretoria count centre, untied his tongue and started performing for the cameras. A journalist challenged him to have a public debate with Lindiwe Mazibuko, an African woman of roughly his age who heads up the opposition Democratic Alliance (DA) in parliament. The DA is widely regarded as a white, liberal party, both of which are anathema to members of the former liberation movement. His response was quick and quirky. He told the reporter he had no interest in taking on Mazibuko: she was only the 'tea-gal', in his view, and she should stay in the kitchen serving 'the madam'. It was the madam he wanted to meet. The madam was Helen Zille, the white leader of the party.

'The madam' was, and regrettably still is, the title the 'black maids' use for their white bosses, at the request of the white women. (Equally unfortunate is the title of 'the master' that is reserved for the white men of the household.) For millions of South Africans, no other title could have been more apt for Zille.

Though she has earned her stripes in the opposition ranks and grown her party's base phenomenally, Zille is a hardened woman with a strong, authoritarian streak. She leads the party with an iron fist and can be woefully patronising, and has let slip a number of gaffes that have made many people question her real social and political outlook. In the eyes of black nationalists, she is a dirty relic from another era and by referring to her as 'the madam', Malema scored an ace on behalf of his people.

Zille, whom Malema on other occasions referred to as a 'political toddler', has regularly been the butt of his debased sense of humour. A few years previously she had had Botox treatment on her face and openly admitted to it, because many believed her stern look was undermining her political profile. Malema was quick to pounce, accusing her of 'using Michael Jackson tactics'. He later warned the public that 'she is plastic' and 'If you can fake your own face, what about the policies?', a comment that got the whole country laughing.

The bite of his wit was as legendary as his extreme and radical politics. In the run-up to the 2009 general elections the running commentary was questioning the ANC's ability to secure a two-thirds majority under Zuma's leadership, to which Malema responded with a memorable blasé line: 'We are tired of a two-thirds majority. Our aim is a three-thirds majority'. He talked about how the Youth League was like a factory that churned out great leaders like Nelson Mandela, but how Mangosuthu Buthelezi, the leader of the black opposition Inkatha Freedom Party, was nothing but 'a factory fault'.

Wit to one side, though, there was also a very threatening and dangerous side to Malema, and there always had been. In 2002, during his COSAS days in Johannesburg, he kicked up a political storm in the centre of the city when he led the student movement in a violent march through the downtown area.

The Education Department had said it wanted to enforce a ruling that the gates to all schools be locked during teaching hours to try to keep crime from their doors as a safety measure for the students. COSAS was against the move and decided to stage a protest in response. The authorities forbade the march, but the thousands-strong student movement defied the order and went on a rampage. Their marchers looted shops, smashed windows, turned hawkers' stands upside down, damaged parked cars and left an unsightly trail of destruction in their wake.

Malema was its ringleader and the leadership of the ANC called him aside a few days later, demanding that he do something about what had happened, but he shrugged off their request, gave them his back and walked in the opposite direction.

In the meantime, he had been drawn under the wing of Madikizela-Mandela, who began to groom him in the art of politics and rebellion. He would spend hours in her company, and often days at her Soweto home, where he found shelter through thick and thin, and he was quick to return the compliment when she, as a member of parliament, was convicted of fraud and theft in 2003. He told the courts they were being racist towards the Mother of the Nation, as she is widely known.

'We are prepared to do anything in our power to ensure that she is not in jail,' he touted at the time. 'If that means burning the prison she is locked in, so be it.'

She didn't forget him for it and sat by his side throughout the hate speech trial in 2011.

'He is my product,' she now claims.

'She taught me public speaking and confidence,' he says in response.

'His rebellious attitude is part of the process of growing up,' she adds. 'He will make a great leader one day.'

★

Malema was not thinking beyond his future in the ANCYL when he returned home to Polokwane in 2003 after his tenure as COSAS president ended. His friends had been lobbying for him to come home and run for the position of provincial secretary of the organisation.

'We wanted a more militant Youth League to bring about change in Limpopo because we had entered into a slump,' says Lehlogonolo Masoga. He had been a close friend of Malema's since the mid-1990s when their paths first crossed, at a time when Masoga was rising through the provincial ranks of the South African Students Congress (SASCO), the university-based ANC-aligned student organisation, while Malema was working his way up through the provincial structures of COSAS. Though the two young men were different in character, they both opted for a militant style of politics. When Malema began to emerge as a national figure, he and Masoga had a bitter falling out, but even so his erstwhile friend remembers the side of Malema that kept them together.

'I liked his bravery,' Masoga says. 'And I liked his fearlessness. He stands by what he believes in. He is never afraid to put words on his views and not everyone has the kind of courage that he has. Very few can think on their feet like he does. And he had what we were looking for in a provincial secretary back then. We were looking for change and we knew we would have to put up a fight.'

'You see, at that time the Youth League had become a trans-mitter belt for the ANC,' says David Masondo, who was a member of the ANCYL as well as the Young Communist League then. Today he is Limpopo's provincial minister for finance.

'We were concerned about the macro-economic policies that were being introduced by Thabo Mbeki, but they were not really being contested by the Youth League. So we had to shake it up,' says Masondo.

Julius Malema was nominated to do the shaking. He ran for

the position of provincial secretary at the end of 2003 and he won the race comfortably.

It was a position Malema held for several terms and with each passing year his power base began to grow. He did not confine himself to the ranks of the youth but began to mingle closely with the provincial leaders of the ANC, and through them slowly became exposed to the possibilities that came with party politics.

'You will respect me. You will. Because I am a leader of the ANC,' Malema told me in a heated moment in the course of writing this book.

We were in the middle of a telephone conversation and I had questioned him about something or other, the detail of which I cannot now recall though I do know that I was neither trying to bait him nor taunt him in any way.

Until that day, I had been saved the sulphurous side of his character that he reserved for the rest of society and I had little desire to change that. But as he unleashed his outrage that morning and ranted for a good 30 or 40 seconds down the phone line before I cut the call, I was reminded of Abraham Lincoln's words: if you want to test a man's character give him power. And to that I would add, 'especially at a very young age'.

Malema was in his late 20s at the time but that outlook had been coloured many years earlier. Though he was early in understanding the whole concept of power, his choice of words that morning showed me how shallow his understanding of himself really was.

5

Malema becomes a man

As fast as Julius Malema's political life was changing, so too were his personal circumstances, and 2006 marked one of the best and worst years of his life: he fell in love, fathered a child, lost his mother and at the heel of it all, he found his true place in the ANC.

While he was living in Johannesburg, Julius dated a woman named Trudy. He was a young, wild thing enjoying city life but she remained his steady girlfriend throughout it all. But not long after he returned to Polokwane, he met Maropeng and in her he met his match. That was the end of Trudy.

'Maropeng is from Seshego,' Malema told me. 'She's a township girl and she has a township mentality.' By that he meant she had a fiery personality, and that, like him, she was never afraid to fight her corner. She gave him a run for his money and he loved her.

I remember once, long after they broke up, sitting with him in his Johannesburg home chatting about something or other that was entirely unrelated to his personal life, and while we were talking he reached for his laptop and brought up a photograph of her that she had sent to him. 'This is her,' he said as he handed the laptop to me. 'This is Maropeng.' They had been separated about four or so years at that time, but there was no doubt about the soft spot he still had for her.

When they first started dating, Maropeng wasn't as much of a political activist as he was, though she didn't mind accompanying him to political rallies or wherever else his politics would take him. One evening, early in 2006, he arranged to pick her up at the house where she lived with her parents in Seshego. They were going to an ANC event.

He was running late and when she got into the car and told him she wanted to talk, his response was curt.

'Later, later,' he said, as he manoeuvred the car out onto the street.

'We need to talk,' she pressed.

'Sure,' he told her, 'but later.'

'I'm pregnant,' she told him.

He felt as if every drop of blood began to drain from him in that instant. He needed something to hold on to and he pressed his palms into the steering wheel, but his hands were already wet with the beads of sweat that were pumping from his palms and he couldn't keep his grip. He was in a state of complete shock.

'That night I got so drunk,' he says. 'Yo, I didn't know what to do, or who to tell. I never thought it would happen like that.'

The first person Julius turned to was Cassel Mathale, a man twenty years his senior and who was then the provincial secretary of the ANC. (Today he is the premier of the province, having continued that steady climb in parallel with Malema on the back of the Zuma victory.) Despite the age gap, he and Julius became good friends after Malema returned home to Polokwane, and as one of his main confidants it was to him Malema turned the following day.

It was no big deal, Cassel told him. He was to stand by Maropeng. She would have the child. Everything would turn out okay.

He then turned to his grandmother and the old woman gave him similar words of advice.

As the weeks passed Julius began to settle into the idea of becoming a father. Then one evening a few months later, as the couple were sitting together on the sofa in the living room of his house, Maropeng put his hand on her belly as the baby began to kick.

'Hey, what's the problem?' he asked her, in that distinctively gruff manner of his, instinct telling him to pull his hand away. But the two feet kicking inside Maropeng touched him in every respect, 'and then I started to demand to touch,' he remembers. 'And I thought something was wrong if I was no longer called to touch, or if he didn't kick.'

When Maropeng was about seven months pregnant, Florah, Julius's mother, died. It was a sudden death and it tore him apart. He had sailed through life without any real check on his emotions and his mother's death left him reeling. Hence when Maropeng began what turned out to be a drawn-out labour a couple of months later, Julius feared the worst. He took her to the hospital and remembers seeing her writhing in pain and gasping for breath, struggling to bring the baby into the world. The doctors put an oxygen mask over her face and he began to panic.

'I thought she was going to die. I thought: "No, man. Not again. Not two deaths: her and the baby, just after my mother."'

He sped home to relay to his grandmother what was happening at the hospital and she quickly put his mind at ease.

'She's not ill,' the old woman assured him. 'She's not going to die. She's giving birth. That's natural.'

A few hours later Maropeng gave birth to a baby boy and the couple named him Ratanang, the Pedi for 'love each other', he says.

It was 14 October, exactly two months after his mother's death.

The couple weren't married but they quickly settled into family life. Julius adored his son, his only child, and he enjoyed every minute he had with him in those early days.

But the bigger family, the ANC, was also beginning to call on him at that time. The landmark Polokwane conference was only a year away and the party had a battle on its hands to unseat

Thabo Mbeki and Malema was being called to task. He began to spend more and more time away from home, attending rallies, visiting branches, plotting the Polokwane putsch, and it wasn't long before Malema's political life took a toll on his relationship with Maropeng and the pair eventually split.

Ratanang continues to feature prominently in his life and he co-rears him as best he can and maintains a good relationship with Maropeng. He has never left a doubt in my mind about the big place the small child occupies in his life, and it is when he speaks about Ratanang that he reveals that softer side of his character, when there is not a trace of aggression or bitterness in his voice.

Though he makes space in his life for fatherhood, Malema hasn't had a steady girlfriend since he and Maropeng separated. There have been lots of women in his life, but no one else has come close to him.

That year, 2006, marked the period when the ANC took over Julius Malema's life. He had graduated from youth politics to the big league and there would be no turning back.

He began to develop a deep sense of self-importance that far outweighed his station in life and an arrogance that began to cost many people their standing in the party. Some of his oldest friends became his foes as he began to say and do as he pleased in the provincial ANCYL. He was a sharp political operator, but he was also a conceited political bully and those who dared stand up to him were dealt with, either by him or his henchmen.

Some branches, and even entire regions, across the province of Limpopo that began to question Malema's leadership style were disbanded. The first to go was the region of Sekhukhune and later Waterberg, both of which were later reformed in accordance with the way Malema wanted them structured, complete with his chosen comrades in the positions that mattered most.

By then, Fikile Mbalula was president of the ANCYL and

had become the face of the anti-Mbeki lobby. Members of the mother body had become concerned about what they perceived as a steady erosion of the party under Mbeki and the over-centralised and ossified leadership he had put in place. When the rank and file began to question the state of democracy within the ANC in 2005, Mbalula emerged as one of the leading voices of the discontent, in pretty much the same way as Malema is doing today.

Mbalula has a fiery character and is a no less able politician than Malema. He is also an excellent speaker and despite the dark and dubious side of his political dealings, he oozes gravitas and charisma and is one of the more popular leaders among the ANC's million-plus membership. Today he is a minister in Zuma's cabinet, but then, in 2005, he was neither a public office holder nor did he hold a position within the mother body, and it gave him the freedom to lobby the party membership for change.

Initially the pair didn't see eye to eye. During the early days of Mbalula's presidency of the ANCYL, Malema questioned his hard-line approach to the union federation COSATU and the SACP. Malema was more left-leaning then than he is today, and he and his provincial peers would openly question Mbalula when he put pressure on the alliance partners, or if he wasn't harsh enough in opposing Mbeki's macro-economic policies.

'There was a time when Mbalula wanted to disband us,' Malema remembers.

Malema and Mbalula eventually found common ground on Zimbabwe, when the latter expressed his staunch support for Mugabe's ZANU-PF party, and they became particularly close when in 2006 the lobbying for Zuma's comeback began.

Malema was only 25 at the time and he was about to become a prominent member of the posse that would cut short Mbeki's career in what would turn out to be a tough and dirty leadership battle that would be settled in his hometown of Polokwane at the 2007 party conference. It was fought long and hard for more than two years and caused a nasty and lasting split in the party, with all those who supported Mbeki entrenched on the one side and all who opposed him (rather than necessarily supporting Zuma) on the other. Neither faction was going to budge; there would be no compromise.

Thabo Mbeki had been groomed for leadership from an early age and appeared reluctant to step down any time soon, even if he had served his fair share of years at the top. But perhaps more important than maintaining a grip on power was his belief that this was a motley crew who wanted to step into his shoes and start pulling at the strings of the transition he had been orchestrating for so long.

In the run-up to the party conference in Polokwane, Mbeki watched a worrying tide rise up and gush towards him, comprising old enemies, some corporate chiefs, the trade union movement and factions from the left whose hopes of a mass insurrection against apartheid he had crushed towards the end of the struggle era in the 1980s.

All these years later, they were now about to crush Mbeki and riding on their shoulders was Zuma, the erstwhile deputy president of the party and the country whom Mbeki had sacked in 2005.

Zuma had been dropped because the corruption charges that were stacked up against him were beginning to weigh heavily on the Mbeki presidency. They were linked to the US$5 billion arms deal scandal from the late 1990s, a hugely fraudulent and controversial contract that the ANC has managed to keep buried this past decade, despite numerous investigations into it in South Africa, Germany, Sweden, England and elsewhere.

It is still the biggest scandal in the history of the democracy, and it started shortly after the ANC came to power and during Mandela's presidency. In 1996, the White Paper on defence acknowledged that the country faced no conventional military threat, there was no shortage of armaments (if anything, there was excess supply from the apartheid era) and that there was a real need to reduce defence spending and divert all available resources to the social reconstruction of the country.

Yet two years later, the government backtracked and decided to modernise its defence equipment. An affordability study was carried out that warned the cabinet against the expenditure and the ludicrous promise of a return of US$4 for every US$1 spent on armaments, but the deal went ahead a year after Mbeki became president. Hundreds of millions were paid out in kickbacks to a number of senior party and government people by the various international arms dealers that made up the winning consortium, which was not the most cost-effective or efficient of the contractors that had bid. In essence, the offsets were vehicles through which many of the bribes were channelled and the deal unleashed a culture of corruption in the country. By not allowing the case to be investigated fully, corruption became institutionalised as well. In the years that followed, sleaze began to escalate and spiked during the later Zuma presidency.

The truth about the arms deal began to trickle out in 2001 and within a few years Zuma's financial advisor, Schabir Shaik, was implicated in it, which eventually exposed Zuma's involvement. By then, he was deputy president of the country.

Most certainly Zuma was not alone, but Mbeki decided to fire him, fearful that if he didn't act decisively and remove him from the cabinet, they would all fall under scrutiny and the glare would go all the way to the top.

Mbeki was foolish if he didn't expect a reprisal in some form, but it is unlikely that he would have foreseen Zuma demand his pound of flesh in so spectacular a fashion as he did in 2007 when he challenged Mbeki for the party leadership, and that it would be Malema, a born foot soldier, who would appear at his side, ready and willing for action.

It was a tough battle, and though Zuma won the leadership in that Polokwane conference, it was only with 60 per cent of the votes: slightly less than half of the ANC's voting members were either still with Mbeki or solidly against Zuma in one of the most spectacular fallouts of the arms deal.

There was still a second hurdle to climb, though. The corruption charges against Zuma were still hanging over him and they would have to be removed somehow if he was to have a good run at the general elections that were to follow in April of 2009 and secure the ANC the comfortable majority it needed to rule in the heavy-handed manner it desired. If Zuma were to fall at that last hurdle, the chances were that all the colourful characters who had propelled him back to power would fall as well. There was no option but to pull out all the stops, at every level, to ensure that their man would walk free.

This second round of battle was not for the faint-hearted. It called for manoeuvres of an unorthodox nature and only the fearless could pull it off – Malema was about to prove himself an ideal candidate for the job for a second time.

In the meanwhile, Mbalula's term as ANCYL president was drawing to a close and he had decided on Malema as his successor. Mbalula's ambitions cannot be underrated: in 2007, as the curtain came down on the Polokwane conference, he was already thinking ahead to 2012 and his plans to become secretary general of the ANC. At his age, that was no small hope and to pull it off he would need to put the right people in the right places, particularly in the ANCYL, one of the party's key lobbying forces. Malema was his man.

The Youth League set their election for April 2008, to be held in Mangaung. Yet despite Malema's rise to prominence at Zuma's side in the comeback fight, he still didn't have majority support among the youth delegates at that time and he went into the conference with only a couple of provinces behind him.

'But if I didn't have provincial leadership structures behind me, I had a lot of delegates with me,' he says of that 2008 conference.

It was the COSAS conference from many years earlier all over again, and it is a feature of his following that has remained constant ever since: Malema doesn't always have the support at the top, but he has it on the ground, where it matters most.

Saki Mofokeng was the preferred candidate and he had the majority of provinces behind him. However, Malema was Mbalula's preferred choice and he won the contest by a very narrow margin of 1,883 votes to the 1,696 of his main challenger. The vote was disputed, though not settled, and the conference was adjourned until June.

When June came round and the second round of voting was about to take place, Mofokeng surprised the members by accepting early defeat. He called on his backers to support Malema and his team and toasted his opponent's win. It was the happiest glass Malema ever drained.

Mofokeng then carved out a successful niche in business.

Some delegates who supported Malema at the Mangaung conference a few months earlier are adamant that the vote was rigged and that Mofokeng would have sailed through if he had taken on Malema that June. Malema may have had support, but the numbers simply didn't add up.

One version of what happened in Mangaung was explained to me in the following way by a man who was a pro-Malema delegate at that time.

'We knew the numbers were tight, so we caucused (or gathered) all of the Malema supporters outside the conference hall. And we did a head count. And with that, we knew how many supporters he had, give or take.

'And as we were caucusing outside, all of the other delegates were inside the hall. They were told to go and register, but then we, the Malema camp, stood in line to vote. So by the time all the other delegates joined the queue, the top of the line was full of Malema people.

'Based on the count we had taken outside the conference

centre, we knew what we were dealing with in numbers. So when roughly that same number of people cast their vote, we knew that we would have to "manage" the rest of the delegates that followed, who weren't Malema supporters, if we were to ensure a Malema win. So at a certain point, we stopped the voting,' when they could technically assume a marginal victory in Malema's favour, he told me. And that's how they came up with a narrow margin that favoured Malema.

I have heard other versions of what happened. I have also been told that a group of youth approached Gwede Mantashe, the secretary general of the ANC, with evidence of a twist in the vote but that he refused to entertain their claims. It was still early days in the Zuma presidency and Malema and Zuma were then still very tight.

Lehlogonolo Masoga, Malema's chief campaigner that year, scoffs at any suggestion of vote rigging. Though the pair have had a bitter falling out since then, in the run-up to the Mangaung conference Masoga had travelled to every corner of the country drumming up support for his friend. A leg-up for Malema would have served Masoga well.

While Malema knew that his friend was loyal to him, he was also aware that Masoga was becoming hugely popular among the delegates he lobbied – and it bothered him. There was only one place at the top and that was his, and for the first time he saw competition where until then he had seen an old friend. A few months after he became League president, Malema saw his chance to make his move. He had retained his post as Limpopo provincial secretary until the disputed Mangaung vote for president was settled in that June, and then he prepared to resign from the Limpopo structures.

The provincial youth elected a young man by the name of Goodman Mitileni, who had been Malema's deputy and therefore was the natural choice as successor, yet despite the fact that Malema no longer belonged to the Limpopo League, he felt he had the right to choose who would succeed him and he wanted his childhood friend Jacob Lebogo to step into his shoes.

It was the South African spring of 2008 and by then Malema was settled in Johannesburg, but he was a regular visitor back home in Limpopo where he would see his former League peers. Malema's life rotates around the ANC and his friends are drawn from party circles or party benefactors and business people who have managed to find their way into the 'golden circle'. When the core of the provincial youth leadership decided to meet in Polokwane one Sunday afternoon in October, it was only natural that he would join them.

Malema expressed his objections to Mitileni's appointment, saying that he had wanted Lebogo to take that job. But the leadership managed to talk him down, pointing out that Mitileni had served his time and was the preferred candidate. Malema retreated.

He then tried a different tack, saying he wanted Lebogo to be Mitileni's deputy, but his comrades explained that there were other more senior and experienced people who should be considered. The Youth League couldn't be reduced to an organisation for friends, he was told. They pointed out that Lebogo had served less than a year as a regional secretary in the province and that it was unthinkable that someone with so little experience could leapfrog to the top in so short a period of time.

With that, Malema hit the roof. He pounded on the table, pushed back his chair as he stood to his feet and addressed his colleagues in angry terms.

'If Lebogo is not elected, then what brought us together . . . is over. And we will meet on the streets.'

All of those who were present that day can relay those words with ease, because they knew they were witnessing the end of an era and the beginning of a resurrection within their own ranks. Malema stormed out of the room, slamming the door behind him and a big freeze set in amongst the local youth. Though

Malema was living in Johannesburg, he had started an ugly spat amongst the locals in his name.

The saga dragged on until 2010 when Malema eventually got his way: Lebogo was elected as provincial Youth League secretary in a disputed vote and Masoga spoke out and began to cry foul. Only a very few, if any, had the courage of conviction to take on Malema, who was by then a very big player in South Africa's politics. But by daring to do so, Masoga quickly earned the support and respect of many in the province who had begun to tire of Malema's style of rule, and the stand-off between the two became entrenched.

Suddenly Malema was in trouble because Masoga's support was real. It wasn't enforced or imposed, as some of his was, and there were no stooges in Masoga's camp, which was beginning to swamp Malema's base in his home province. Malema eventually expelled Masoga from the party, but only after the debacle had been hauled through the courts.

By and large Zuma and the other ANC leaders turned a blind eye to their junior president and left him to his own devious devices. I remember sitting with some of these people in Polokwane one evening when they tried to reason with the ANC leadership in Johannesburg through Mantashe by phone, but there was neither the will nor the appetite on his part to deal with it. It was blatantly evident that something was going horribly wrong and that Malema was behind it. He was beginning to govern the Youth League like a fiefdom, and with a deadly iron fist, yet Mantashe and his peers refused to entertain the notion or examine the evidence that was brought before them.

The dereliction of duty on the part of the ANC leadership was staggering. It still is. And it is little wonder that Malema's arrogance began to take on life-size proportions from then on.

'You have to go back, you have to go very far back in the history of the ANC if you want to understand what is happening today,' Joe Matthews argued.

Before his death in 2010, at the age of 81, Matthews gave generously of his time to assist with the research for this book, recalling and interpreting the early chapters of the ANC's history.

A respected member of the party, whose affiliation stretched from the early Youth League days in the 1940s, through the struggle era and right through to post liberation, Matthews also hailed from a family with strong ANC roots and he was widely regarded as a custodian of the movement's liberation history until the day he died.

Before then, and drawing on his extraordinary capacity of recall, he added insightful comments and anecdotes about those earlier years. But above all, he gave a sharp interpretation of the past as I was trying to figure out the present.

'There are many events over the last 100 years that you must first understand before you can really appreciate all of the changes that are taking place today. Things take a long time to happen in the ANC.'

Julius Malema was also going back in time and re-interpreting the party's past so that it would help him in his plans to reshape its present and determine its future. In his political rallies, public statements and general utterances, he forever harked back to the past, more than anyone else in the ANC, because it was the only way he could really justify himself in the new South Africa.

6

(Re)writing history

As suggested earlier, Julius Malema became a deep 'scratch on the mind' from early on in his Youth League presidency. To some blacks, he was the embodiment of the nightmare they knew could happen but hoped never would; while to some whites, he breathed life into the nightmare they were always anticipating, the one that would finally vindicate them in their hardened beliefs that black politics would be disastrous for the country, and they dined out on his menacing gibberish on a regular basis.

'See, we told you this is what they are like. Look at him.'

'This is it. The rest are coming. It's over.'

'I said it, many times. That Mandela stuff was just a front.'

'I knew we shouldn't have agreed . . .'

On it went. But while South Africa tried to make sense of the scrofulous black 'boy' who had appeared in their midst, Malema and his main allies – all of whom belonged to the mother body rather than the ANCYL – began to hatch their plans to take over the ANC. Jacob Zuma had served his purpose by bringing Malema and his cohorts into the fold in return for their efforts during his comeback campaign, but the next stage of their plan was now upon them: to gain control of the party. To do that, they would call upon an era in ANC history when the youth took the lead.

Malema is well versed in the history of his party and knows how his forebears, the founder members of the ANCYL, hijacked the ANC during an ebb in its fortunes in the 1940s and transformed it into a movement that would serve its own aims. He is acutely aware of how the founding leaders of the Youth League – among them Nelson Mandela, Oliver Tambo and Walter Sisulu – managed within a few years of the League's formation to take hold of the reins of the ANC and dictate its course during the early years of apartheid. As he looks back today, what appeals most to him is how they kept their hands firmly on the leadership and effectively became the new ANC.

Today, Malema insists he is repeating history when he attempts to steer the ANC on a course of action that will reinvent the party, except that this time, he says, his plan is to complete the steps of the so-called National Democratic Revolution.

'We have three areas of strategic influence, which the NDR seeks to attain: political power, economic power and social power,' he once told me while at his peak.

'We are at the beginning,' he answers, when I ask him to rate the progress of the so-called revolutionary project on a scale of one to ten.

'Nineteen-ninety-four was the ushering in of one of the aspects of the NDR, which is political power,' while social power towards 'a non-sexist, non-racial, democratic South Africa' is still a work in progress. The big one, economic power, is where his mind is now focused. This, he believes, can only be achieved through the nationalisation of the country's assets, above and beneath the ground, and the general sharing of the country's wealth.

'Is socialism the end stage of the NDR?' I ask.

'Yes,' he replies.

Yet the ANC insists it is a multi-class, broad-church structure and rarely describes itself as a socialist party, or certainly not to the exclusion of other political faiths.

'We have a responsibility to safeguard the identity of the ANC as multi-class, an organisation that seeks to liberate our people.

Our immediate task now is the liberation of our people in an economic sense. As to what happens after, we will decide.'

Though some form of socialism would be the inevitable consequence should Malema's project see fruition, it is the part of his political plan that he keeps couched for now.

'You see, people are afraid of the word socialism and you must not pronounce it a lot,' he said as he became engrossed in one of our chats sometime around 2010. 'It will scare them. I might have houses. I might have watches. That's what the economic system dictates now. But when we've got an economic system that says that everything we have we need to bring together and share among ourselves, I will be the first one to surrender. I've got no problem with socialism. I've got a problem with socialists who want to hijack the ANC and without giving this phase of our revolution a chance to unfold. They want to take us immediately to socialism. That will have serious consequences.'

Malema's reference here is to the communist party of South Africa, whose members have become more powerful under Zuma's leadership than ever they were under Mbeki's. Blade Nzimande, the leader of the communist party, is currently the minister of higher education, while his deputy in the party, Jeremy Cronin, is the deputy minister of transport. Other communist notables are dotted throughout the cabinet, not least Pravin Gordhan, the minister of finance. While the likes of Malema are fond of warning of a rise of the communist flank, it is also true that by co-opting the communists into government, Zuma has weakened their presence in their own party and the SACP as a whole.

Either way, the end game for Malema is socialism and in his mind it is not a matter of if but when the socialist flag will be hoisted.

'In our lifetime,' he says, harking back to the era of Mandela, the fight for a free South Africa and the famous words of the former president.

As I say, that was a conversation I had with him in the first half of 2010, by which time the bitter spat he was about to have with Zuma was beginning to become apparent. Yet, even today, from the party's fringes, he still believes he was put on this part of the Earth for one reason only: to shake up the ANC, as his predecessors had done in the 1940s. However, the shades of difference that set him apart from that generation are vivid.

He does not have the formal education or social sophistication of his political forebears, and his style of militancy makes that of his ANC ancestors pale in comparison. Nor does he share their political orientation. Though he likes to call himself a national revolutionary democrat with a solid grounding in African nationalism, a political ideology advocated by the ANCYL in the 1940s, Malema is a neo-nationalist in practice and a national corporatist at heart, pushing for a closed political system through which the state will increase its control over the economic, social and all other functions of the country.

In the absence of any access to wealth or means of production, Malema's political forebears in the ANCYL pursued politics for purely ideological reasons, as Joe Matthews argued. They were referred to as the 'hire-purchase class', because given their lack of access to wealth, it was the best they could have hoped for at that time. Their struggle was not about advancing their own economic interests – they couldn't have, even if they had wanted to. They were black outcasts, fighting for basic human dignity.

Today, however, each step is carefully measured in terms of the financial interests and potential gains to be gleaned from resource-rich South Africa, which is why Malema appears to be fighting so hard for party control. His approach to politics, and more importantly his approach to business through politics as well as his conspicuous wealth and greed, show that any concern for the poor is an afterthought.

Perhaps the greatest similarity between the two generations is their resistance to communism. Old tensions between the nationalists and the communists, which lodged themselves in the bosom of South African politics many decades ago, are what Malema is bent on bringing to the fore again. In harnessing that conflict, Malema is taking on the big one: the real battle for the ANC, something that runs very, very deep in the ranks of the Tripartite Alliance and even pre-dates the formation of the ANCYL. (Tripartite Alliance is the term used to describe the co-operation between the SACP, COSATU and the ANC, an alliance that dates back to the struggle era. Though the ANC is the political force of the group, the unions and the communists hold senior positions in the ANC, and through that they also field national election candidates and hold substantial sway over government policy.)

That conflict highlights an even more critical point: the ANC's history is littered with examples of disunity rather than unity and has led to the kinds of factions from which Malema has himself recently emerged.

'It hasn't always been the united front that they will try to present in the run-up to the centenary,' Matthews argued. 'And that is important in trying to understand the faction to which Malema belongs today.'

What is worth noting too is that the ANC when it was formed in 1912 was, in many respects, as far removed from its own society then as the ANC of today is now becoming. In recent years, the former liberation movement has become a means to wealth for many of its members rather than a people-centred party pushing for a better life for all.

The 'gentlemen of our race', as Pixley ka Isaka Seme referred to his fellow founding fathers when they met to form the ANC in January 1912, pledged a break with the past and planned to mould a new kind of Africanism modelled on the politics of the Congress of the United States.

What spurred the move was exclusion from the Union of

South Africa, the new British dominion that had come into effect on the last day of May 1910 in the wake of the Anglo-Boer War of 1899–1902. By the end of it, the Boer republics of the Orange Free State and the Transvaal had been trampled upon by the British. Time would show, though, that it was not the Afrikaner community but rather the majority black population that would be on the losing side. Blacks found themselves politically disenfranchised, while right across the country they were cast to the fringes of social and political life.

Some groups representing black interests appealed to London to consider their protest in the years leading up to 1910 as the groundwork for the Union of South Africa was being laid. When it became apparent that their concerns were falling on deaf ears, they began to unite around the issue of black exclusion. By then there were many so-called 'native' political organisations dotted around the country, though only operating at regional levels, and it was clear their impact would be minimal without a nationwide movement. Hence at the 1908 South African Native Convention in the city of Bloemfontein, which is today known as Mangaung, a decision was taken to fill the void.

On 8 January 1912 and at Seme's invitation, large numbers of well-known African dignitaries and personalities from all over South Africa turned out in formal attire in Bloemfontein to attend the inaugural conference of the new organisation. Despite the writer Sol Plaatje's insistence that it be given an African name, it was launched as the South African Native National Congress, only to be renamed the African National Congress eleven years later. In its early years, it was simply known as Congress.

By and large the founders were an elite, all-male group. Many of them were chiefs or of aristocratic stock. Most of them had studied abroad or were drawn from the *kholwa*, the community of Christian converts who had studied at mission schools and were members of the African middle class.[1]

Among them was Seme, who became the first treasurer-general

of Congress. He had studied first at Columbia University in New York and later at Oxford University before moving to London where he trained as a lawyer. The Reverend John L. Dube, who at the age of 41 became the first president-general of Congress, was also a graduate of Columbia where he had studied to become an educationalist. Dube was the founder and headmaster of the Ohlange Institute in Natal, and was often dubbed the Booker Washington of Natal because of the influence of the African-American preacher on his thinking. He was also the editor of the *Ilanga lase Natal* newspaper.

Plaatje was elected the party's first secretary-general. A one-time court interpreter, he became better known as a journalist and later as the editor of the *Bechuana Friend*, a Kimberley newspaper, before claiming due fame for his 1916 literary work *Native Life in South Africa*. Later fame came with his translations of Shakespeare into Setswana. Thomas Mapikela, a successful building contractor who was also the president of the Free State Native Congress, was elected the speaker of Congress, and George Montsioa became its recording secretary.

Added to that mix were three vice-presidents, a chaplain-in-chief and a deputy, and seven paramount chiefs who bore the double title of honorary presidents of the South African Native National Congress.[2]

That first national executive of Congress comprised 'four ministers of religion, lawyers, an editor, a building contractor, a teacher and estate agent, an interpreter and Native Labour Agent (who recruited African mineworkers)'.[3] They were supported by an equally conservative core membership.

Without exception, the various records, books and accounts of early ANC history agree on one fundamental point: the main goal of the founding fathers of the ANC was to maintain their own social order rather than to challenge the weight of repressive white rule that was beginning to weigh heavily on black South Africa.[4] And yet the criticism that rains down on the ANC all these years later would suggest that little has changed. Today's ANC is scorned for its elitism and the way in which its core members dole out privileges for themselves and among a select few. The challenges of forging an inclusive society against the backdrop of the legacy of apartheid are as enormous today as the fight against white domination was back then, yet it is still an elite form of politics that continues to prevail. In its 100 years of struggle politics, the ANC has, in some respects, still to learn from its early failings.

When it was founded, the ANC was guided by its members' Christian teachings and liberal political outlook on life, as well as by Booker T. Washington who believed the solution to the American Negro issue was economic upliftment and self-improvement – an historic version of Thabo Mbeki's policy of Black Economic Empowerment – rather than political assertion, and it was that liberal outlook that robbed the men of Congress of the foresight that was required when they started out. They were first and foremost loyal subjects of the Crown of England before ever they were activists for the black cause. In his acceptance letter, Dube appealed to his members to believe 'in the sense of common justice and love of freedom so innate in the British character'[5] that would help them achieve their ideal of an African nation enjoying equal opportunities in the new dominion and through which they would contribute alongside Afrikaners and Britons to a better life for all.

That liberal political outlook did not oppose segregation *per se*. If the so-called natives, as one of three groupings in multi-racial South Africa, could enjoy the same basic rights – decent education, increased access to land, social freedom, legislative representation, economic activity, the franchise – as the whites, they would not object to the Union. In their naïveté, they lobbied for a racially impartial political system in a country that for years had tried to stamp out African existence in the interests of white settlers; and which, more recently, had found itself under the rule of the architects of the 1909 South Africa Act which was the forerunner to the unions of South Africa and white supremacy.

As Walshe notes, they were also advocating 'an expansive and outward-looking nationalism which could make little headway against the reality of the South African power structure and the exclusive, ethnic loyalties and narrow nationalism of white South Africans'.[6] They also underestimated the challenges of forming a Union-wide organisation in a largely rural South Africa at a time long before the dawn of technology. However, as Dubow also argues, it is easy to criticise the early movement, but 'to do so is to ignore the fact that the full implications of segregation were not yet clear', in those very early years at least.[7] Even so, they were slow to respond when the full picture began to emerge.

The first hint of what was to come only became apparent in 1913 when the Natives' Land Act, or Black Land Act as it was also known, was ushered in by the South Africa Party. This repressive piece of legislation was initially intended as a temporary measure pending the outcome of a land commission, but it endured for decades and not only resulted in an inhumane slump in the socio-economic conditions of non-white South Africans, but sharpened African nationalism as an ideology.

The overall thrust of the Act was to ensure the territorial segregation of the races by creating African reservations that would house the non-white population. As colour-coded con-tours were drawn across the country, little more than 7 per cent of the land (then measured in units called morgen and which represented 10.4 million of a total area of 142.5 million morgen) was allocated to 80 per cent of the population.[8] A negotiated settlement was not an option and restrictions were put in place for the purchase or rental of land outside the reservations, which resulted in overcrowding, while slum life in the urban areas emerged as an alternative.

Beyond depriving the natives of their land, the Act also severely curtailed their movement around the country and from farm to farm. Those who chose to remain on white property were forced to work 90 days of the year without pay. Earning power was vastly diminished with the termination of sharecropping, forcing blacks to live in squalor and killing that initial hope of Dube's of contributing to the new South Africa as an equal African nation.

That is what sparked Plaatje's famous line in *Native Life in South Africa*, which used apt words for living conditions under the Black Land Act: 'Awaking on Friday morning, June 20, 1913 the South African native found himself not actually a slave, but a pariah in the land of his birth.'[9]

One would have imagined that these new challenges would have given Congress a fresh political outlook, yet it still contented itself with non-confrontational forms of action, which Meli attributes to a leaning towards Mahatma Gandhi and his followers in the Indian community, though that interpretation conveniently overlooks the inherently conservative nature of the early ANC.

Instead, Congress petitioned Pretoria as well as London and sent two delegations overseas to argue its case in 1914 and again in 1919. Back home, the organisation widened its support base, and though it became the most widely recognised voice of black opposition and opinion, it held on to its vision of becoming an equal player in a multi-racial South Africa.

Though opinion against white rule had begun to harden in its ranks by the end of the First World War, in the eyes of the public its constitutional approach to the Union and the Land Act had failed. Furthermore, social unrest was mounting in urban South Africa and living conditions had reached a new low.

Just how low is evident in the following facts and findings of Walshe's:

- in both Natal and the Transvaal, one third of the African population was to be found on European-owned farms
- Africans outnumbered whites by eight to one in many

districts, with no possibility of accommodation in the already overcrowded reservations
- urbanisation was creating slums
- social injustice was creating a new-found cohesion among black South Africans
- there was a marked rise in protest against unjust laws
- a series of droughts increased the flow of migrant workers and added pressure on food prices
- a post-war recession led to increased taxation
- a cut in expenditure on African education followed, even at the time of a baby boom
- by 1924 only 702 African pupils were registered in secondary schools, representing 0.04 per cent of the entire African school-going population
- widespread industrial action and strikes were a natural consequence of socio-economic decline.

Sadly, similar findings exist today that point to an equally low standard of living. Nearly two decades after liberation, the term 'slums' has been discarded for the more respectable label of 'informal settlements', though there is nothing respectable about their living conditions. Worse still is that they now house more than 10 per cent of the entire population, and of the estimated five million people living in such squalor, the overwhelming majority are African. The informal settlements usually crop up on the fringes of the townships as more and more people flock to urban areas in search of something better. But township life can be just as degrading and lacking in basic services such as sanitation, roads, electricity, refuse collection and the like. The phenomenon of 'service delivery protests', which started in 2004 when people began to take to the streets demanding their basic rights, is a modern-day form of activism. Though education has become more accessible, its quality is abysmal. The public health system is heavily burdened by the HIV/AIDS epidemic.

Land reform is behind schedule. Corruption is out of control with estimates suggesting that 20 cents out of each tax rand is currently lost to graft and fraud. Unemployment is rife, and critically high among the young, with estimates reaching as high as 70 per cent. Hope of real social justice is wearing thin in the face of the 'elite politics' that has settled in under four successive ANC-led governments, with no sign of the ruling party taking sufficient heed of the alarm bells that are ringing around them.

Much like today, the early ANC had been napping, and in 1919 Clements Kadalie took them by surprise when he started a nationwide mass movement at the Cape Town docks that he called the Industrial and Commercial Workers' Union (ICU). Trade unionism was then still a relatively new concept in South Africa; the first union had only been established in 1881 in the wake of the gold rush and they were racially exclusive: despite the entry of blacks into the work force, unions had remained largely white in membership.[10]

However, what distinguished the ICU from other unions was not only its black rank and file, but also the fact that it did not have an ideological base and didn't follow trade union orthodoxy. Though it dealt initially with depressed wages and poor working conditions, it branched out to address the general grievances of the people and very quickly became a mass organisation. The initials of the ICU were translated into a powerful slogan, which began to echo throughout the country as a warning to white employers and oppressors: 'I see you, white man.'

'It eclipsed the ANC,' as Matthews put it. 'And it's the one big challenge that really stands out in the institutional memory of the ANC, one that should never be forgotten,' particularly in the light of the tensions today within the ANC itself and across the Tripartite Alliance.

Kadalie's union also showed the power of mass membership. In 1924, the ICU had a membership of 30,000, which more than tripled to 100,000 over the course of the next three years,[11] the kind of membership the ANC did not reach until the early 1950s.[12] Indeed, in 1947, ANC membership stood at only 5,517, according to Lodge.[13]

Much of the ICU's success had to do with Kadalie himself and his approach to politics. He was very different from the elite men of Congress. He was a man of extraordinary gravitas and had an uncanny ability to grip people when he addressed them. A platform trooper of note, he took on the plight of the poor with a passion they had not seen before. Kadalie emerged at a time when the people needed a leader who would be on their side.

In today's South Africa, it was a need for a similar kind of 'leader of the people' that brought Zuma back into the fold. In the run-up to the Polokwane conference, he presented himself as one of the masses, a man who resided on the margins of political life. But once ensconced in the Union Buildings, Zuma's pro-poor message changed, and halfway through his presidency – both of the party and the country – there was little that differentiated him from the Mbeki elite he had ousted.

With the platform vacant, it was Malema who ironically became the trooper, eclipsing Zuma as the man of the people until he was eventually expelled from the ANC in 2012. But until his demise, Malema furiously lobbied the sidewalks of South African life with an appealing pro-poor message, a platform he is still pursuing independently.

But to go back to the 1920s and to Kadalie, while his project was hugely successful, the ICU was wracked by internal tensions and eventually began to fragment by the end of the decade, yet the ANC failed to exploit the opportunity that was presenting itself. Instead, it was the Communist Party of South Africa (CPSA) that stepped in to fill the void. Though the CPSA was only formed in 1921, the political ideology that framed it had surfaced with the discovery of mineral deposits in the late nineteenth century. The diamond and gold fields attracted workers from all over the world who brought with them the idea of trade unionism and a socialist and Marxist outlook.[14]

It eventually led to the formation in 1915 of the International Socialist League (ISL), which was guided by the *Communist Manifesto* of Karl Marx and Friedrich Engels. And though the members were in favour of black social standing, Africans were wary of the ISL.

The ISL's secretary-general, David Ivon Jones, had given them good reason for doubt when he demonstrated a problematic ideological bent in an opinion piece he wrote in its weekly publication *The International* shortly after the ISL was formed. He reasoned along the following lines: if the native question could be tackled head on, it would shake the country's capitalist foundations, thus boosting the ISL's own political project and paving the path ahead. 'Not till we free the native can we hope to free the white,' he concluded.

This was understood by some to mean that the blacks were finally recognised as belonging to South Africa's working class. But the black sceptics' interpretation of those words was that the African could only be freed by the white man, which understandably infuriated many and nurtured mistrust amongst African activists that lingered for almost a decade. Indeed, it lingers still.

The mistrust was often mutual, as many white workers believed their black counterparts were too willing to sell their labour at below the market rate and therefore threatened their own existence.

But despite the tensions, the ISL continued to grow its support base. In 1917, it lobbied support among South Africans for the Bolshevik Revolution and issued pamphlets in English, Zulu and Sotho entitled 'We are South African Bolsheviks'. On the pages of *The International* they argued that Bolshevism was the answer to South Africa's racial problems. In 1919 Vladimir Lenin launched *The Communist International*, or Comintern, to unite communists all over the world according to the Russian orthodoxy. In 1920, as subordination to Moscow deepened, he laid out a list of 21 points he wanted communists all over the world to adhere to.

Meanwhile, Bill Andrews, one of the founder leaders of the ISL and a follower of instructions from Lenin, had begun to gather various political organisations under a single banner. In 1921 the CPSA was formed in Cape Town, though headquartered in Johannesburg with Andrews as its secretary.

There was not a single black delegate present at the inaugural conference and the CPSA remained a whites-only party until 1924, when it eventually opened its membership to blacks. Some far-sighted thinkers and leaders in its ranks finally acknowledged that 'the problems of the working class can only be solved by a United Front of all workers irrespective of colour'.[15] Jones's earlier remarks had finally been laid to rest. What also influenced the annual conference that year was the Young Communist League, which had been pushing for pro-African policies across the CPSA.

Within a few years the complexion of the CPSA had significantly changed and the negative perception harboured by many blacks had diminished. This eased the overtures the party was making to the ANC on Moscow's instructions, which wanted close ties with the black political movement.

In 1927, it began to make its mark when Eddie Khaile, who was a member of the CPSA's central committee, became the secretary-general of the ANC. At the end of that year the communists invited the then ANC president, Josiah Tshangana Gumede, to visit the Soviet Union. He returned a couple of months later armed with red rhetoric that has never been forgotten.

'I have seen the world to come, where it has already begun,' Gumede told his comrades. 'I have been to the new Jerusalem.'

Gumede was also the bearer of a militant message from Moscow that called on the communists and the nationalists to form a united front so that South Africa could become 'an independent Native (Black) Republic as a stage towards a workers' and peasants' government'.[16]

But the Soviet leaders were thinking beyond the tip of the African continent. They looked upon Britain, a bastion of the free market, as their main capitalist enemy and the only way to kill the enemy was to attack the British Empire by gaining ground in the colonies.

'Moscow thought that organizing liberation movements in the various British colonies, including South Africa, would greatly hasten the demise of capitalism,' according to Norval. 'The ANC fitted perfectly into this scheme'.[17]

Joseph Stalin, who was by then the leader of the Soviet Union, took it upon himself to openly reorganise the South African movements from Moscow. He demanded that the CPSA appoint blacks to all its top executive positions and in a piece he penned in *The Communist International* towards the end of 1928, he urged the party to 'pay particular attention to the embryonic national organizations among the native, such as the African National Congress ... Our aim should be to transform the African National Congress into a fighting nationalist re-volutionary organization against the white bourgeoisie and the British imperialists, based upon the trade unions, peasant organizations, etc., developing systematically the leadership of the workers and the Communist Party in the organization. The Party should seek to weaken the influence of the native chiefs ... by developing peasants' organizations and spreading among them the influence of the Communist Party.'[18]

If there is any credence to the theory that the communists tried to hijack the ANC, something that still sits sensitively with Malema and other members today, then it started around this time, but their best attempts bore few successes and the fate of Gumede marked one of their first failures.

Gumede's call for revolutionary change tapped into a budding militancy and radicalism in the ANC that gravitated towards these first overtures of class struggle that he also wanted to inject into the rank and file. However, a core section of the conservatives, deeply suspicious of the growing influence of the CPSA, stood firm in their objection to Gumede dragging the ANC into a class-based alliance. It eventually forced a contest at the 1930 annual conference and Gumede lost to Seme, one of the founders, by 14 votes to 39. The old conservative guard had returned.

Though Seme had come to prominence in 1906 with his groundbreaking essay 'The Regeneration of Africa' (for which he scooped Columbia's prestigious George William Curtis medal), and later as a founder of the ANC, his term as party president was the less remarkable period in his professional life during which 'Congress sank to its nadir', in the words of Walshe.[19]

Similarities between the ANC's state of affairs 70 years ago and those of today shouldn't go unnoticed, and the challenges facing the party under Zuma are practically mirrored in that earlier chapter of the ANC's history. According to Walshe,[20] Seme's presidency was characterised by a series of political sins. It was a time of organisational weakness and ineffectiveness, and Seme appeared unable to rein in radical elements emerging in the ANC's ranks. He neglected his national executive and attempted to grant the presidency extraordinary powers. Not helping matters was the fact that the ANC's mouthpiece, *Abantu-Batho*, folded shortly after Seme took over the reins and this further stunted the fragmenting movement.

Seme's name had also become tarnished outside the ANC with charges of corruption, for which he was struck off the Supreme Court's roll of attorneys in 1932 (though he was reinstated as a lawyer ten years later). And so it was that under the watch of one of its founding fathers the ANC sank to an all-time low.

In the words of the respected communist, activist and journalist Govan Mbeki, Thabo Mbeki's father, Congress was 'politically in midnight slumber'[21] by the end of the 1930s. The promises the founding members had made to one another and their people had yet to transpire.

When the ANC celebrated its jubilee in 1937, it was decided that a more aggressive anti-government direction was required and Seme lost the presidency to the Reverend Zaccheus Mahabane. One of Mahabane's first moves was to travel throughout South Africa, with his secretary-general, Reverend James Calata, to try to shake up the party's dormant structures and branches and revive the ailing movement.

A year earlier, then Prime Minister J.B.M. Hertzog had enacted the stringent Hertzog Bills, which were the next best thing to ethnic cleansing in their attempts to fine-tune the decades-old project of social segregation, yet Seme's ANC had failed to mobilise their members and supporters against the Bills, leaving a void that was filled by some non-ANC activists when they started the All-Africa Convention (AAC). Though it was never meant to challenge the ANC, but instead to create an umbrella-like structure for all black political organisations, the AAC was a warning that complacency within the ANC was no longer an option if it was to regain its pre-eminence in black South African politics. By the end of the 1930s, with the revival campaign in full swing, the ANC began to attract new blood with characters such as Z.K. Matthews (a cousin of Plaatje's and father of Joe Matthews), Reverend Tema, J.B. Marks, E.T. Mofutsanyana, Govan Mbeki and Gert Sibanda becoming members.

The party was showing signs of improvement when at the 1940 conference Calata encouraged 47-year-old Dr Alfred B. Xuma to stand against Mahabane. Xuma won by a hair's breadth – 21 of the 41 votes – 'so beginning, by the narrow margin of one ballot paper, a decade of leadership which was to transform Congress'.[22]

However, it was not for his radicalism that Xuma won the race, and it would not be for his militancy that the ANC turned over a new and critical leaf. Eight years before he stepped into office, he had claimed in an interview that he was 'neither a politician or agitator or racialist. I am merely an interested student of human relations.'[23]

'Xuma also presided over the era of delegations, deputations, letters and telegrams,' as Nelson Mandela recalls in *Long Walk to Freedom*.[24] His talents did not extend to the 'popular touch', as Lodge puts it. 'He was no orator and preferred the atmosphere of the committee-room to that of the mass meeting.'[25]

Yet it was time to shake the ANC out of the political slumber of which Mbeki had talked, and if Xuma was not going to do it, a group of young men who had been standing on the sidelines would do it for him.

They were a new and educated breed, many of them graduates of the University of Fort Hare, one of the oldest black universities in South Africa. They were less conservative in their ways than the older traditionalists and more forthright in their approach to politics. They had watched the ANC remain mute in the face of the Hertzog Bills. They had read about fascist Italy destroying the Ethiopian empire, or Abyssinia as it was called, yet only heard the AAC, and not the ANC, speak out about it at the time.

These young men also came of political age at a time when the demand for black labour had begun to increase with the onset of the Second World War as white industrial workers were called up to fight against Germany and its allies. But rising inflation also meant a drop in the real value of wages and a marked increase in material deprivation. This new black urban class was not content to sit back, and in the early war years its appetite for protest soon became a source of inspiration to the would-be founders of the ANCYL, among whom were Anton Lembede, Ashley Peter Mda, Tambo, Mandela, Sisulu, William Nkomo, Lionel Majombozi and Victor Mbobo.

'Here for the Youth Leaguers was the potential source of mass support which the Congress movement had so shamefully neglected to exploit,' writes Tom Lodge.[26]

'Many felt, perhaps unfairly, that the ANC as a whole had become the preserve of a tired, un-militant, privileged African elite more concerned with protecting their own rights than those of the masses,' Mandela wrote.[27] 'The general consensus was that some action must be taken, and Dr Majombozi proposed forming a Youth League as a way of lighting a fire under the leadership of the ANC.'[28]

'And that's when the shock troops came in,' as Matthews put it.

The ANC Youth League was founded on a staunch faith in black African nationalism and a narrow mistrust of white-led communism. An early tale from that era shows just how deep-seated it really was.

The 'Votes for All' campaign was rolled out by the Communist Party and the (South African) Indian Congress ahead of the 1948 general election — which ushered in the apartheid regime — to remind the public about racial discrimination in the run-up to a whites-only vote. The ANC was asked to join the campaign, but three young nationalist die-hards — Oliver Tambo, Nelson Mandela and Walter Sisulu — were opposed to it on the grounds that it was a veiled attempt to 'substitute the ANC', as Sisulu put it at the time.

In 1948, the three young Turks were requested by their provincial ANC executive leaders to decline the invitation politely but to set up a meeting with their communist counterparts, which took place in downtown Johannesburg, at a venue close to the intersection of Diagonal and Market Streets.

But instead of standing his ground, Comrade Walter was seduced by the able communists.

'They were able to put up very sound — and looking now with the help of hindsight — very sound and progressive views,' Nelson Mandela later told Luli Callinicos when she was writing Tambo's biography.[1] 'And Comrade Walter was now persuaded by their argument [to support the campaign]. Whereas Oliver and I were keeping in mind the mandate that was given to us by our executive.'

So annoyed were they with their comrade that when the meeting ended, they turned their back on him and walked away along Market Street towards Park Station.

'We left him behind and wouldn't talk to him at all,' Mandela remembered.

7

The shock troopers come in

Though it was Lionel Majombozi who first mooted the idea of forming a youth wing of the ANC, it was the outspoken and idealistic Anton Lembede who drove the political project on the back of African nationalism. Ironically he had been mentored by Pixley ka Isaka Seme, in whose practice he worked as a lawyer: he who had failed to inject the same kind of militancy into the ANC when he had the chance to do so some years earlier.

Lembede was a different political character to Seme entirely. He was an educated young man who spoke well and with great zeal, but he kept his message simple. In *Long Walk to Freedom*, Nelson Mandela remembered Lembede preaching to his peers, telling them 'Africa was a black man's continent, and it was up to Africans to reassert themselves and reclaim what was rightfully theirs. He hated the idea of the black inferiority complex and castigated what he called the worship and idolization of the West and its ideas. The inferiority complex, he affirmed, was the greatest barrier to liberation'.[2]

It was also Lembede who began to push the idea of a racially assertive nationalism, a political ideology he felt had benefited his Afrikaner brothers. If it had worked for the Boers, it would surely work for the blacks.

'Nationalism has been tested in the people's struggles and the fires of battle and found to be the only antidote against foreign rule and modern imperialism,' the young up-and-coming politician wrote in an African newspaper around that time.[3] Lembede wanted the ANCYL to 'place its emphasis on indigenous leadership and national self-determination'. 'The leaders of the Africans must come out of their own loins,' he wrote, because 'Africa is a black man's country'.[4]

In the four or more years that Malema had had a place in national politics, he continually preached this kind of black African nationalism in various contexts, but all too often in a way that placed white South Africans in a politically vulnerable spot.

Malema was also suspicious of communists, black and white, something that also formed a critical part of the 1940s militant brand, not only because, in their view, communism was an expression of white paternalism, but because there was an enormous gulf between a political analysis based on class and one which made ethnicity the crucial determinant.

When a delegation of youth paid a visit to party president A.B. Xuma in 1943 to explain to him their plans to start a youth league, they based their reasoning on the imperative for change. Their thinking was by then well advanced, because the idea to start a youth wing had been hatching for quite some time. It first surfaced in 1940 at a provincial meeting of the ANC in the former Transvaal and two years later, and on the initiative of William Nkomo, it was taken to the annual conference where it was endorsed by the executive. When they met with Xuma, the youth element presented their case in a coherent and convincing manner.

The ANC needed to become a mass organisation, they told him. A growth in membership was imperative. They would do what the Young Communist League had done since the 1920s and mobilise on the ground. An overhaul of the ANC's politics was necessary and a radical plan of action was required. They would become the foot soldiers and they were at the ready, with a manifesto in hand, just waiting for it to be implemented.

Mandela remembers how Xuma was wary of the proposal, seeing it as potentially politically dangerous.

'He enjoyed the relationships he had formed with the white establishment and did not want to jeopardize them with political action,' Mandela recalled,[5] a line Malema repeatedly echoes today in his criticism of Zuma.

In response to a mass-based organisation, Xuma told the young men that 'Africans as a group were too unorganized and undisciplined'.[6] Furthermore, 'we should be careful about Africa for the Africans because we can make ourselves isolationists like the government we are opposing,' he cautioned.[7]

He felt their programme of action was rash and 'what was really wrong with the manifesto was the tone of the criticism and expressions used. The committee should start off without antagonizing anyone.'[8]

However, what Xuma may have lacked in radicalism, he made up for in pragmatism, which he had in abundance. It was his ambition to build up the ANC and 'the men of the Youth League were precisely the kind whom Xuma was attempting to bring into the organization: creative, committed, well qualified young professionals'.[9]

Later that year the youth delegation travelled to Bloemfontein for the annual ANC meeting, where the idea of a youth wing was tabled and accepted. The ANCYL was formally constituted four months later on Easter Sunday, April 1944, at the Bantu Men's Social Centre in Eloff Street, Johannesburg, though the current-day Youth League insists it was started in September of that year. Regardless of whether it was a spring or autumn dawn, it began to breathe life into 'the emerging spirit of African nationalism', as Mandela recalls, with Lembede at the helm as president, Tambo as the secretary-general and Sisulu as the treasurer.[10]

The watershed moment that so many talk of in black South African politics had begun, a period in history that is central to any understanding of today's political state of affairs and of Malema's place in politics. Though the Youth League was started as a power structure within the ANC – or as Walshe puts it, 'a disciplined pressure group that would give direction and vigour to the fight for African freedom from within the movement'[11] – today it is like a fault in the broader structure of the party, by virtue of the power that is vested in both its leader and in the youth wing's broad mandate. What was evident during Malema's tenure was that a strong Youth League leader serving under a weak ANC president is anathema for the broader party.

Not since 1990 has the ANCYL been so prominent in political life as it is today, and with the exception of the late Peter Mokaba, Malema stands out as the most powerful youth leader in peace-time South Africa, at least until his expulsion. Nothing changed in the structure of the ANCYL or the powers vested in the position of the president to give him that profile. It was simply a combination of Malema's character and the weakening of the ANC in recent years that allowed the current ANCYL to rise to the heights it did in its attempts to treat the ANC as if it were a blank canvas upon which it could stamp its mark.

None of the ANC members recall the past in the way that Malema does, or as often as he does, as he weaves the events of history into the present to explain these changing times. He regularly flags the militancy of the 1940s and the Freedom Charter of the 1950s (see p. 272) as a means to explain and justify his actions in the new South Africa, but always in the name of ANC tradition. It is a clever move on his part, because there is no one in the 'family' of the ANC who can frown upon him for calling on party tradition.

There are few today who can still remember the events of the 1940s, but among those who could was the late Henry Gordon Makgothi, who lived in Orlando, on the outskirts of Johannesburg, at that time. Before he passed away in 2011, Makgothi had spoken to me about that era and how Mda began to canvass the township's youth, explaining 'the situation of the African people and we liked what he said. It was a troubled period and for young people who had the consciousness, we wanted change'.

By the time 1944 dawned, and the ANCYL was formed, they were ready converts.

At that time, Makgothi was a student at St Peter's High School where Andrew Mlangeni (who would later become one of the eight Rivonia Trialists to be sentenced to life imprisonment, along with Mandela) and Joe Matthews were also students, and where Tambo was a teacher of Maths and Science.

Matthews was no stranger to politics, and by aligning himself with the new youth wing, he was extending his family's political bloodline. His father, Professor Z.K. Matthews, the son of a Kimberley miner and café owner, was a renowned intellectual, a prominent and respected ANC leader and the cousin of Plaatje, one of the ANC's founders. (Joe Matthews' daughter, Naledi Pandor, currently the minister of science and technology, later rekindled the family tradition, picking up where her father left off after he made a political home at the Inkatha Freedom Party in the 1990s, though he died a close friend, if not a son, of the ANC in 2010.)

'We already called Matthews professor by then, because of his father,' Mlangeni recalled as he cast his mind back 60 or so years.

Mlangeni was not initially drawn to the ANCYL and joined the Young Communist League instead, only turning to the ANC youth wing in 1950 after the communist party was outlawed. Matthews, however, was in the new movement from the outset and started a branch of the ANCYL at St Peter's school, becoming the branch chairperson.

He remembers Lembede coming to talk to the pupils during class time and pushing his left-wing politics. 'As Karl Marx said, "A pair of boots is better than all the plays of Shakespeare." '

The ANCYL membership was largely male. One of the exceptions was Ellen Moloto, who later became president of the

ANCYL and a well-known activist under her married name, Ellen Kuzwayo. The other prominent female face from that time was Albertina Sisulu, the new wife of Walter.

The stage trooper in the early days was Mda, long before he defected from the ANC and joined the breakaway Pan Africanist Congress (PAC). It was he who preached political ideology, explaining why African nationalism was the only answer to South Africa's problems.

Though the youth were outspoken and often criticised their seniors, their loyalty to the ANC was always unwavering. After all was said and done, they were acutely aware that the 30-year-old Congress was the only worthwhile political party to belong to and their allegiance, like their militancy, they wore on their sleeves.

They were obsessive about communism and what they perceived as a 'foreign ideology' at a time of rising African nationalist sentiment in the face of extreme Afrikaner nationalism. As they observed the socio-political events of the late 1930s, the youth also watched the CPSA make a comeback. It had gained in popularity in the wake of the call for the Black Republic in 1927, so much so that its membership ballooned from 200 that year to 1,750 a year later, peaking at 3,000 in 1930. However, as the black influx overtook the rank and file, it resulted in the loss of some of its core and most able leaders who walked out in protest, hence it was unable to take political advantage of the dire social consequences that came about as a result of the 1930s Depression, which should have been its natural hunting ground. By the end of the decade, it had dropped the Black Republic slogan and was forced to rethink its approach.

A lifeline was thrown the way of the CPSA in 1939 with the start of the Second World War, which it initially opposed on the grounds that it was being fought to preserve the British Empire. However, when Hitler invaded Russia in 1941, it found its natural stance in opposing fascism and began to tap into the patriotic sentiment that had engulfed South Africa by extending its support for the troops who had been dispatched to the front. Membership over the next two years quadrupled and the Party (as the communist party is referred to, distinguished with the upper case P) seized the new opportunity to infiltrate political organisations and trade unions, placing its emphasis now on a non-racial, class-based struggle.

This was an ideal to which the African nationalist youth were strongly opposed and two years after the Youth League was founded, they tabled a resolution at the ANC annual conference in Bloemfontein to expel all communists from the ANC.

'We were suspicious of the white left,' Mandela conceded in his memoirs, 'wary of white influence in the ANC' and 'concerned that the communists were intent on taking over our movement under the guise of joint action'.[12]

'With a few of my colleagues in the League, I even went so far as breaking up the CP meetings by storming the stage, tearing up signs and capturing the microphone,' the former president admits.[13]

'Those suspicions about Mandela the nationalist, who was anti-communist, you know, they never really went away,' says Ronnie Kasrils, who was a staunch communist throughout the struggle era, a respected ANC comrade and later a minister in Mbeki's cabinet. 'And if you talk about Mandela the legacy, you know you are looking at Mandela as essentially a black nationalist.

'I would say Mandela is really leading that key group of Turks against the communists,' Kasrils continues, slipping into the present tense as he thinks back to that time. 'Lembede, Robert Resha is coming in on the scene. Certainly Walter himself. And Oliver [Tambo].'

The move to ban the communists started in 1945, when Mandela, Tambo, Sisulu and Lembede proposed to the provincial wing of the ANC that the communists be expelled. They pushed through a motion that 'members of political parties or other political organizations should forfeit their membership of Congress unless they resigned from these bodies so as to devote themselves wholly to Congress'. And they won it comfortably by 31 votes to 24.[14]

They then pushed the motion to the annual conference in Bloemfontein a year later, but the young nationalists were heavily defeated by the traditionalists.[15] The move by the youth was an affront at a time when many of the ANC's senior leaders were also CPSA members.

'Well, communists are quite formidable,' says Kasrils, his mind still rolling over the 1940s. 'It's not now simply white communist leaders who will always be vulnerable in a nationalist struggle in Africa, because apart from Bram Fischer and Joe Slovo and Rusty Bernstein, who were very eminent revolutionaries, and women like Hilda Bernstein and Ruth First, you've also got Moses Kotane and J.B. Marks,' both of whom were on the ANC's executive team, the NEC.

'I mean these are really formidable communist leaders. They have a following. They are very charismatic. And I think if the Party didn't have people like that on its side, the nationalists would have taken hold of the liberation movement and of the ANC as they are trying to do now,' he says in reference to Malema and his fellow factionalists.

They failed in their 1946 attempt but, not content to stop at that, another attempt was made a year later by some of the youth at the provincial conference, but they were defeated for a second time and agreed to lay the dispute to rest, for the time being at least, as a shift in the political climate was telling them they would have to begin to choose their battles more carefully.

In the meantime, D.F. Malan's Purified National Party had been gaining ground on the promise that South Africa was no country for black men, a pledge that became reality on the back of their victory in the election of 26 May 1948, which ushered in the ideology of apartheid.

'Well, I like this,' Walter Sisulu said as he picked up a news-paper the following morning at Park Station in Johannesburg, 'because it is going to put further momentum to the resistance movement. We now know that we have an enemy in power, and difficult days are coming for us, and I think that we are going to have a better opportunity of mobilising our people to resist this development.'

It was now apparent to the ANC that it could no longer remain docile in the face of oppression, though it would be the party's junior members rather than its senior leaders who would push for a radical break with the past. At the party's conference at the end of 1948, the youth presented their plans in a document called the Programme of Action. During the following twelve months the vision was discussed at branch level, some modifications were made to it along the way and the final draft was presented to the conference in December 1949.

Its ideological thrust was Africanist-inspired, though there was nothing particularly original about the thinking behind it or the plan it proposed, which mapped out a forceful course of militant action through which the Youth League believed it could recruit greater support for the ANC and set the movement on a mass footing in its fight against the new white regime.

What was different about the Programme of Action was its call for mass action that would radically change the ANC's approach to fighting racial segregation. However, the emphasis on action was also its weakness, as it focused on the means at the expense of a clear definition of the ultimate goal, which would leave the ANC vulnerable in terms of broader ideology in later years.

Indeed, Malema focused on the ultimate goal when he pushed for nationalisation of the country's mines, and should he succeed it will likely be at the expense of the means, which would have dire consequences for South Africa's future.

Like the youth of the 1940s, Malema was securing support

for his plan through the branches of the ANC as he rallied them ahead of the 2012 conference, but he found the biggest resistance to the move at leadership level.

Though the 1940s youth had secured backing for the programme from many party members who had become frustrated with the lack of change, like Malema they did not have the support of the leadership, particularly that of President Xuma. Mandela, Sisulu and Tambo decided to try to engage him at his Sophiatown home in a bid to bring him on board, but Xuma refused to budge.

If he didn't support their plan, he could no longer count on their support for re-election, they told him (in a tone that Malema would later try to echo until his removal in 2012). Xuma accused them of blackmail and 'unceremoniously showed us the door', as Mandela recalls.[16]

At the December conference, Xuma lost his presidency to James Moroka, a medical doctor from the Free State. The youth's preferred candidate in the meantime was Z.K. Matthews, but his refusal to stand forced them to seek out Moroka at the eleventh hour. He agreed that in return for their endorsing him as president, he would support the youth's programme and allow them to have greater control over the executive.

Three years earlier the youth had prevailed upon the ANC to double the executive membership base to 22, in the hope of creating space for some young blood, or a 'generational mix' as Malema calls it today. But the move backfired when three notable communists (Marks, Kotane and Dan Tloome) were elected.

However, the upshot of the 1949 conference was that Sisulu, then aged 37, was elected to the strategic position of secretary-general, while five of his ANCYL colleagues – Tambo, Mda, James Njongwe, Mbobo and Godfrey Pitje (Lembede had died suddenly in 1947) – were also elected to the executive with Mandela joining them during the early months of 1950.

The Youth League also lobbied the ANC to adopt the raised

clenched fist as the party's official symbol, and it succeeded on that score as well.

That year, 1949, is a key year in the ANC's history as it marked a before and after moment in its politics of struggle. The youth have long claimed it as one of their own big victories, the year when they took control of the party and moulded the 'new ANC', and in most respects they did. However, as Lodge points out, its leadership remained eclectic in the years immediately after 1949, composed as it was of a mix of African conservatives and liberals, a crop of radical youth, as well as the two respected communists – Marks and Kotane.[17]

Immediately after 1949, the young nationalists were forced to modify their rigid, anti-communist stance. Though they continued to harbour suspicions of what they perceived was a threat to African nationalism and African leadership, they could not but acknowledge the Marxists as unexpected allies when the CPSA endorsed their call for mass action. Nor could they deny the positive outcomes of the Defiance Campaign of 1952, when millions of black South Africans from all political walks began to peacefully resist the unjust laws of apartheid by marching into white-only towns and cities around the country without their permits. Other political events from that decade were only made possible by virtue of the wider involvement of all anti-apartheid activists, not only narrow nationalists.

When six of the youth joined the ANC's executive in 1949, they shared a bench with a small but significant group of Marxists who began to influence their thinking at the same time as some of the ANCYL's leadership positions were filled by graduates from the University of Fort Hare, who slowly instilled a Marxist analysis into thinking about African nationalism among the ANC juniors.[18]

However, in 1950, when the CPSA liquidated itself just days ahead of the enactment of the Suppression of Communism Act by the apartheid regime (which was intended to outlaw them as a political organisation anyway), the communists were also forced to the change their tack. The move left them with no option but to work through the ANC, where there would be no place for inter-party conflict or anti-nationalist posturing if they were to succeed in sowing the seeds of communism. It was not an attempt to take over the ANC but instead to influence the direction the nationalist movement would take.

'The Communist Party hoped that South Africa should go through a two-stage process of change. The first would be a so-called National Democratic Revolution ... in which socialists or communists (they don't make a strong distinction between the two) should ally themselves with progressive nationalists, such as the ANC,' explains Lodge. 'They were hoping to work within the ANC in such a way that the ANC would be a progressive nationalist movement, predisposed to a socialist society. And what would come next would be a move towards a communist society.'

Hence in its 1949 annual report and ahead of its disbandment, the CPSA's central committee agreed on the following. It's a long quotation, but one worth repeating for the thinking on the part of the communists towards the ANC at that time:

> The national organizations can develop into powerful mass movements only to the extent that their contents and aims are determined by the interests of workers and peasants. The national organizations, to be effective, must be transformed into a revolutionary party of workers, peasants, intellectuals and petty bourgeoisie, linked together in a firm organization, subject to a strict discipline, and guided by a definite programme of struggle against all forms of racial discrimination in alliance with the class-conscious European workers and intellectuals. Such a party would be distinguished from the Communist Party in that its objective is national

liberation, that is the abolition of racial discrimination, but it would co-operate closely with the Communist Party. In this party, the class-conscious workers and the peasants of the national group concerned would constitute the main leadership. It would be their task to develop an adequate organizational apparatus, to combat chauvinism and racialism in the national movement, to develop class consciousness in the people, and to forge unity in action between the oppressed people and between them and the European working class.[19]

The communists and nationalists, along with their allies in the Indian Congress, worked closely together in opposition to apartheid throughout the 1950s. However, efforts on the part of the communists throughout to ensure that the ANC adopted positions that would lead towards a more egalitarian, socialist society hardened mistrust among the nationalists.

'Men make their own history, but they do not make it as they please,'
Karl Marx wrote in The Eighteenth Brumaire of Louis Bonaparte.

'The tradition of all dead generations weighs like a nightmare on the brains of the living. And just as they seem to be occupied with revolutionizing themselves and things, creating something that did not exist before, precisely in such epochs of revolutionary crisis they anxiously conjure up the spirits of the past to their service, borrowing from them names, battle slogans, and costumes in order to present this new scene in world history in time-honored disguise and borrowed language.'

8

From underground to above ground

In 1960, the apartheid government banned all black political parties and the ANC was forced into exile, with its leadership headquartered in Tanzania and members scattered in various other countries on the continent and elsewhere in the world, as well as at home. However, the centre of the ANC failed to hold and by the end of the decade discontent was growing among the exiles who felt that the revolution was failing them. This was raised at the party's conference in Morogoro, Tanzania, in 1969, which became another flash of tension between the communists and the nationalists.

In the run-up to that conference Chris Hani, a staunch communist who was a member of both parties, put his head on the block when he challenged the ANC by lending his name to a document that aired the grievances that he and seven other men shared. Hani was a well-respected figure and the ANC was forced to take note of the matters to hand. 'The Memorandum', as it later became known, bared some home truths that the movement could not disown; not least the financial greed that had crept into the executive (the ANC was receiving a lot of international funding by then) as well as the disconnect that had developed between the leadership and the party's members, both internally and externally.

In June 2011, COSATU drafted a document with a similar tone that talked of the withering character of the ANC, the 'predatory' nature of some of its corrupt members, and the concern that South Africa was steadily veering off track. A few weeks later, a faction within the ANCYL released an even more detailed memorandum outlining the resentment that was rising in the ranks of the Youth League, though it quickly disappeared when Malema threatened to take action against its authors.

Malema's actions had echoes: the eight men who drafted the 1969 Memorandum were initially suspended for raising dissenting voices. However, unlike the youth of 2011, their concerns were acknowledged and the fact they had raised them ensured that organisational reform featured prominently on the conference agenda.[1]

The 'Strategy and Tactics' document that came out of that seven-day meeting at Morogoro (which was heavily influenced by the communist Joe Slovo) outlined the ANC's military theory, but it made one other fundamental policy shift: it opened up membership, though not leadership, of the ANC to non-African freedom fighters in exile.

The document was resolute in this thrust that the 'liberation of the largest and most oppressed group – the African people' was the single focus of the struggle, but it argued strongly that 'there can be no second-class participants in our movement' and that 'our nationalism must not be confused with chauvinism or narrow nationalism of a previous epoch. It must not be confused with the classical drive by an elitist group among the oppressed people to gain ascendancy so that they can replace the oppressor in the exploitation of the masses.'

As Slovo put it years later, 'Morogoro asserted the right of the rank and file to have a say as to who would lead them.'[2] However, there were hardliners who resisted the move, and though they were not in a majority, it showed a lack of unanimity over basic policy questions at senior levels of the ANC and 'might therefore be a cause for more important and debilitating divisions in the future', Lodge argued.[3]

The divisions eventually surfaced when the ANC rank and file collapsed around two factions in 2007: one led by Thabo Mbeki, the other by Jacob Zuma. But the factionalism started long before then and current ANC members trace it back to 1990, when the movement was unbanned, something that brought with it a sea of challenges and changes.

After 30 years as a secret underground structure, it was about to become a mass organisation and embark on a process of transformation nearly as profound as that which South Africa itself was about to undergo. The metamorphosis from liberation movement into ruling party was about to begin.

'That shift fundamentally changed the ANC,' Joe Matthews believed. 'And we have never fully appreciated just how much it has changed the ANC until now.'

'We used to talk about it in exile when it was becoming apparent to us that we were coming home,' says Aziz Pahad, former deputy foreign affairs minister in Mbeki's cabinet, as he thought back to that era. 'We knew that managing this concept of the broad church would be difficult once we were back home. We knew it would bring change. But like any change, we would just have to see what kind of change it brought and then learn how to manage it.'

What February 1990 initially brought was the return of all the exiles, but it also brought a rush of new members from within South Africa, and while it attracted thousands of individuals who were eager to help take the country to the next level, among the new members were plenty of opportunists laden with ambitions that had little to do with politics. Many who had feared activism throughout the struggle era were now quick to flock to the ranks of the would-be ruling party in the hope of fine things to come.

Rather than be influenced or changed by the ANC, many of these 'come lately' members began to change the ANC instead, and the early years after unbanning saw the emergence of a new kind of ANC cadre.

The transformation of the ANC has become more pronounced under Zuma's leadership and there is widespread concern about the calibre of the senior leaders who guide the party with him. As a ruling party that sits on two thirds of the vote, there is also considerable concern across society about the kind of men and women who are now governing South Africa.

Concerns that are being raised today began yesterday, says Pahad. 'Since 1991, at the [ANC] conference in Durban, all the subsequent documents have been picking up on the issue of the calibre of the cadres, be it at policy conferences or general council meetings. It is there. The concerns around the reasoning and values of our cadres are there . . . We called it the decay of the cadre,' he recalls. 'And I often say to people, why are you surprised now? It has been there in writing for a long time.'

The transformation of the liberation movement affected seniors and juniors and the ANCYL underwent as much change as the ANC itself. During the period in which the ANC was outlawed, the League had practically collapsed, though a youth section existed in exile but with more direction and guidance from the ANC than was the case prior to 1990.

Jackie Selebi, the former head of the South African Police Service who was convicted of corruption and sentenced to fifteen years in prison in 2011, was the head of the youth wing in exile and he too points to 1990 as the fateful year.

Shortly after he went into exile in 1976, and on the instructions of Oliver Tambo, who was then the president of the ANC, Selebi was appointed to lead and train the hundreds of younger members who were flocking to the exile camps on the continent in the wake of the Soweto uprising.

He was to instil in them the importance of learning, producing and fighting 'and each of these three things was equal to one another. Not one was superior to the other, and you could not do one without the other.' The idea was to produce a new kind of cadre in preparation for a free South Africa.

Selebi travelled between Lusaka and the camps in Angola, as well as the Solomon Mahlangu Freedom College in Tanzania, to oversee the growing population of youth in exile. When all parties were unbanned in 1990 he returned home and Peter Mokaba took over the leadership of the Youth League, when it was formally regrouped in 1991.

'Until then, I was head of the youth section of the ANC. I was not a "president",' which is the title that was given to the head of the movement when it was re-established in 1991, a title 'that's more about power and less about policy.'

His words are critically true. Malema often commanded the treatment he received partly because he was the 'president' of the ANC's youth rather than a representative of them, and in that presidency is vested the kind of power that a person of Malema's character was only too well able to manipulate.

Vuyiswa Tulelo, a strong, fiery though likable woman who Malema brought in as secretary-general during his first term, draws out the significance of that power when she talks about how the Youth League lobbied for voting rights in the ANC in the late 1990s. Until then, it had no official say in organisational or policy matters of the senior movement.

In 1999, Tulelo was elected to the League's executive, under the presidency of Malusi Gigaba.

'But when I was under Gigaba the Youth League was dormant,' she says. 'It had a strong presence in the institutions of higher learning, but the people who are the backbone of the Youth League did not feel a part of it then.'

Yet the youth remained silent.

'We had to,' she says. 'We were lobbying the ANC for voting rights and to do that we had to present a stable and united front.'

Gigaba, now the minister for public enterprises, gave the ANCYL the respectability it was looking for in the eyes of its seniors and in 2001 it was granted the right to a block vote.

Though it is only a small percentage of the overall vote, it finally allowed the youth to have some say and become minor decision-makers.

Gigaba was then succeeded by Fikile Mbalula, and in Tulelo's mind, 'That's when the ANCYL found its voice.'

During the Mbalula terms, which ended in 2008, the ANCYL became more militant, more vocal and more confident about lobbying support in the townships and away from the universities and institutions.

'And with Malema, we have found our place in the ANC. We are now an integral part of ANC life. And they can no longer say, "You can't do that." We have an opinion and we are not afraid to express it. Now they take us seriously.'

It has been a slow process, which the youth has steered with strategic steps until they got to the point they wanted to reach. It is not clear whether the ANC was aware of what was unfolding, or if the decision to grant them more power within the party came at a time when there was stronger leadership in place.

Mbalula, a wily politician and a man of strong character, could not have risen in the way Malema did under Zuma leadership. Mokaba, who was more radical than Mbalula ever was, was taken under the wing of Mandela until his tone slowly softened. However, the ANC under Zuma, widely regarded as the weakest the party has been for quite some time, indulged Malema for way too long.

It's trite to say that Malema is radical, but the sheer militancy of the Youth League during his tenure and its bold departure from the ANC in both policy and practice points to fundamental failures within the ANC, particularly a lack of political vision and discipline right across the board, from junior to senior members, as it tried to make the transition to a ruling party.

Thabo Makunyane, the former executive mayor of Polokwane, who in 1990 was appointed the ANC's provincial convenor in

Limpopo while the movement began to formalise and organise its structures, believes the transformation was unguided in most respects.

'We were focusing on going into government and preparing to become a ruling party, and political education and discipline suffered. In hindsight, this was critical – it was a mistake we made at a time when the party was undergoing unprecedented growth.

'Another factor at play was the black business sector, which was largely associated with the Bantustans,' and therefore regarded by their own communities as doing business with the apartheid regime. 'What many of these business people began to do was to align with the ANC or join the ANC, to show their communities that they were "on the right side", if I can put it like that,' Makunyane adds. 'They would go as far as flashing their ANC membership cards out of fear of such things as consumer boycotts, which were happening at the time and which ruined many businesses.'

What did not help was the understandable fact that genuine leadership was slow to emerge. There was still a fear associated with black politics after three dark decades of underground life, and taking politics and activism out of the closet again was still a big challenge.

As these factors played out throughout the country, they were particularly acute in Limpopo, Malema's home province, where the ANC began to fracture from very early on.

Until 1994, South Africa had four provinces that increased to nine under the new demarcations, from which Limpopo emerged. Ever since its formation, the province has been beset by political infighting and bickering. Though not very pronounced then or now, it was to be expected to some degree in a province that is home to so many ethnic groups.

Of South Africa's ten former Bantustans, Venda, Gazankulu and Lebowa were fully incorporated into Limpopo, while parts of KwaNdebele and Moutse (from Mpumalanga) were also brought into the province alongside people from the former northern Transvaal.

Ngoako Ramatlhodi, a returned exile and the province's first premier, was therefore faced with a delicate balancing act when it came to assembling the first cabinet. It was widely expected that Sothos would outnumber all others in his team, not only because Ramatlhodi was himself Sotho, but because they represented the largest ethnic group in the province. And while he could have opted for an even spread of groups across his cabinet, he chose to recruit from a skilled rather than an ethnic base and ended up with a bench that was weighted with Shangaans from Gazankulu, because the former Bantustan was credited with an education system believed to be superior to the rest of the region at the time. The Shangaans accounted for less than a quarter of Limpopo's population, yet they were disproportionately represented in top positions in the provincial cabinet and the selection started a rivalry that has continued ever since.

Alongside the chauvinism was the opportunism, mentioned above, and some of those newcomers were quick to sow seeds of factionalism when their demands were not met.

All things considered, Ramatlhodi's first term as provincial premier was characterised as much by division as it was by the challenge of steering a brand new province through the early years of the democratic dispensation. What often exacerbated those challenges was Ramatlhodi's style of leadership. Though he was a respected comrade in the eyes of the senior ANC leadership – a former speech writer for Tambo, a Mandela appointee and an old associate of Mbeki (who was then the deputy president of the country) – he lacked the confidence and skill to rise above the schism that was developing in the provincial ranks of the ANC.

Despite this, he held on to the premiership for a second five-year term and was succeeded in 2004 by Sello Moloto, a man of his choosing who was also a staunch supporter of Mbeki. However, Moloto turned out to be as insecure as his predecessor and the erosion of provincial party unity that began under Ramatlhodi accelerated during the Moloto era. By the time he left office in 2009, the Limpopo wing of the party had fragmented. Many of the ANC-appointed municipal managers and provincial leaders pledged their loyalties to competing factions and ran their patches accordingly, as if there were two centres of power at play. It was a prospect that raised the very legitimate question: who in fact rules the ANC or the (provincial) government?

The fracturing of the ANC was not restricted to Limpopo. Throughout the country, the former liberation movement was beginning to rupture around that time, and would continue to do so in the Zuma era that was to follow. However, Limpopo was exceptional, so pronounced was the extent of the divide and many were of the view that it was under Moloto's watch that Limpopo truly began to slide politically, socially and economically.

Malema liked to refer to Moloto as *'digata-marokgwana'*, a popular Sotho term to describe a small man trying to fit into a big man's pants. Literally translated it means tripping over one's trousers. And when he took a swipe at Moloto, as he often did, he would refer to the 'government of *digata-marokgwana'*.

That Limpopo's political terrain was forever in a state of flux suited Malema and his politics that have forever oscillated around a 'them' versus 'us' mentality. He had been inducted into the ANC from boyhood as a fighter and like any fighter he needed an enemy. In 1990 he still had one – the white-led regime and the population of white South Africans. As a student activist in the late 1990s and early 2000s, he found his enemy in 'the system' as he fought for transformation in education. From 2004 onwards, he ironically found his enemy within the ranks of his own party, challenging leadership structures around him.

By then, Limpopo's two centres of power were well defined: Moloto led the provincial government while Malema and Cassel Mathale, who was then the provincial secretary of the ANC, controlled the party and most of the municipalities throughout the large province.

That divide became even more entrenched a year later when the senior structures of the ANC decided to support Jacob Zuma's comeback plan. It sparked a wave of anti-Mbeki sentiment all over the country as the various provinces began to fall behind one or other of the two men. Malema had his new enemy in Mbeki.

As time wore on, it was a divide that became less about Mbeki and Zuma. It turned into a standoff between nationalists and communists, between young and old cadres, between the so-called left and whatever it is that sits at the other extreme. It unfolded as a new kind of battle for the ANC, a race amongst comrades to the top.

It is a push towards the narrow nationalism and elitism that the old ANC warned of more than 40 years ago in Morogoro. It is a fight for total control of the ANC, but unlike the 1969 push for control of the party, the soul of the ANC is different to what it was then because the ANC, post-liberation, is markedly different from the party that fought for freedom.

As Joe Matthews pointed out, the challenges the ANC overcame throughout the struggle were based on ideology, 'before governmental power, before access to resources'. But 1994 'transferred a party of idealistic people into interests. They changed from a liberation movement into a party of government, and not only a party of government but a party that has the potential to lay its hands on resources . . . This is the struggle for resources and against all those who might pose an obstacle to appropriating those resources.'

Turning and turning in the widening gyre
The falcon cannot hear the falconer;
Things fall apart; the centre cannot hold;
Mere anarchy is loosed upon the world,
The blood-dimmed tide is loosed, and everywhere
The ceremony of innocence is drowned;
The best lack all conviction, while the worst
Are full of passionate intensity.
Surely some revelation is at hand;
Surely the Second Coming is at hand.
The Second Coming! Hardly are those words out
When a vast image out of Spiritus Mundi
Troubles my sight: somewhere in sands of the desert
A shape with lion body and the head of a man,
A gaze blank and pitiless as the sun,
Is moving its slow thighs, while all about it
Reel shadows of the indignant desert birds.
The darkness drops again; but now I know
That twenty centuries of stony sleep
Were vexed to nightmare by a rocking cradle,
And what rough beast, its hour come round at last,
Slouches towards Bethlehem to be born?

(W.B. Yeats, 'The Second Coming', 1919)

9

The second coming

Julius Malema was about to usher in a new chapter in the country's history. He belonged to a generation that still relished the thought of a bloody revolution and a section of society hell–bent on fighting a war that had ended a long, long time ago, one that was settled through dialogue and not bullets.

Though there is a degree of romanticism attached to his induction into the ANC while he was still very, very young, it is important to remember that his earliest instructions were to fight, to attack, to take up arms, the only real solutions that were explained to him then as a means to end apartheid. In his mind, he was plucked from a life of poverty and misery and drawn into a small secret unit of would-be soldiers who would have marched into the country's streets in the event that armed resistance became necessary. Even if there is more fantasy than fact to that story around his early years, it is how he sees himself, how he understands the way the ANC door was opened to him, why he was 'being called upon' to enter the party's ranks and take to the streets of South Africa and complete the National Democratic Revolution.

Apartheid ended with the first free and fair elections in 1994 that followed a series of sensitive negotiations over the space of two years. The Convention for a Democratic South Africa (CODESA) was a forum that brought 19 political groups to the table to try to thrash out a peaceful end to the regime, but the talks collapsed halfway through when 46 people were killed in the bloody Boipotong massacre, a reminder of the delicate balancing act the two sides were attempting. The talks resumed on the back of a compromise: a sunset clause that would ease the transition from white minority rule to democracy through a coalition government, essentially an assurance to whites that there would not be a backlash from the black majority.

Though it was the only means to avert a bloodbath at the time, there are many black South Africans who now feel that they ceded too much in the 1990s, the consequence of which is a white-dominated economy and a society that is still skewed in favour of minorities. They believe that only a revolution would have truly overhauled the institution that was apartheid. Malema is one of them and to this day he tries to re-enact the war he feels he missed out on.

I remember him once getting some of that sentiment off his chest when he began to articulate some of the anger and resentment that is pent up inside him. It never made much sense to me, because Malema had just entered his teens when Nelson Mandela became South Africa's first democratically elected president, promising his people that 'never, never and never again shall it be that this beautiful land will again experience the oppression of one by another,' as he was sworn into office in Pretoria on 9 May 1994. It was over, apartheid had ended, and though the success of the immediate future would depend on the delicate balancing act of the transition, and would take time – a lot of time – Malema's generation had a lot to look forward to. Furthermore, it was up to the ruling party, his own party, to make the changes that were required. Yet in his mind, then and now, is the strong feeling that those who had oppressed South Africa had been given too light a sentence through the CODESA talks, to which he and others would not have agreed. He is still bitter that he never had a chance to pull the trigger.

'We weren't around during the negotiations,' he told me, his voice a deep growl. 'But we are here now.' And twenty or so years on, he wants change.

As philosopher Achille Mbembe puts it, there is a problem with certain segments of black South Africa not having won the war through the gun. 'There's a feeling of castration that comes from the idea that we couldn't terminate this war with a bullet and put the whites down by stamping our boots on their throats, as was the case in Zimbabwe. And Malema's war envy suggests he wanted that and almost still does. It's what feeds this kind of lumpen radicalism that has always been a part of South African political culture, but it is now found moving from the margins to the centre.'

Days after Malema's presidency was confirmed in 2008, he addressed a rally on 16 June, which is Youth Day in South Africa and a national holiday to commemorate the young men and women who were killed in the 1976 Soweto uprising. With a general election only nine months away, the national focus at that time was on Zuma's corruption charges, which were being challenged in the country's courts. It was Malema's first public appearance as president and he wouldn't get a second chance to make a good first impression. He stepped up to the microphone and in a rasping voice told the tens of thousands of youth gathered in front of him that he would not only die but he would 'kill for Zuma' if the charges were not dropped. That was his introduction to the South African public, his first big sally as youth president. It's a statement that best summed up Malema – he wanted a fight.

A whole anthology of political outrage now survives his four or so years at the top, each one worse than the last. On the subject of rape, he tried to defend Zuma, who had been tried for raping the daughter of a family friend in 2005, and though Zuma was acquitted, the public jury has kept an open mind on the matter ever since.

'The woman stayed until the sun comes out, requested

breakfast and asked for taxi money,' Malema said a couple of years later. 'She must have had a nice time,' words that landed him before the Equality Court for hate speech in a case that he later lost.

His most hateful words were directed at Helen Zille, the white woman who heads the official opposition party, the Democratic Alliance, which governs the province of the Western Cape.

'You have put a cockroach in cabinet and we need to remove that cockroach by voting the ANC into power,' he told an all-black gathering in the Western Cape.

The awful shame in Malema's words related to the 1994 Rwandan genocide in which 800,000 were killed in the space of 100 days, the majority of them Tutsis who were referred to as 'cockroaches' that had to be 'exterminated'. The minority Tutsis had a monopoly on power in Rwanda, precisely the point Malema was making about the white-led provincial government in the Western Cape, though he denied the link. When he was pressed on the matter in parliament, Deputy President Kgalema Motlanthe thought it was 'just downright simple bad manners'.

That was in 2010 and a year later, at the height of local government elections, and while sharing a stage with Zuma, Malema told his followers that whites were 'criminals' and demanded that they must be 'treated' like criminals. Zuma didn't possess the civic fortitude to stand up to him so he threw his head back and laughed while the crowds cheered Malema on. As he began his second term as League president, he called on the youth to go to 'war' against the ANC.

That's Malema, a man who was born standing up and talking back, to borrow Roy Buchanan's lyrics.

'The Diabolical' is how a friend of mine refers to him.

Malema had well and truly departed from the spirit of 1969, the promises of 1994 and the non-racialism that had guided the ANC over the years. Moreover, his leaders were standing on the sidelines, watching the spectacle unfold, and for more than three years they did little to halt his show. It was as if, as one ANC official put it, 'the small president had become bigger than the big president'. To be sure, the strain of decency had long left the ANC, but it was hard to know who really epitomised its passing: Malema or his seniors. What was clear, however, was that in the absence of proper leadership, the ANC was now on autopilot.

It's quite remarkable that for 24 years, between 1967 and 1991, Oliver Tambo had led the party from exile and directed its operations against the apartheid regime from bases in Tanzania, Zimbabwe and London and yet as a ruling party, Zuma's ANC were unable to lead themselves.

Despite their weaknesses, the liberation movement had once been disciplined and 'once upon a time, that discipline was so rigorous that even Mandela had to crook the knee,' writer Rian Malan points out. 'When Madiba emerged from the prison gates in 1990, comrades insisted that he tear up his prepared speech and deliver one that stuck to the party line in every respect, including the need for ongoing class struggle and armed insurrection. The great man knuckled under and did as he was told.'

Yet Mandela also expected others to do as he did. When a few years later the ANC ventured into neo-liberal economics, communists, trade unionists and radicals saw this as a betrayal of everything they'd fought for.

'But when Mandela, who was then state and party president, said, "The leadership has decided," they zipped their traps and fell into line, at least in public,' Malan adds.

That steely discipline gradually eroded over the years and gave way to a party characterised by excesses, crass greed and corruption and inured with hypocrisy. It was never so marked as when Zuma took power, both of the party and the country, and promoted scores of hundreds of like-minded cadres to senior positions. It was so dramatic it could have been carnivalesque, Mbembe argues, leaning on the term that was coined by Russian literary theorist and critic Mikhail Bakhtin, who explained it in the following way:

'Carnival is not a spectacle seen by the people; they live in it, and everyone participates because its very idea embraces all the people. While carnival lasts, there is no other life outside. During carnival time, life is subject to its laws, that is, the laws of its own freedom.'[1]

When the carnival comes to town, the solemnities, etiquettes and formalities disappear and are overtaken by those who normally reside on the fringes of society. The carnival liberates them. For them, hell becomes heaven and fantasy becomes fact.

'The carnival only lasts for a short while,' says Mbembe. 'It is a small window of opportunity during which everything is turned on its head. And in that short space of time, you can swear, and you can fuck and fart and spit and all of that.

'But the problem here is that the carnival has become the permanent. We are now living in a permanent carnival. This is the last chapter of the transition and this is the point at which we have arrived.'

It is the end of a century of struggle politics and the liberation movement, one of the oldest and most respected in the world, is celebrating that milestone in the context of the carnival that Mbembe so aptly depicts.

'And the engineer of the carnival was Zuma. Remember he brought the song "Bring Me My Machine Gun" ["Umhsini Wami"]. He brought some outrageous activities into the political domain. It was he who brought the carnival to the centre of everyday South African life.'

Halfway through his term, Zuma began to wake up to the folly he had brought to bear, but he struggled to contain it. He had allowed the taste of the carnival to linger a tad too long, and those he brought with him were reluctant to leave.

'They are saying no, we will sit here and we will break the pot.

And when there is nothing to eat, then we will fight each other,' says Mbembe.

At a party political level, Zuma had gathered an eclectic group around him when he was fighting to come to power in 2007, men and women from the unions, from the communist party, from business, the Youth League, even some of Mbeki's more conservative followers who also wanted change, and many of them he rewarded with good jobs or positions of relative power. When it came to business, though, Zuma's circle was small and intimate and when in power he looked after his family and close friends, and in particular the Gupta brothers, a munificent Indian business family that had taken Zuma under their wing.

Naturally this qualified the attitude of many of Zuma's followers, many of whom felt hard done by, while others simply helped themselves without him.

Limpopo was then under the stewardship of Cassel Mathale, though it was common knowledge that he ran the province with Malema. As daft as it sounds, the Youth League leader had an equal say in all of the public contracts that were awarded, business deals that were struck and any other public expenditure worth talking about. By then, 2009, Malema was already a big player in business in the public and private sectors, though until that year he had operated on the wings of a provincial leader who was hostile towards him. But with Mathale as premier, Malema was able to feed his bigotry and his greed, which had become two aspects of the same rampant disorder.

It was because of Malema that the portmanteau word 'tenderpreneur' was slipped into the South African lexicon half way through 2009, a pithy, if not pathetic description for the politics of patronage that had come to define the African National Congress and through which its entrepreneurial members were increasingly tapping into lucrative state contracts, or tenders.

Though not alone in his endeavours, Malema wore his wealth on his sleeve and it was for him the crude term was created, and hardly a reference was made to him after that time that did not feature the title.

10

Teething on tenders

'Do you think Malema is mentally stable?' a respected friend once asked me. 'I do,' I answered. 'He can be volatile. He can be a bit rough around the edges. He can be many things, but he's definitely not tipping towards the insane side of life.'

'So what is it, then, this attitude of his?' he wanted to know. 'It's a mix of things,' I told him. 'But above all, I think it's the fact that he has very little life experience and way too much power; a lethal mix that has completely gone to his 30-year-old head.'

It is this mix that made him believe he is invincible but it blinds him to boundaries. Possibilities are enormous in his world but he can't see that today he might be the big man and tomorrow some kind of hapless hero. He ploughs through life without a care in the world for the repercussions of his words and actions.

'But surely he must know it's not going to last,' my friend suggested, that Malema's excesses will eventually get the better of him.

I thought back to a conversation I once had with Malema in the wake of a heated political moment, sometime late in 2010. I can't remember what it was he had done – no doubt spouted off an insult of some sort, but whatever it was, he found himself with a suspended sentence hanging over his head, yet he knew, or at least he thought he knew, he was untouchable amongst his peers.

'They can't get me,' he said as he laughed heartily. 'I'm the one with the nine lives. They can't bring me down.'

He was ahead of the game at the level at the party, but he was embroiled in a war with the media who were digging into the dark areas of his life. Back off, was his standard response, 'I'm a private citizen.' It was the shield he believed made him untouchable in the eyes of the law as well, and which forced him to seek an urgent interdict against *City Press*, a local Sunday newspaper, when they tried to expose his slush fund halfway through 2011. The newspaper was about to publish some damning allegations when he instructed his legal team to send a senior counsel to the court and argue his case as a man entitled to privacy. To his dismay, he lost that battle: the court granted the newspaper permission to reveal all.

In an ironic twist of fate, I had sent Malema an extensive list of questions that same week (see p. 279). A couple of weeks earlier I had met with him and told him to expect the questions, which would give him his right of reply to allegations this book would make before it went to press.

They were drafted by me but sent with a covering letter from the law firm acting for my publisher and myself, and they were hand-delivered to the ANC headquarters shortly after lunch on 20 July. He was asked to respond within ten days.

Two days later Malema called me, wanting to know if I was behind some of the information that *City Press* had revealed. I wasn't and I told him so.

'This is very suspicious,' he suggested. 'You came here two weeks ago and told me you would send me questions. And now they do it instead.'

'But surely my questions are not identical to what they might have sent you,' I argued.

'What questions?' he demanded. 'Where are your questions?'

That's when I became aware that he hadn't received them and he quickly sent one of his aides in search of them. I didn't expect to hear from him again, as the letter had instructed him to respond via the lawyers, but that didn't stop him from calling me. Shortly after 19h30 that same evening the phone began to purr.

He had the questions. And he wanted to talk. I appealed to him to liaise with the lawyers directly, as the letter had stated.

'I have some things I want to say to you first,' he said.

Here we go, I thought.

He told me he didn't like the fact that I was now communicating with him via a lawyer's letter when I had always engaged with him in person. He reminded me of the extraordinary access I had had to him, which was true.

'You know, for nearly two years you could phone me and meet me and talk to me. And now you end it like this,' he exclaimed.

I reminded him the move was procedural. I told him it was also in his interests; it was his opportunity to set the record straight.

'But why a lawyer's letter?' he wanted to know. 'Why can't we just sit down and talk?

'You can bring your little notebook and your pencil,' he continued. 'And you can bring a recorder. It will all be on the record. I have no problem answering these questions.'

'So what happens if I raise an issue about some incident or other that you deny, what then?' I asked.

'You stay with your story and I stay with mine,' he responded.

With the lawyer's go-ahead, I decided to take Malema up on his offer and I met him at an up-market restaurant in Johannesburg the following afternoon. 'Wall Street' is located in the plush business district of Sandton, not the most natural of hideouts for a self-styled economic freedom fighter, but that was his choice of venue, and over the course of a couple of hours we went through the long list. What follows is the upshot of that conversation.

'The ability to make business is one's willingness to go and kick doors,' he told me. 'That's what I have done in the past when I was young.'

He began to dabble in public contracts, or tenders, when he was still a teenager and attending the Mohlakaneng High School in Seshego. Malema and his friends competed against the teachers to provide the school uniforms for the few hundred learners and the teenagers won the bid.

'But we underpriced and we didn't make a profit,' he claims, adding that he didn't influence the outcome in any way. 'I was only at the SRC level then,' a suggestion that perhaps his powers of sway only came later.

Not long after that he began to rise through the ranks of COSAS and along the way he met Pule Mabe, who was a journalist for the local newspaper, the *Mail & Guardian*, covering some of Malema's rallies. Their paths continued to cross when Malema, at the age of 20, moved to Johannesburg after he became the president of COSAS. That was in 2001 and around the time that Mabe began to give up on the idea of journalism. He secured a stint in one of the local government departments before landing a job at the state-owned Passenger Rail Agency of South Africa (PRASA). By then Mabe was involved in many business deals. He and Malema had a lot in common and they established a good rapport.

Malema was like 'Jimmy who comes to Jo'burg', as Patti Nkobe says of her old friend. He was the farthest thing from a city slicker when he first arrived and he wouldn't have had the polish or the plush outlook of the rising black middle class. Mabe wouldn't have been much better. He was another young man from the provinces trying to melt into the metroscape of Johannesburg. Two kindred souls fixed on the city's bright lights. Two of a kind out to make a quick buck.

'Pule at that time was a bit advanced in business,' Malema says. 'He had a Golf, a Jetta, a Combi [mini-bus taxi]. And he started introducing me to those types of opportunities.'

But he insists that it was Mabe who was eliciting most of the tenders and that he was just helping out. He was not involved in all of them, he wanted to point out. Only a few.

One of those was a tender they won to brand plastic water bottles for Lepelle Northern Water, the water board in their home province of Limpopo.

'This was not me [who got the tender]. Pule came with it. He included me,' Malema says. On that basis, one might assume that he was brought in to do some work for a fair fee in return, but Malema claims he did it for nothing: his version is that his toil and troubles did not earn him anything at all.

Another deal that came their way was the co-ordination of entertainment for the inaugural ceremony of a mayor of the Waterberg District Municipality, in the southern stretches of Limpopo.

'Pule was involved in entertainment,' he explains. 'And we needed to market his company. We were literally knocking on doors from one comrade to the other. That's how we got that tender in Waterberg.'

He cannot remember the year – 'I was still COSAS president at that time' – nor does he remember the amount of money it made for them, though on this one he admits he did rake some in. Some time back, I remember him throwing out a figure of R30,000, but this may not be accurate. But it wasn't the money he was after.

'When the money was paid, I asked Pule to give me his car,' he said. So Mabe pocketed the money and Malema got his first car, a second-hand white Citi Golf.

No doubt there were numerous other business deals that the pair pulled off around that time, but towards the end of 2003 Malema packed up his bags and piled that small Golf high with his possessions and headed home to Polokwane after his term as COSAS president came to an end. That December he was elected as provincial secretary of the Youth League, based in Polokwane, but he maintained his ties with Johannesburg all the while.

I wanted to know more about the lure of Gauteng and I ask if it had anything to do with the ties he might have developed with the state-owned South African Rail Commuter Corporation (SARCC), or indirectly with them through PRASA. The corporation was trying to clamp down on fare-evaders – or train surfers as they were called – and it rolled out the 'Sparapara' campaign to curb the growing trend of non-paying passengers. Through that Malema allegedly won a few tenders on the back of a bid to communicate to the public that train surfing had to stop, tenders that were linked to PRASA, where Mabe was working.

'They were not really tenders,' Mabe had once told me when I talked to him about them. 'I just brought him in to talk to people. I saw him as a voice of reason.'

Malema trots out the same line all these months later.

'No money,' he says. Just motivational speaking – 'talking to the young ones' – which was in turn raising his political profile. And he casually writes it off as more of a political project than a money-making venture, though that too is hard to believe.

'You know, we were suffering financially at that time,' he says. Sello Moloto had replaced Ngoako Ramatlhodi as premier of Limpopo 'and the government was not so available to me. I was not so powerful then.'

We had already hit the spot where he would have to stick to his story and I to mine, because he was not far off his 23rd birthday when he started out as the provincial secretary of the League and despite what he says, friends remember how he began to live life to the full around then, making a name for himself around the city as he scaled the social ladder.

He had started to spruce himself up. Gone were the T-shirts and shorts. Gone were the sandals. The Afro was shaved off. He developed a taste for nice shoes and good clothes and before long a fetish for designer labels. That was also when his waistline began to bulge as he feasted off his new lifestyle. Malema was becoming a new man.

So if there wasn't a second income, where did the money come from to fund it?

He admits he belonged to an important clique of key players – 'leading politicians and high business people in the province' – who opened doors for him in all directions. 'We lived like a family. We took care of one another. But no tenders. It was comradeship,' he insists. 'That's how we are.'

Then I broach the thorny subject of SGL, the firm of consulting engineers that is based in Polokwane and that has become infamous through its links to Malema and is now being investigated by four of the state's prosecutors for fraud and corruption.

The history of SGL was explained to me in the following way by people close to its operations: In 2004, Malema met the two directors of the firm – Lesiba Gwangwa and Jonathan Khedzi – at the home of well-known businessman Matome Sathekge. Sathekge owned Bakgaloka Holdings, and the two men had done some work for him in the past. When they tried to get their own firm off the ground, Sathekge told them Malema would help put some tenders their way. Whatever arrangement they came to would be their own.

Infrastructure projects were plentiful in the province, which at the time was undergoing major restructuring. Civil engineering was a good business to be in, but for a young company starting out, with a track record that only spanned a few years, SGL needed a leg-up and Malema was going to provide it, they were told.

Malema had failed his end-of-school exam and hadn't any further education or training in any kind of technical discipline, and yet he was going to push some major engineering contracts the way of this small firm.

Malema flatly denies this.

Sathekge says there was no such suggestion on his part, Khedzi refused to comment on the matter and Gwangwa denied it outright. Malema, however, admitted he was introduced by the well-known businessman to the two young directors, but he says it was for reasons very different from what I was led to believe.

'What was central in me being introduced to these young chaps was for them to help the Youth League. SGL was donating money to the Youth League programmes,' he argues.

I talk him through the alleged deal as it was explained to me. Malema was to help SGL win tenders and in return he – rather than the Youth League – would earn 10 per cent of the value of each one he put their way. Therefore, the bigger the amount of the tender, the better for Malema and the more tenders he put their way, better still. For the directors of SGL it was a workable agreement. These tenders were crucial for their growth and survival.

I was told that the brokering fees were allegedly paid out in one of three ways: in cash; in cheques made out to one of his cousins; or in cheques made out for cash. The cheques would either be collected by his cousin or cashed on Malema's behalf by one of the directors who would then deliver the cash to him at his home. Sometimes he would collect the cash himself, though the pick-up point would rarely be at the office.

'How would I do that?' Malema asks.

'You tell me,' I say in response.

'You should have asked the fools who told you to explain [it],' he shoots back.

The sources stick to their guns – that's how it was, they say, though Gwangwa won't entertain it for a moment. Nor will Malema, who says that even if he had wanted to, the political climate was not conducive to it at that time.

'The doors were closed,' he persists, arguing that he was on the wrong side of Moloto and times were lean.

'So no tender kickbacks?' I ask. 'No cash payments or cheques made out for cash but for your benefit?'

'No, no, no.'

I recalled a conversation I had had with him in the spring of 2009. We were talking about his lifestyle and when I asked him what or who was footing the bill for it all, he told me what his ANC salary was. He led me to believe he was taking home something in the region of R40,000-plus a month at the time, when the various deductions were totted up. And it was inconceivable that that amount could sustain Malema's lavish ways, though he insisted at the time, 'I don't have any other income. This is it.'

So when his business interests began to trickle into the public domain towards the end of that year, I asked him in which field he felt he excelled: politics or business.

'Do the two have to be mutually exclusive?' he asked in response.

'That would depend on the nature of the business,' I replied.

But even with the correct separation of interests, did he feel he was a better politician or businessman?

'I'm a good deal broker,' he answered. 'That's what I am.'

I remind him of that conversation as we try to get the record straight and I turn to the other companies to which he has been linked and on behalf of which he is alleged to have helped to drum up business deals, according to former associates. I ask again if it is possible that there was a budding broker in him all this time.

'You know, in that process there was a point when one registered companies in his name and tried to do some jobs and was not successful,' was his careful response. 'And the companies became dormant.'

Was he not a shareholder in Ever Roaring Investments?

'Ja, but I was not always there,' he says.

'Did he and his fellow shareholders ever venture into a multi-million rand deal linked to Vuna Health Care [which in turn is linked to ANC-owned Thebe Investments] to provide medical supplies across the province over a three-year period?'

'I don't know if they had a business with Vuna,' he says in reference to Ever Roaring. 'I never did.'

I put it to him that the deal allegedly earned him – and the other three main shareholders who were with him in Ever Roaring Investments at that time – some R250,000 between them. The tender should have earned them far more, but they scuppered the chance of that at the bidding stage.

He denies this, saying, 'There have never been financial benefits coming from Ever Roaring. It actually took money from us.'

(I would later learn that payments continued long after that initial payout.)

The same applies for Blue Nightingale Trading 61, he suggests, the company to which he appointed himself as a director and some family members as fellow directors.

Yet it was through this company that he secured a 3 per cent shareholding in Tshumisano Waste Management, the consortium that won a R200 million public tender in 2005. Though it had been reported that Malema was bought out a year later, I put it to him that my information shows that he remained as a shareholder until the five-year deal wound down in 2010, the books for which were being settled at that time.

'Definitely not,' he says, arguing that he wasn't a director of Blue Nightingale in 2005 when the tender began (though I point out that would not necessarily preclude his involvement as a shareholder).

In addition to his dividend payouts, my information is that Malema received a payout from the consortium in 2006 that was just shy of R270,000, which financial insiders claimed was a loan, but which in practice was essentially a financial gift.

'What loan?' he asks. 'I don't owe anybody.'

If not a loan, then perhaps a gift.

'No,' is the flat response.

He is equally adamant that Blue Nightingale was not involved in Beta Projects and the consortium that won multiple and hugely lucrative cleaning tenders throughout Limpopo in recent years. Then I tell him I have the financial records that show a 10 per cent shareholding in the Beta consortium.

'But have you seen the money go into my account?' he asks.

I haven't, but surely the financial statements speak for themselves?

'No, it's not true,' he says.

I was fortunate to get my hands on the company's records, or in the case of SGL and the other companies above, to have had access to those who were closely linked to it all, and I was satisfied that I knew how the various deals were done. When the state investigations are concluded, Malema will find it hard to sustain his denials.

What is remarkable about it all is that his businesses and wealth were blossoming at a time when he was on the wrong side of the provincial political divide that had emerged in the ANC. What is evident now, with hindsight, is that Moloto had lost control on the ground and over his municipalities where Malema and his men were making inroads, in business and political terms.

All told, he was becoming a man of many means but he was also building a powerful political profile, as one of the leading figures in Zuma's comeback plan. In the run-up to the party conference at the end of 2008, a friendly businessman advised him, for the sake of some privacy and tax benefits, that he should establish a trust, which he named after his son, Ratanang.

When I ask him about the nature of the trust, he sticks to the same line that he has been trotting out ever since the trust was exposed some weeks earlier: it's a charitable trust; it's for the good of society; it's doing no harm; and it's earning him no wealth.

However, he claims that in addition to himself and his grandmother, there are many other trustees.

'There are people from outside [the family] as trustees,' he says, 'but it remains a family trust.'

Who are they and when were they appointed?

'I'm not going to tell you that,' he shoots back.

Is the trust in order?

'The trust is tax compliant. Because to buy properties, you have to have a tax certificate and pay tax on property as well. So there is no problem there.'

Malema has a good laugh to himself when I ask to see the finances.

'Nobody will see the financials of the trust,' he says.

Yet, the South African Revenue Services (SARS) are currently knee-deep in an investigation into Malema's tax affairs and are probing an extensive record of multi-million rand payments that have been made to him over the years. Malema has so far insisted that the payments were gifts, and that he did nothing in return for his benefactors, which therefore makes it difficult for the revenue collectors to collect their dues. They were then forced to start an inquiry, calling on all of his benefactors to explain the payments, a process that is still unfolding.

Tokyo Sexwale, a senior figure in the ANC, is reported to have part-settled one of Malema's tax bills that apparently ran into millions of rand, though Sexwale denies this. Should that be proven true, or indeed if the SARS inquiry throws further light on the alleged money-making racket that Malema appears to have been caught up in these past few years, the modus operandi of South Africa's ruling party would be blown wide open. Sexwale is a man with big ambitions and with business ties right across the party.

I often pity Ratanang Ramohlale. Ratanang is not a common name, and one can't begin to imagine the shame that will be heaped upon him when he becomes a teenager and is recognised as the namesake – and the beneficiary – of the most controversial trust fund in South Africa, which by then will most likely have been the subject of various court trials for the fraud that appears to have been channelled through its accounts. When it first came to light and the state investigations began, the child would have been about five years old and I ask Malema if his son was aware of what he had done in his name.

'No, he knows nothing,' Malema says, looking more awkward than I had ever seen him before. He is uncomfortable and within seconds he shifts the topic.

He talks me through the property investments that started in 2006 when he bought a plot of land in the up-and-coming residential area of Ster Park in Polokwane, which the locals dub 'Tender Park' today. It sits on the lip of a swathe of land on the eastern side of the city that has been earmarked to house the legislature when it is eventually relocated from Lebowagomo to Polokwane, and which will add to the value of the area when it does.

Malema bought the site for R222,000 from the municipality, but in a deal that was ironed out in the following way: A friend of his called Matane Mphahlele – the advocate whose name would later surface in a scandal of alleged company hijacking by the official company's register CIPRO – bought the site in August 2006 for R222,000, though he did not register it until the following April, but as soon as he did, it was immediately re-registered in Malema's name in a dubious 'double transfer'.

What was odd about the deal was that the price didn't change when the site changed hands. Is this not a tad suspicious? I ask him. Was he not effectively buying off the municipality but shielding such a move by putting Mphahlele up front?

'No, the municipality was about to take the site from him,' when Mphahlele failed to raise the funds to secure the purchase. 'And I said, give it to me, and he agreed. And I went to the municipality and said "I'm going to pay the land for Matane, but it must be a double transfer." They said, "No, this is his site. And it must be like he is paying for this site and then he can legally transfer it to me."'

If what Malema says is true, then the response on the part

of the municipal staff raises questions. The double transfer also sounds odd, if not illegal, and I tell him it's as if Mphahlele may have defaulted so that Malema could move in, secure the site at the same low price, but save himself some scrutiny about securing prime municipal land as a rising political figure.

But he rejects that notion outright.

He tells me he took out a loan from Standard Bank to buy the site, which was then sold on his behalf by a real estate agent a few months later for R680,000. How much Malema actually got for it he will not say. But with the proceeds he put down a deposit on a modest house in nearby Flora Park, for which he paid close to R1 million, rolled by a bond – which has since been cleared – and he immediately pumped a further R500,000 into the house in renovations.

He had the existing walls raised quite high around the perimeter for privacy. He installed a swimming pool and a 'lapa', or thatched entertainment structure. He changed the windows throughout the house and he renovated the front entrance.

When Malema won the presidency of the Youth League in 2008, he moved back to Johannesburg. He had a short stay in a Sandton penthouse, before moving to a house owned by Lembede Investments, the League's own investment vehicle, which has also been the subject of various cases of corruption. In April 2009 he moved to a three-bedroomed house in Sandown, on the edge of the plush Sandton area, the rent on which was R18,000 a month.

The owner, Kenneth Hollingsworth, was approached by a real estate agent who told him she had a tenant who wanted to rent it.

'He's a good tenant. And he will pay cash up front,' she told him.

'Great,' Hollingsworth said.

'You won't have any problems with him,' she continued. 'Great,' he said again.

'Would you have a problem if the tenant was Julius Malema?' she asked.

'Not at all,' he said. 'I don't care who it is so long as it's a good tenant.'

True to his word, Malema paid cash up front for the rental for the entire year, complete with the two months deposit. The payments came in a couple of tranches.

'I approached Pule and different comrades and asked them to help me pay the rent,' Malema suggests when I put it to him the afternoon I sat with him to go through the questions. 'We asked for up-front payments so that we don't go around every month knocking on doors.'

But two months after Malema moved into the house, he decided he wanted to buy it. It was in an ideal location, in a quiet residential estate just off the N1 motorway, accessible both for work in downtown Johannesburg and to the route to Polokwane. It was surrounded by high walls, which appealed to him for security reasons. It was modest-sized, though with plenty of room for expansion. There was also ample room for parking, which he also liked.

So he put pressure on the owner until he relented.

'The house wasn't for sale,' Hollingsworth told me. 'But he wasn't giving up. So in the end, I put a figure on it that was way above the market rate.'

At the time, the house was worth about R2.8 million but Hollingsworth threw the price of R3.6 million at Malema. Without a moment's hesitation, Malema accepted.

Again he says he asked for contributions to help him put down a deposit. 'And then they started contributing.'

I ask who 'they' are, but he refuses to say.

I tell him that I heard there were four men who contributed to the down-payment.

'No, different people,' he says. 'There were more than four.'

The one name that keeps coming up is that of Sexwale and I

ask Malema if he was one of those behind the house or if he was funding his lifestyle in any way at all.

'Tokyo – he has never given me money,' he says.

'Has he ever given the trust money?' I ask.

'No, Tokyo has never given the trust money.'

So why does his name keep coming up?

'They try to discredit me by saying I've been bought by Tokyo.'

With or without him, Malema continued to build his property portfolio. A year later the trust bought a farm in Palmietfontein, on the outskirts of Polokwane. According to the deeds records, it was a cash purchase for R900,000. Not long after that the trust purchased another property, a residential home in Polokwane, where his son, Ratanang, and the mother of the child, Maropeng, now live.

That house was purchased through Gwama Properties, of which Gwangwa is the sole director but in which the Ratanang Trust has a shareholding.

Another property, in Quinn Street in Polokwane, was added to his portfolio a few months later. I ask Malema how many more might follow and he tells me there might be some more. And he leaves it at that.

He was certainly in the money around that time and ploughing it back into properties. His wealth was conspicuous in other ways, not least through his cars. From the Citi Golf he drove home to Polokwane in 2003 he graduated to a white Colt double cab later that year. Then he bought a black Audi A3.

'And I had to raise money for that too,' he claimed. 'My car subsidy as secretary-general was not enough to cover it. So I asked the comrades to help me,' careful to embroil as many others as he can in his transactions.

Not long after that, he was driving a top-of-the-range black Audi A3 Quattro 3.8. Around the middle of 2008, he bought his first Mercedes. A superior Mercedes followed a year after that again. As 2011 began, Malema took possession of another sleek

Mercedes, this time an S600 V12, one of the most expensive models.

In the meantime, other cars featured among Malema's possessions, mostly Land Rovers and Range Rovers. One belonged to businessman Raymond Matume.

'What's wrong with that?' Malema asks. 'We are comrades. He's a businessman. He gives lots of money to the ANC.'

What about the political favours this begs?

But Malema insists it is not he who doles out the tenders. He may be a public figure, but is not a public official, is his line.

Other cars that have featured in his mix have belonged to Lesiba Gwangwa, the director of SGL.

'Lesiba is a friend. He can help me if he wants.'

But Lesiba is also a business partner and a director of a firm that has secured a number of public tenders since Malema began to feature in his life in 2004. In 2010 the Public Protector was called upon to investigate SGL and the possibility that Malema's involvement in it was influencing the multiple tenders the company was winning.

What Advocate Thuli Madonsela, the Public Protector, concluded was that as far as she could gather, there was no real evidence pointing to irregularities in the tenders. She pointed out that Malema had only joined SGL a year earlier, and during his tenure as director the company had only been awarded three public contracts. However, she also acknowledged that much of the paperwork required to carry out the investigation could not be found, and with some unusually minor recommendations about record keeping and transparency, the chapter was closed.

'I denied it,' he says, when I ask about his directorship. 'I don't know how my name got there . . . That's what I said. And that's what it was'.

Which, a denial of the truth or a statement of fact?

'Yes. The issue ended like that. My directorship was not confirmed by me. There was never any other issue.'

Yet he openly admits to having a shareholding in On-Point, which is held by the trust.

'I've got a relationship with On-Point from a family business point of view, not as an individual,' he says, though he refuses to declare the level of shareholding and, once again, denies any allegations that he influences the many tenders the company has been winning.

'I do not know what happens at On-Point. I just queue when the dividends are due.' Then he quickly corrects his slip adding, 'And not me, the trust does that.'

It was the first proof that Malema was directly trading off the public purse. As a result of that revelation, On-Point is now the main focus of the four state forensic investigations into his financial affairs, as the company had won a lucrative tender at the Department of Roads and Transport in Limpopo in 2009. The company was appointed to administer all of the department's public tenders over a three-year period, effectively controlling expenditure to the tune of R3 billion. Documentation that I was given, which listed all the companies that had been awarded contracts, showed how On-Point favoured all of the usual political suspects in the province, and even awarded tenders to itself.

The kickback agreements were quite sophisticated and in some cases drawn up on legally binding documents highlighting demands on the part of On-Point in excess of 20 per cent, but in one case fetching as much 70 per cent, of the tender amount.

The young man who was tied into that particular deal was a civil engineer who worked at On-Point, drawing a mediocre salary. With the work that passed over his desk, he could see that a lot of the companies were not sufficiently qualified or experienced to be involved in the projects. Often it was the case that he would do the drawings for them or assist in other ways. Eventually he asked his boss if he could also 'have' a tender. Gwangwa agreed, but demanded a 70 per cent stake. If that's what it took, the young engineer thought, then so be it. Gwangwa had come a long way from the days of SGL, the forerunner to On-Point, when he would pay Malema a 10 per cent cut. That was only seven years earlier.

But by the spring of 2011, practically every one of the country's media houses were investigating Malema, his companies and his cronies. Granted, the focus was very one-sided, but Malema had come to represent the worst of ANC politics and though he wasn't the only one draining the public purse dry, the spotlight was fixed upon him. He also gave good mileage as there seemed to be enough damning evidence to satisfy all of the newspaper houses for a number of months, each with their own exclusive take.

At the same time as these exposés were being splashed across front pages, the ANC was attempting to introduce a punitive media bill that would have prevented the publication of these same stories and the bravery on the part of the country's journalists was commendable. The Sunday newspapers in particular, along with the weekly *Mail & Guardian*, report excellent, in-depth, forensic-like investigations with a frequency that I doubt exists anywhere else in the world.

Yet despite the public glare, Malema continued to live as he had always done. The cash flow remained steady and at the beginning of 2011 he razed his Sandown residence to the ground and started to build a luxurious home in its place, at a cost of R8.5 million (though the construction work came to an abrupt halt early in 2012 as the state investigators began to close in on Malema).

Around the same time, his grandmother's home was demolished and in place of the small bungalow a two-storey house rose up.

And yet he was becoming increasingly difficult to find on paper, operating instead in what he thought was the safety of the Ratanang Family Trust and elsewhere.

'But it's not a secret trust,' he says. 'It's private.' And another outburst of hearty laughter follows.

While he does his level best to justify it all in the name of comradeship and charity and whatever else, Malema has put the spotlight on a way of ANC life that could have serious consequences for him and a number of other party members who lurk behind trusts and blur the lines between business and politics.

But therein lies Malema's saving grace, perhaps. If the authorities attempt to bring him down, he will surely threaten to bring his peers down with him.

Corruption is only not a problem when it doesn't exist, and there are few, if any, places in the world that are free of the scourge.

'But you know you've got a real problem with corruption when those in the know, those at the top, sit back and do nothing about it,' John Githongo, the fearless Kenyan whistleblower, told me.

For a number of years he had kept careful watch over Nairobi's administration as an anti-corruption fighter and in 2002, when President Mwai Kibaki came to power on an anti-corruption ticket, his administration asked Githongo to come into government to fight graft from within.

Though initially reluctant, he eventually said yes, but he was to be sorely disappointed soon after when he realised the rot was continuing rather than being rooted out.

'But, John, it's our turn to eat,' one of his government peers told him when he began to ask some difficult questions. It was said to him in a tone that suggested he should have known better, that his disquiet was perhaps unreasonable, if not naive.

That was when he decided to root out corruption himself and over the course of a few months he gathered incriminating information until he had enough damning evidence to blow the whistle on one of Kenya's biggest scandals. His story became the subject of a book that bore the title It's Our Turn to Eat.

'When you know corruption exists, and you know that the chiefs know, and you know that they know you know, yet they look the other way, then you've got a serious problem,' he continued. 'Because the message that is coming from the top is that it's OK. And that kind of message can do big damage in a society, it can rip a society apart. That's when corruption becomes difficult to root out, very, very difficult.

'And that's when society forms its own perceptions, and that too can be dangerous. People will expect the worst and will begin to see corruption and graft both where it exists and where it doesn't. They will begin to lose trust in the officials, in their ruling party. And then everything becomes difficult.'

11

Fear and loathing in Limpopo

Julius Malema was a man-child living like an aristocrat, enjoying himself to the full. He mingled with powerful people and moved in all the right circles. He was paraded about town with his bodyguards in tow. He had drivers who drove his expensive cars – some of which were his own though mostly they were gifts or were on some kind of favourable loan. He wore only the best labels over his short, stocky frame and was often dressed by some of the country's top designers. He threw wild and raucous parties at his homes in Johannesburg and Polokwane and would ply his guests with champagne and expensive whiskies and turn his 'house' music up full blast. He liked to be the DJ, but when he wanted to get down and dirty, he would hire a music mixer and party hard until the sun came up.

It was fun and frolic for many years and his peers were in awe of him. He was powerful and he was wealthy. In addition to the properties were the acres of land he added to his name, a name that was linked to an array of deals all of which played out alongside a political career that was going from strength to strength. He was the latest thing out of Africa.

But Malema was far too conspicuous for his own good. He was leading a life no different from that of many other prominent cadres of the ANC, the 'new' and 'old' alike. He just lacked the kind of discretion necessary to ensure he could keep it going. So when the lid was eventually lifted, Malema carefully reminded his party peers that he was not alone, and in the weeks following his financial showdown, he went viral on radio call-in shows and other media outlets to present himself to the world as a product of the ANC, throwing his hands up in the air as if to say, 'What have I done wrong? You taught me how to do it.'

Meanwhile, many of Limpopo's residents were clapping their hands in hearty appreciation at the prospect of Malema going down, and if he did, it might put an end to the style of govern-ance that had been crippling the province in the past few years.

From his Sandown home he directed much of Limpopo's day-to-day affairs with the assistance of the trusted men and women whom he had appointed to key provincial government posts, and a premier who was amenable to his ways. Though it is rich in minerals, the province is one of the poorest parts of South Africa and has been crippled by the spectacular rise in corruption and graft since 2009.

If provincial Gross Domestic Product (GDP) per capita is taken into account, the province would rank amongst the poorest in the country, but it would not languish at the very bottom of the pile. But poverty in itself is a big word and if it were taken in its broadest sense – to include an erosion of rights, security, dignity and so on, in addition to economic deprivation – then the provincial rankings would alter pretty rapidly. If the cost of corruption, poor governance and political factionalism were to be factored in, Limpopo would most likely fare the worst of all provinces.

It is all but impossible to put a figure on how heavily corrup-tion weighs on the lives of those who live in the province or on the provincial purse. If national calculations are accurate in suggesting that 20 cents of every tax rand is lost to fraud and corruption nationwide, it can be safely assumed the loss is far greater in Limpopo. Consider for a moment the structure of the province and then it is easy to see how quickly corruption can take hold.

Government services is the second biggest sector of the provincial economy, after mining, and contributes 15 per cent to the provincial GDP. Construction, often an indicator of economic growth, is the smallest sector (2 per cent of the total), followed by agriculture and manufacturing, which contribute only 2.9 per cent each to the total value of production, according to Glen Steyn, a local economist who compiles most of the provincial data. All told, the dependence on government rather than the private sector appears sharp in Limpopo. And therein lies the danger political analyst Moeletsi Mbeki so often warns of when he says that as a nation, South Africans consume too much and produce too little.

Government – municipal and provincial – is also the biggest employer by far, particularly in Polokwane, the seat of local and provincial government. The public sector salary bill currently swallows 65 per cent of Limpopo's annual budget, while it is estimated that 60 per cent of the local active workforce is employed by the provincial government.

In a province with a low rate of manufacturing and production, the government budget is looked upon as a big revenue spinner. The competition for public tenders is high, a situation that creates an ideal breeding ground for graft, to which the current administration appears to have fallen prey.

Since 2009, it has found itself under intense public scrutiny as the media continues to expose fraudulent deals involving high-profile politicians and politically connected individuals who are trading on the public purse. But neither the treasury officials in Pretoria nor in Polokwane can put a figure on the revenue that may have been lost to graft or the percentage of public tenders that may have been negotiated on corrupt grounds.

Late in 2011, when the province's R43 billion allocation had run dry, five of the eleven provincial departments were brought under the administration of the national government, at the request of Finance Minister Pravin Gordhan. A team of investigators was swiftly drafted in to try to find out where the money had gone and when early reports pointed to widespread misuse of public funds, particularly in the departments of roads and transport, education and health (not surprisingly where Malema and his cronies have been winning a lot of public contracts), Gordhan appointed accounting firm PwC to begin a forensic investigation, which is currently ongoing.

Consider again Malema's company On-Point, which won the contract at the provincial department of Roads and Transport to effectively manage and administer all of the department's tenders, through a so-called Programme Management Unit. The PMU didn't exist until the change of government in 2009 when the new administration decided to introduce it in a move that effectively outsourced government work to the private sector, at the same time as Malema had crowned himself the country's economic freedom fighter, pushing for nationalisation of the country's assets.

Around the same time as the department announced plans to create the PMU, a company called On-Point was started by Lesiba Gwangwa, Malema's business partner, who had started SGL many years earlier. At the time it bid for the tender, On-Point was only a few days old. As a company it had no track record and did not possess the skill required, nor did it have a qualified civil engineer among its staff, a core requirement for the bid application. To fill the void, it simply attached the name of a civil engineer who had once worked for the company and who is currently caught up in a legal battle trying to disassociate his name.

On-Point won the bid. The tender value – in the region of R50 million – was not the main draw. It was the fact that Gwangwa could now decide who got what deals in the province.

It is a dangerous business to be in, trading in tenders in this way. It is not only potentially fraudulent but it doesn't always put the right people in the right places to provide badly needed essential services.

SGL – the forerunner to On-Point – was already a case in point. In the past couple of years the company has been flagged for poor workmanship many times. There was a taxi rank in Sekhukhune that collapsed. There was a water reticulation system, also in Sekhukhune, that went so badly wrong it cost many times the amount of the initial contract value to put it right.

'Why wasn't the company who did the work held accountable?' I asked one man who was involved in the damage repair on that particular one.

'Because certain people do what they want around here and no one will ask questions,' he replied. 'They are above everyone else. They are not treated like anyone else.'

The municipality was forced to dip into its budget instead to repair the damage at the expense of other essential projects and the overall project of service delivery.

'It's a phenomenon that has become widespread across the country,' says Sydney Mufamadi, a former minister in Mbeki's cabinet. 'Those who don't have the skills or the entrepreneurship to produce are buying access to politicians so that they can access the tendering system that way. And our society is not only becoming one that consumes, but we are now in the early stages of a dangerous kleptocracy.'

Limpopo is also a province that attracts a lot of overseas aid money, yet two diplomats – one from Europe and the other from Latin America – say they cannot spend the amount of money they would like to in the province because the accounting structures are not in place. Hence it is those who are at the bottom of the pile, those in need of development aid, who lose out.

Of course the fiscus also suffers, though many will try to tell you that it doesn't. They argue that the public purse is not affected if state tenders are doled out amongst pals, insisting that if a bribe is paid, it does not affect the tender amount in any way.

It is merely a transaction between two people – like a fee – that has no bearing on the cost of the tender or the public coffer that is awarding the contract and it therefore becomes a private arrangement.

That's an argument that's a tad too convenient because the person on the receiving end of the kickback is unlikely to declare the extra stream of income to the taxman. How could he or she? And whoever lurks behind the 'front man' will surely opt for silence too.

A company I have referred to elsewhere in the pages of this book found itself in a tight spot when it became embroiled in the practice of paying out kickbacks in return for tenders. Like any company doing business with the state, it was registered for tax purposes and therefore was obliged to declare all payouts over a certain amount to the taxman. But the firm of accountants employed by the company in question was unable to settle the company's books. The accountants could not make any sense of the frequent payouts or the gaping holes that cropped up when the payouts were not declared. When the owners of the company were pushed to explain themselves, they simply couldn't and were eventually removed from the books of the accountancy firm. That was in 2008, but it didn't stop what was going on. An accountancy firm that was prepared to cover SGL's tracks was brought in instead.

However, bribes, fees, payouts and donations, or whatever one might call them, are not always paid in cash or cheques. There is one case in Limpopo where a high-flying businessman struck up a friendship with one of the most senior politicians in the province when the ANC changed its leadership in 2007. The businessman was of the view that five years of such friendship could be worth millions in tender revenue and he did what it took to cement the alliance.

It often meant funding their parties, purchasing designer clothes at top-end boutiques, buying alcohol or settling restaurant bills, not only for the politician in question but for his associates as well.

The businessman and the politician eventually bought a property together and though it was only the businessman who put up the capital, they were equal partners in the deal. The men agreed that the politician would facilitate public contracts for the businessman and with each transaction the politician would increase his equity in the property. It was explained to me as 'political capital'. And it worked. The businessman in question did exceptionally well, though he too now finds himself subject to the forensic inquiries.

Yet, the taxman says he benefits from these kinds of deals in a very roundabout way. Black money doesn't last long in anyone's hands as it has to be spent as soon as the palm is greased. Underground cash leads to spending sprees and the kind of boost that every economy thrives off. What was a coveted item yesterday is within easy reach today, or what was never even coveted at all is within even closer reach. In the last few years, the small city of Polokwane has opened a number of high-end restaurants and hotels, shops and other spending outlets, through which revenue is returned to the taxman.

While there are many benefiting from this form of arrangement, it creates a very vulnerable and fearful society in which to live. Since 2009 tens of senior public servants have been purged from their positions as the new government in Limpopo began to close ranks. And in doing that, a strong message was sent out to all public servants that job security is based on political allegiance rather than performance. The indirect message that is being communicated is that it is pointless trying to find a job, as the current requirements call for political connections above all else.

Hence the number of discouraged work seekers is rising steadily. According to the South African definition of unemployment, if one is not actively seeking work, one is not counted as being out of work. Therefore 'the labour force participation rate in Limpopo is consequently very low at 36.7%, compared to 54.2% for the country as a whole', while 'international comparisons indicate that many countries have labour force participation rates in excess of 60%', according to Steyn's research.

Those who do have jobs hold on to them dearly, because under this administration, job security has been severely eroded. Many contracts have not been renewed and often for no good reason, while others have found themselves under the most extraordinary and unnecessary pressure.

One civil servant who managed a department that oversaw sensitive property deals and who was not part of the new clique talks about the harassment she endured when they tried to force her to resign. She eventually cracked under the pressure and was signed off by her doctor for a month on stress-related grounds. Her employers refused to accept her doctor's certificate, demanding that she be examined by a doctor of their choice instead. When she refused, they simply cut her pay.

Another civil servant, Matlala Maremane, tells of how he showed up for work one Monday morning to find that his office at the Polokwane municipality had been broken into and the hard drive from his computer removed. The offices are monitored by CCTV cameras and when he checked the footage, he found senior staff accompanied by the municipal manager, breaking into his office and tampering with his computer. Within hours of reporting it to the local police station, he was suspended from his job, a battle he is still fighting.

'But it doesn't really matter,' Maremane says. 'They will fire us anyway. We will appeal. The case will drag through the courts. And then there will come a time when I won't be able to pay the legal fees and I will have to drop it. They will eventually win this one. And by the time they do, I will have lost a lot of money, my livelihood and my future. I'm not the first and I won't be the last.'

That was true. The purging of staff right across the province was openly talked about. The provincial government employed the same lawyer who returned the same guilty verdict against each person who was brought before him.

I was often reminded of John Githongo's words to me:

'When you know corruption exists, and you know that the chiefs know, and you know that they know you know, yet they look the other way, then you've got a serious problem.'

South Africa is condemned by geography to share a border with Zimbabwe and the two countries meet at the border town of Beitbridge, a small low-lying town in the north of Limpopo. In the run-up to the Fifa World Cup in 2010, the people of Polokwane liked to joke about the African soccer fans who would make the journey to South Africa overland and would surely think they were still in Mugabe's country when they entered Malema's home province, such was the deterioration of their lives. It was a sad attempt at satire.

'I don't care,' was Julius Malema's short answer when I asked him how he felt about the criticism that rained down on him throughout 2010.

The laughter had gone out of his relationship with the ANC and the story about the falling out was a favourite for the political hacks. His irregular business affairs were another hot topic, keeping some of the country's top investigative journalists frantically busy.

No one could sell newspapers quite like Malema, and for the media he was their perfect match. Be it on a good day or bad, the ANC Youth League president made it on to their front pages more than any other South African figure, political or otherwise. The fact that most of the coverage was biting bothered him not at all.

'I am not made by newspapers and I will not be destroyed by newspapers,' he snapped.

'I don't even read the news. Why should I? I make the news.'

12

Powerful and fearless

He was little more than a year in the job as ANCYL president and the short and portly rebel was puffed-up and full of self-importance. His following had grown, the League's membership had dramatically increased and he was appealing to constituencies well beyond the youth. There hadn't been any real strategy and there were no advisors or spin doctors guiding Julius Malema's moves. Because he was only in his late 20s and mingled with men and women in the ANC rather than in the League, people initially saw Malema as a puppet whose strings were being pulled for money in return, but as he found his feet and his voice as 'The President', it was apparent that he was leading from the front.

'This is me. All me,' he used to tell me. One hundred per cent Malema.

'He understands politics but he also understands his own people,' says Cassel Mathale of his friend. 'He understands their needs and he knows how to talk to them.'

Malema was touching on all of the hot political issues by then. He spoke about land reform and the need to share the country's wealth. He was pushing nationalisation of the country's mines and addressing the need for the African majority to be involved at the centre of all decision-making processes right across the board, be it in government, business, the judiciary or elsewhere.

'He's talking to the country – straight talking – and pronouncing on some very critical issues that we are all struggling with,' his predecessor Fikile Mbalula told me late in 2009 when Malema was gaining in prominence.

Jacob Zuma foolishly added to the praise-singing around the same time, telling Malema he was 'a leader in the making' and one who was 'worthy of inheriting the ANC'.

That endorsement took place in Seshego, Malema's township, when the state president was unveiling a church that Malema and his moneymen had erected in honour of his late mother, Florah. To the right of the main entrance they hung a marble plaque upon which was etched her name, the date the church was opened, and that it was bequeathed to the community by the controversial Ratanang Family Trust, an unwitting move that identified where he was stashing the money.

'I don't know,' Malema said when I asked him why Zuma had decided to give him such a hearty clap on the back that spring day. 'But I'm not complaining.'

Malema was obviously doing something right and he decided to continue doing what he had been doing all along – being as radical, militant and daring as he possibly could. The odd political outrage was doing no harm either.

Then, early in 2010, when the ANC celebrated the twentieth anniversary of the unbanning of the party and the release of Nelson Mandela, Malema decided to resurrect the old struggle song *'Dubula iBhunu'*, or 'Shoot the Boer' (or white Afrikaner farmer):

The cowards are scared,
Shoot, shoot.
Ayeah,
Shoot, shoot.
The cowards are scared,
Shoot, shoot.
Awu yoh,

Shoot, shoot.
Shoot the Boer
Shoot, shoot.
Shoot the Boer
Shoot, shoot.
Shoot the Boer
Shoot, shoot.
Shoot the Boer
Shoot, shoot.

It was his political mentor, Peter Mokaba, who coined the modern-day version of *'Dubula iBhunu'*, which he used to chant at political rallies during the tense years immediately before and after the end of white rule in 1994. But as the country settled into democracy, the song faded into the background and was sung only very occasionally until Malema decided to trot it out again that year.

'Why now?' I asked him at the time.

'Why not?' he answered, with a casual shrug of his shoulders. 'We are in charge now. It's our song. We sing it when we want to.'

Within weeks, the country's most notorious Boer, Eugene Terre'Blanche, the 69-year-old founder of the minority separatist group the Afrikaner Weerstandsbeweging (AWB), was beaten to death by two of his farm workers on Easter Saturday afternoon.

Malema was not in the country when Terre'Blanche met his death, though that didn't stop all fingers pointing in his direction as the one who had incited the murder. He was in Harare, visiting Mugabe and learning about the nationalisation of Zimbabwe's mines and its criminal land reform plan. The afternoon Terre'Blanche was murdered Malema was on the outskirts of the capital addressing a youth rally, at the end of which he sang *'Dubula iBhunu'* to his heart's content, as he had been banned from singing it in South Africa by the Pretoria High Court two days earlier.

When news of Terre'Blanche's death reached Malema in Harare he was the guest of honour at a gala dinner attended by some 500 of the country's top business people. The news did little to distract him. He simply proceeded with his schedule. South Africa, meanwhile, was simmering with tension, fearing a backlash by the extreme wing of the Afrikaner community, and throughout that Easter weekend the country was nervous.

The following morning a VIP motorcade pulled out of the Sheraton Hotel in Harare where he and his fellow ANCYL members were staying, as if nothing at all had happened. The 23-car convoy started out with a visit to some small land holdings in Mashonaland that had been returned through Mugabe's land reform programme to the local folk to farm. Then they visited a platinum mine owned by Zimplats, one of the early targets of the country's indigenisation plan to force foreign investors to cede 51 per cent of shareholdings to black Zimbabweans. The majority of its shares were owned then by South Africa-based Implats, along with a 13 per cent shareholding in the hands of independent investors, and it was listed on the Australian stock exchange. Its foreign composition made it a prime target, and it was forced to hand over the majority share two years later.

Next stop was Harare's main football stadium where Malema was billed to walk onto the pitch at the start of a game between the local top team, Dynamos, and Lupopo, from the Democratic Republic of Congo. But by the time the convoy crawled through the gates of the stadium, the match was long underway, so the South African youth and their Zimbabwean hosts settled into some VIP seats and watched the game for a while.

Half an hour or so later, the enterprising group was back on the road, headed in the direction of New Donnington Farm in Norton, which is about 60 kilometres south-west of the capital and owned by the country's controversial Reserve Bank governor, Gideon Gono.

In the absence of any other viable farms to showcase, most

high-profile visitors to the country are usually taken to Gono's. Spread over an area of 4,000 hectares in a district where farm size is limited to 400 hectares for everyone esle, New Donnington comprises two farms that were merged into one when the governor acquired them some years back.

New Donnington was the last stop of the day and Gono had decided to throw a party in honour of the South Africans. A marquee was erected on the lawns of the main house and as the convoy made its way down the farm's 10-kilometre driveway, the slaughtered beasts were turning tender on the spit.

I was travelling in a car with Pule Mabe, Malema's old friend who by then was the treasurer-general of the ANCYL as well as a private business partner of his boss, and it was then, as we reached the farm, that Malema's grand plan finally became apparent to me.

'You see, South Africa is the biggest producer of platinum in the world,' Mabe told me. 'Zimbabwe is sitting on big reserves of platinum as well.'

Southern Africa's reserves were discovered in the mid-1920s, but exploration proper only began many decades later as the multiple uses of platinum group metals became apparent. Industrialists now say that one in every five manufactured items either contains or is produced with platinum, making it one of the most strategic metals in the world. In the past decade, the price of the precious metal has almost tripled from US$500 per ounce in 2000 to US$1,500 in 2010.

Platinum is very rare with below-surface deposits accounting for only a minute fraction of the Earth's crust, occurring at only 0.003 parts per billion, according to one estimate. Above-ground reserves would only meet a year's demand, and if all the platinum in the world were poured into an Olympic-size swimming pool, it would apparently just about cover one's ankles, according to mining speculator Greg McCoach.

Between them, the two southern Africa countries are sitting

on the bulk of the world's deposits. So large is South Africa's platinum wealth that it now supplies in excess of 80 per cent of global demand. Zimbabwe's deposits and potential sources are not insignificant, though production has not been as high as its neighbour's. What makes Zimbabwe so attractive for mining houses and investors, though, is the fact that the metal is closer to the surface than it is in South Africa, making operations less costly and profits and returns more attractive.

'So if we can work together, we can create a superpower,' Mabe went on. 'Africa's first big superpower. And then we will be fully independent and we will stand up to the world. Africa can't do that without a superpower.'

His train of thought began to unfold as he told me how easy it would be to pull it all off. He grinned as he snapped his fingers. Malema's revolutionary thinking would capture the African imagination and it would build up momentum as it worked its way up through the continent from the southern tip.

There was no talk of sovereignty, or independence, or likely and logical resistance to the grand plan, just a rousing rendition of why it must happen and how 'we never realised the responsibility we were being given when we were elected as the leaders of this Youth League. But we need ZANU-PF to do it.' And their hosts were giving them all the right signals that night.

Malema, Mabe and his ZANU-PF friends were seated at the top table in the marquee, facing onto the gathering of about 150 or so guests, the majority of them ZANU youth.

As the evening began to draw to a close, Malema rose to his feet to give his hosts a lecture in political survival. As the youth of ZANU-PF you may be down, but you are not out, he assured them, promising that the ANCYL would help them get back on their feet. But they must be relevant to the people of Zimbabwe – be a part of them rather than fight against them. And if they can do that, then ZANU-PF has a future. Malema warned them against violence. It could have no place in driving their political project, he told them. But that did not mean that they must surrender. They simply had to find another means to fight their battle.

'This is war,' Malema blasted into the microphone. 'Arm yourself now, like you did in the past giving us AK-47s to go and fight the regime. But today the struggle is different. You are arming us to prepare ourselves for another confrontation. Because the struggle today is a struggle for economic emancipation. And we shall overcome . . .'

There aren't too many people who are prepared to bring ZANU-PF back to life and that Malema had travelled to Harare to throw them a lifeline made him a hero in their eyes, the new big man of Africa. They sang and danced and ululated when his speech ended.

'The winds of change are blowing across Africa,' Saviour Kasukuwere, Zimbabwe's minister for youth, indigenisation and empowerment, said as he took his turn at the podium after Malema stepped down.

'His coming to Zimbabwe has changed the mood of our country . . . Your speech tonight is a watershed speech here,' he told Malema. 'This political education will forever remain in their ears.'

Kasukuwere likened Malema to Alfred Rogers Nikita Mangena, the Zimbabwean guerrilla chief who was killed in battle in 1978. He was on his way to becoming the commander-in-chief of the Zimbabwean army, Kasukuwere continued. 'And he was only 33.

'He is the commander of southern Africa at 29,' he said, pointing at Malema.

Zimbabwe needed to regain control of its economy and the mineral assets of the country and stop the flow of the country's wealth overseas, Kasukuwere argued.

'We need to intervene,' he said. 'And that's why we salute this brave young bull,' he said in reference to Malema.

Earlier in the evening he had told the South African youth leader and the seven ANCYL members who had travelled to Zimbabwe with him that their hosts wanted to give them a gift to mark the 'historic visit'.

'A heifer. For each of you,' Kasukuwere said. That was their take-home prize for befriending ZANU-PF. That's how the Zimbabweans wanted to show their appreciation.

Malema's face was expressionless at first, as was that of Mabe who was sitting next to him at the top table.

'A heifer. A virgin cow,' Kasukuwere explained to the two city slickers.

'And a bull as well for you, Comrade Julius.'

They were then taken outside to a patch of land where the bovines were grazing in a cordoned-off area of grass, waiting to be vetted. They were healthy-looking heifers, but not a patch on Comrade Julius's bull. He was a prize-winning beast and had scooped the country's top awards in 2007, 2008 and 2009 at Harare's Agricultural Show. He had the badges to prove it, all of which were neatly displayed on a small board that was hanging off the fence.

Not to be outdone, Kasukuwere said he would personally match the gifts and pledged to give each of the South African youths a heifer 'as well as a bull for Julius'. Gono nodded. He would do the same. All told, Comrade Julius would take home three heifers and three bulls, while his colleagues would take home three heifers each.

The underlying message was not to be missed, they were told: the animals were to graze on the land that rightfully belongs to the people of South Africa.

And the bulls are equally symbolic. 'They are a mark of strength and bravery. And you must never behave like a castrated bull,' Kasukuwere told his guest.

March on, he ordered the young South African. And be brave. 'You can shoot Malema tomorrow, but you can't shoot the idea,' he continued. 'Anyone who thinks they can stop Malema, they can't.

'You are free,' he told Malema. 'That song must be sung. "Shoot the Boer".'

The audience rose to their feet for a second time, chanting the lyrics from the bottom of their bellies. As the only white person in the marquee, I was conspicuous enough as it was and I dared not defy their moment of jubilation by sitting it out for the dance of the night, so with reluctance I rose to my feet at the table where I was seated, but stood like a ramrod as they pounded the ground beneath them.

Two years earlier I had been forced to leave Zimbabwe when Mugabe's spin-doctor, George Charamba, devoted his Saturday morning newspaper column to a piece I had written in South Africa just days earlier about the peace deal that Mbeki was trying to broker, and how Mugabe was being offered amnesty for the atrocities he had committed, if he would only step down. In cold print that Saturday morning, Charamba wrote that I was an 'agent' who had done 'wonderfully well to become the poke-and-probe stick for the British' and 'a serial rapist of the truth'.

I digested his words while I drank my morning coffee in my hotel room in Harare. It was early, not long after seven, and when the time seemed respectable, I put a call through to my editors in South Africa, read the piece to them, and asked them to get me out of the country.

Charamba is a malicious thug who wears the suit of a respectable official and on his orders more journalists have been picked up and tortured in the past few years than one would care to imagine. My concern that morning was not the fact that I didn't have a visa – it was my third time to travel into the country as an undercover journalist in the space of two years, something that's not all that difficult. When I went through immigration on the Wednesday, three days earlier, and the dour official demanded to know the purpose of my visit, I told him I was attending the well-known cosmetic surgery clinic in Harare's city centre, a favourite for not an insignificant number of South African women looking for a cheap alternative to Johannesburg's upmarket outlets. I had even made a booking a day earlier to cover my tracks, which I had printed out and the official waved me through after only a cursory glance at my appointment card.

On one of my previous visits I masqueraded as an Irish missionary. In an earlier incarnation I was the wife of a diplomat who was attending a conference at Victoria Falls and I was joining him for the weekend in the tourist town. A well-known media acquaintance who works for one of the world's leading newspapers had sailed through the previous year with a tennis racket slung over his back.

As tough a country as it is with its heavy ban on foreign journalists, Harare's borders are more porous than even Mugabe would care to imagine.

No, what bothered me, if not petrified me, that morning was the fact that Charamba had chosen to write about me and print my name in the headline of *The Herald*, the government mouthpiece. My name meant nothing to the people of Zimbabwe and my fear was that he knew I was already in the country and the piece was intended to tell me so. Nothing scares me more in this world than Zimbabwe's torture police.

My editors pulled out all the stops. Mbeki was jetting in that afternoon and his presidential jet was scheduled to land at 14h00. A commercial flight was due to depart 10 minutes before that and we knew the Zimbabwean police wouldn't dare arrest me with the South African president about to touch down in the country. Though I am Irish, I was a member of South Africa's media then working for one of the biggest newspaper groups in the country.

The flight arrangements were made from the Johannesburg side, from where plans were also made for me to leave my rented car at the hotel and the keys with the hotel manager. A human rights lawyer was contracted to pick me up, escort me to the airport and stay with me while I checked in so that he could record anything that might go wrong. Nothing did and I vowed to myself as my plane took off that back I would not go.

But when Malema announced he was heading off to Zimbabwe two years later, I asked him if he would watch my back if I went too. It was the early days of this book and my research had only begun, but if he had support in Harare, then I wanted to see it. I would make my own way and stay in a local guesthouse, all I wanted was his backing. When he agreed, I knew I was in good company, though I remained stiff with apprehension the entire weekend. Not Malema. He was having a fine time of it.

On the Monday morning, Mugabe cleared his diary to meet with Malema at State House and laid on a grand and warm welcome. As the pair shook hands and posed for the cameras, I was struck by how short they both were. Mugabe in person is not half the man he presents himself as in public. He is quite possibly the shortest dictator in the world. Malema is also a small man and the pair were identical in height and it was quite a sight to see Africa's two big men together.

When Malema jetted out of the country around noon that day, he was feeling every bit as big a man as Mugabe. When I cast my mind back over his spectacular rise and no less spectacular fall, for me that weekend in Harare was the turning point for him. He was so totally and utterly high on the power he felt he had, a crash of some sort was inevitable. He was totemic on the streets of South Africa and now he was about to spread his wings on to the continent. I truly believe he felt he was unstoppable and when a halt was eventually put to his gallop, he simply couldn't believe it, or accept it. He was incapable of shattering his new image of himself.

That big man feeling was still with him when he called a press conference at Luthuli House three days after he arrived back in the country. Members of both the local and international media were quick to accept his invitation as the country was still tense in the wake of the murder of Terre'Blanche, and though his politics were for most people a throwback to another era, his killing had rocked South Africa and left its racial wounds raw and gaping once again. Malema was standing squarely in the firing line of the latest divide and the media wanted to hear what he had to say for himself.

He offered few concessions to social or political pressure that Thursday morning as he opened the press conference. Remorse was the furthest thing from his mind.

'He died before changing his racist behaviour,' Malema had said of the AWB leader in the immediate wake of the killing. 'His death should not be linked to the ANC struggle song . . . Our hands do not have blood.'

Instead, Malema wanted to brief the media about his four-day trip to Zimbabwe during which he had lauded Mugabe for his leadership, hailed Gono as a financial genius for his creativity at the Reserve Bank, and pledged to breathe political life back into ZANU-PF at the expense of their unity government partners, the Movement for Democratic Change (MDC).

The MDC was quick to criticise Malema as a prominent member of the ANC for taking sides at a time when the South African government was keeping watch over their fragile transition as a supposedly neutral neighbour and broker.

But Malema ignored what they had to say and instead chose to restate and reinforce his views as the press conference got underway. 'We want ZANU-PF to be retained in power. That's what we want,' he told the media contingent in his opening remarks. 'We are not going to relate with some Mickey Mouse we don't know. We relate with people we've got history together [sic].'

'They will never find friendship in us,' he continued. 'They can insult us here from air-conditioned offices of Sandton. We are unshaken. They must stop shouting at us. They must go and fight for their battle in Zimbabwe and win. Even if they've got ground, and they are formed on the basis of solid grounds in Zim, why are they speaking in Sandton, and not Mashonaland or Matabeleland?' he asked.

Malema has never addressed an audience of any sort, big or small, public or private, without an opponent of some sort as his focus. It is always them versus us. If you are not with him, then you are against him. The MDC started out as the enemy that Thursday morning.

'Let them go back and go and fight there,' he went on as he settled into his pitch. 'Even when the ANC was underground in exile, we had our internal underground forces fighting for freedom. And . . .'

'You live in Sandton,' Jonah Fisher of the BBC cut in before Malema could get the rest of the words out of his mouth.

Why this fact irked Fisher was not entirely clear, nor was it apparent what it had to do with the MDC. Malema was making the point that some members of Morgan Tsvangirai's party were based in South Africa while there was work to be done on the ground in their home country. Why he didn't point that out to Fisher was poor play on his part. But that's when the fun started.

'. . . and we have never spoken from ah, ah, ah, ah exile,' Malema continued, as he stuttered through to the end of his sentence, evidently thrown by the unexpected interruption.

Malema hadn't anticipated Fisher's challenge. His excesses had not only gone unchecked by his own party for quite some time, but the 'big man of Africa' feeling that he was endowed with in Harare was still with him. He was still on a political high.

'You see, here, let me tell you before you are *tjatjarag*,' a Pedi word that means to 'go ballistic', Malema said, turning to Fisher, his pudgy forefinger pointing in the direction of the journalist as he leaned across the table that separated him from the media pack. 'This is, this is a building of a revolutionary party and you know nothing about the revolution. So here . . .'

Fisher interrupted him for a second time.

'So they're not welcome in Sandton, but you are?' he asked.

Fisher's tone and his line of questioning riled Malema no end. There are not many people who challenge the young Turk in public and here was a white British male, of all people, ridiculing him in front of the media, of all groupings.

'. . . so here, here, here you behave or else you jump,' Malema shouted, reminding Fisher in a grisly tone and heavy-handed manner that they were on the eleventh floor of Luthuli House. 'So here you . . .'

Fisher cut in for a third time, this time laughing at the young man's ranting.

'Don't laugh,' Malema hollered at him.

'This is a joke,' Fisher responded.

'Chief. Can you get security to remove this thing here?' Malema said to whoever of his comrades was standing near the door.

'If you are not going to behave, we are going to call security to take you out,' he said, turning to Fisher once again.

The sound of clicking cameras was nearly as loud as Malema's voice by that point as photographers jostled to capture the moment on film.

'This is not a newsroom, this. This is a revolutionary house. And you don't come here with that tendency,' he continued, his finger wagging furiously at Fisher. 'Don't come here with that white tendency,' he shouted, his voice rising to fever pitch.

'Not here. You can do it somewhere else. Not here. If you've got a tendency of undermining blacks even where you work, you are in a wrong place. Here you are in a wrong place.'

Fisher dared interject for a fourth time before Malema's last few words could be heard. 'That's rubbish,' he said as he began to pack up his bag.

'Then you can go out. Ja, you can go out,' Malema said as he watched his new foe prepare to leave.

But as the journalist walked to the front of the room to retrieve his microphone, which was set up right in front of Malema on the table at which he was seated, the ANCYL leader decided to lower the tone of the spat.

'Rubbish is what you've covered in that ah, ah, trouser,' he remarked fatuously, pointing at the journalist's genitals. 'That is rubbish. That which you have covered in this trouser is rubbish.'

What Fisher's private parts had to do with anything remains a mystery, but Malema had reached boiling point by then and it was all downhill after that.

'OK?' Malema continued in a provocative tone, prodding a reaction. 'You are a small boy. You can't do anything.'

'I didn't come here to be insulted,' Fisher shot back.

'Come out. Go out,' Malema roared, tongue-twisted mid-sentence amidst the frenzy.

'Bastard. Go out. You bloody agent!' he shouted at the top of his voice as Fisher walked towards the door.

For a fraction of a second a deathly silence hung over the room. There were no more clicking cameras. No more sniggering journalists. Not even the sound of a single member of the media walking out in solidarity. Just the deafening sound of shock, which was only ruptured a moment or two later when Malema casually proceeded with the event as if nothing had happened, returning blithely to his views on Zimbabwe and why he felt the neighbouring country was a misread success story.

Within minutes of Fisher walking out of the door, the journalist became a news story in his own right while the youth leader quickly earned himself the nickname Kidi Amin, after the former Ugandan dictator, as footage of the sordid drama was uploaded onto websites and social networks all over the world. One of the first of South Africa's post-1994 leaders had just stepped up to the podium and bared his true colours.

I was at home in Cape Town that day and listened to the drama unfold on the radio. A while later I watched the footage on the internet. I watched it over and over again that afternoon, not quite believing what I was hearing. It was the most outrageous outburst I had ever heard and my only regret was that I wasn't there in person to see it all unfold. That evening, as the dust began to settle, I spoke to Malema by phone. I wanted to know why he had done it.

'No man. You don't get it,' he said.

Perhaps I didn't, but I still wanted to know what could have provoked such an extreme reaction on his part.

It could be argued that Malema was not alone in his bad behaviour that day. Though he was without doubt the worst offender, Fisher had also stepped out of line. The BBC journalist and all the other members of the media were at the so-called revolutionary house at the invitation of the ANCYL, after all. Malema was giving his spiel about his four-day trip to Zimbabwe and protocol suggested that he should have been allowed to have his say, regardless.

Fisher mustn't have liked what he was hearing and chose to dismiss the Youth League leader's words mid-sentence, without signalling or excusing his interjection. And in doing that, he touched on a very raw nerve.

Malema's behaviour was wholly unacceptable. But it is hard to imagine Fisher adopting the same tone of gusto with senior politicians such as President Jacob Zuma or other cabinet ministers.

It is equally difficult to imagine one of South Africa's black journalists addressing the Tory youth leader at Millbank in London with the same kind of bravado and getting away with it. Or, for that matter, Fisher addressing one of his own politicians in the same manner.

All that said, Fisher's behaviour still didn't warrant Malema's outburst. Could he not simply have asked the journalist to leave,

I wondered? Could Malema's spokesperson, the unlikeable Floyd Shivambu, who was seated next to him, not have called the house to order? Did he really have to get personal with Fisher?

'Why the extreme anger?' I asked.

'You don't know what it's like to have a white man tell me what to do in my own house,' he responded.

There was not a trace of anger in Malema's voice as he explained this. He was reeling after the day's events and was merely putting words to something very heartfelt, something that runs very deep in his thinking.

What happened at 'revolutionary house' that Thursday morning should have sounded the alarm bells in Malema's mind. But if they did sound, he was not about to heed them. He continued to walk a fine line.

The ANC chiefs began to mull over whether or not to slap him with disciplinary charges on three counts: defying the ANC's line on Zimbabwe; singing '*Dubula iBhunu*'; and his treatment of Fisher.

Zuma was scheduled to leave the country for a state visit to the United States from where he would travel on to Brazil for an Ibsa summit, and on the eve of his departure South Africa was still firmly focused on what Malema might do next. So Zuma decided to call a snap press conference during which he publicly humiliated the young man by telling the media that Malema's behaviour was 'alien' to the ANC. This was no laughing matter and Zuma left Malema in no doubt about it as he boarded the state jet and headed out of the country.

Sarah Malema was left reeling from Zuma's words. Her grandson must really have stepped out of line for Zuma to speak out like that, she thought. She immediately reached for her phone.

'Tell me, what did you do?' the old woman wanted to know when she got through to her grandson.

He tried to dismiss her question lightly, but she was having none of it.

'You must have done something very wrong for Zuma to speak about you on the television like that,' she said. 'Zuma is a good man. He doesn't fight with people like that.'

'Do you hear me?' she continued. 'You will lose your job. They are going to fire you. Zuma is complaining about you.'

Malema didn't try to challenge his grandmother, but continued to listen.

'You are the first person we know that Zuma is fighting with,' she said in a stern tone.

'Yo,' he thought as the call came to an end. 'This was serious. This woman stood by me always. And she only ever phoned me twice to give out: once about Naledi Pandor and now about Zuma.'

Malema thought about her words carefully, 'Because when I hear her talk like that, that's where you get the feeling of the last ordinary people and how they feel about [what you do].'

Granny was a good barometer and he knew he would have to make up for the lost ground if he was to hold on to whatever popularity he had among his 'people'.

But as if he couldn't help himself, Zuma had no sooner left the country than Malema stepped onto the nearest platform and started to taunt his boss. Thabo Mbeki would never have done what Zuma had just done, he told his gathering, as he began to compare the incumbent to his predecessor.

It was his most treacherous move of all as it drilled right down into Zuma's insecurities. Zuma was about to complete his first year as president and the reviews were not going to be good. He was seen as weak, underperforming and incapable. News had broken a few months earlier that he had fathered another child with the daughter of one of his old friends, a woman who was half his age and allegedly HIV-positive, and the public had not forgiven him his shameful behaviour. The conservative block within the ANC was still deeply horrified. Zuma knew he was not living up to standards and that his moment of victory had long left him. He was acutely aware that he would never be as able as the two presidents who had gone before him, but to compare him unfavourably and publicly to them, especially the one he loathed, was blasphemous.

Some of Zuma's ministers and senior party loyalists felt just as aggrieved. These were the core men and women who had supported his comeback and who had been paid off with senior cabinet or government posts in return. Some of them were good, if not excellent, but mostly they were a bunch of arrogant and inefficient individuals dressed up as the new nobles and they knew what Malema was trying to say. He was going to pay.

Within a few days the party charged him, adding the Mbeki incident to their draft list.

Malema did his level best to prevent the charges from sticking and in a subsequent meeting of the ANC's executive, he told his fellow comrades why they couldn't possibly charge him for aligning with ZANU-PF. At the most recent party conference, a resolution had been passed to extend support to the neighbouring liberation movements, ZANU-PF being one of them, and he reminded them of that.

'I was simply doing my job,' Malema told the meeting.

He read the resolution to them.

'I then repeated [it],' he told me. 'I said, "I want to repeat: You must have a structured relationship with ZANU-PF." And then they laughed.'

He also reminded the executive that it was party protocol to protect the various resolutions. So the Zimbabwe charge fell away.

It didn't take much effort on his part to point out why it wouldn't be a good idea to side with the media. Though Mandela had been a genius at handling reporters and ensuring the most amazingly positive coverage during his presidency, Mbeki developed a brittle relationship with the country's journalists. However, since coming to power this new ANC has been hell-bent on silencing the Fourth Estate at all costs, so the charge of spitting fire at the journalist was also struck off.

For all the reasons that would later play out in a courtroom, they couldn't possibly rebuke him for singing a struggle song, which was a part of their history.

The one that stuck was the invidious comparison of Zuma to Mbeki and for that he faced a disciplinary hearing in May 2010.

Before he faced the disciplinary team, Malema went home to Seshego where Sarah slaughtered a goat and performed a ritual, a common occurrence in African life when the living call on the ancestors for protection.

'First I had the slaughtering and then I went to the DC [disciplinary committee]. That's why I'm still here,' he later told me.

Malema had asked Justice Minister Jeff Radebe, a senior member of the party, to represent him at the hearing. Radebe initially agreed, but then closer to the date he thought better of it and withdrew and offered his own lawyer instead.

'But we knew we needed someone with political clout, so we asked Mathews [Phosa].'

Phosa agreed and turned out to provide a solid and excellent defence, but Malema was still found guilty. (Mugabe later dispatched two officials to meet with Phosa in Johannesburg who personally thanked him on the dictator's behalf for defending Malema.)

Malema's sentence was four-fold: he was ordered to apologise to Zuma; attend anger management classes; pay a US$1,000 fine which he was asked to remit to a youth project of his choice; and slapped with a two-year suspended sentence, the most damning part of the ruling, because if he were found guilty a second time in as many years, he would be axed from the party.

Malema duly retreated from the public eye for a while to allow the dust to settle and have the time to rethink his steps. But his silence must not be misunderstood, he told me when I saw him a few weeks later. That he was brought before the disciplinary committee didn't bother him much, he said.

'The disciplinary charges are politics. Politics was coming to me now. It's what I have done to other people before. Now it was my turn. I've always been a problem, so what's the problem?' he shrugged.

He scoffed at the idea of anger management classes.

'It's imposing on me the culture I don't know. In my tradition, if you are angry, they perform a ritual, because it means you have angered the ancestors,' he explained.

Anger management classes don't feature in his world. The fine he could live with. The apology he got out of the way pretty quickly. But the suspended sentence would be a different matter. He would have to be careful now.

What upset him at the time was the behaviour of his colleagues, some of whom assured him they would never allow him to face the disciplinary team, while others opted for silence throughout the saga and didn't utter a whisper of support in public when he needed it most.

'I will never rely on an individual again. I should have learned this from Peter [Mokaba],' he told me that day.

That Cassel Mathale had also kept his silence gutted him.

'Just one word would have . . .' he said as his voice trailed off.

(When Malema was eventually fired from the party two years later, Mathale was the only one to speak out in support of him.)

With the benefit of hindsight did he regret what he had done, I wondered.

It wasn't what he did that he regretted, but what he hadn't done, he told me.

'I only regret I didn't put some expensive shoes on his back,' he said, referring to Fisher.

'You know there, I just put politics aside. I saw some young boy who is white, who is demonstrating some white supremacy to me. I wanted to kick him. I was very angry.

'You know, my township character just came out. When you are undermined in the township, you don't negotiate.'

It was what he told the leadership of the ANC when he stood in front of them not long after the incident to explain why his temper had got the better of him that morning.

'That's why in meetings we have tables, to deal with these kinds of problems,' Kgalema Motlanthe told him in jest.

What about the cows he had left grazing in Zimbabwe? I asked.

He laughed in response.

'I will not touch those things,' he answered. 'They got me into big trouble. They can stay there.'

Yet within a year, he was at it again, baiting Zuma by comparing him to Mbeki. He simply couldn't help himself.

'Mbeki is the best leader the ANC has ever produced,' Malema told a rally with all the authority and confidence he could muster in that moment.

'There are those who hated him with a passion but [they] forgot that Mbeki, during his leadership, had produced a two-thirds majority during elections,' he argued, in direct reference to the incumbent president under whose watch the ANC's performance had waned in the local government elections earlier that year.

'Those who hate Mbeki are jealous of his achievements. He was the most educated and clever,' he went on, another veiled reference to Zuma, an uneducated and poorly read person. 'He was the best and I respect him for that.'

Malema would stop at nothing to disgrace and belittle Zuma

and he was playing for keeps, regardless of what it might cost him in the end. He could not forgive the president for making a spectacle of him by disciplining him in front of the whole country.

'Never again. No more tea at his house. No more friends. No more talks. It's purely politics now,' he told me.

'That man,' he tut-tutted as he shook his head from side to side. 'It's over.'

But it wasn't the gash in his pride that was bothering him. His hay days were cut short. That drunken power I had watched in Harare just a year earlier was gone, buried. And he wanted it back.

In late 2010 I meet Sarah Malema for a second time at her Seshego home. There are some biographical details I want to confirm with her as I round up my research for the book and she has kindly agreed to entertain my request. Her grandson, Tshepo, is with her to interpret for us for a second time.

I stick to the family history, but as the conversation draws to an end, I tell her there's something else I'm curious about: the ringtone on her cell phone. The last time I met the old lady was earlier that year in March and when her cell phone rang that afternoon, it was the voice of Jacob Zuma singing his personal anthem, 'Umshini wami', that echoed through the house.

That didn't seem odd to me then. Malema had come to prominence on the back of Zuma's victory and it was only to be expected that Sarah, as Malema's next of kin, would wear her politics on her sleeve in such a way.

But since that day in March, her grandson's animosity towards Zuma has become an open secret and the 'small' president has locked himself into a dirty battle with his senior partner.

So I wonder who is singing on her phone today? Is she still pledging allegiance to Zuma, despite the fact that her grandson no longer is? Or is she with her grandson as he prepares the ground for the 2012 leadership conference when he will try to unseat Zuma? And if it's the latter, she would have any number of revolutionary songs to choose from his repertory.

'It's Zuma,' she says, and asks Tshepo to dial her number so that I can hear it for myself:

Umshini wami mshini wami
khawuleth'umshini wami
Umshini wami mshini wami
. . .

One verse after another, she allows it to play on.
'Must I change it?' she asks with a cheeky smile on her face.

13

Fighting that fight

The ANC Youth League elect their leaders every three years during a national conference, and halfway through 2011 Malema was running for a second term. His fall twelve months earlier had rallied many of the league's hardliners behind him, but it also created a space for some of his opponents to emerge. Four weeks ahead of the election, Lebogang Maile declared his intention to challenge Malema.

It was a tough call, and Maile knew it. Malema was still untouchable, despite all he had been through, and Maile had few illusions about toppling him. He just wanted to make a point to his leader that his base was not rock solid and that his members could not be taken for granted. He would also use his campaign to bare some home truths about Malema's style of leadership.

In a pithy two-page document, his campaigners talked about the 'decline of organisational democracy owing to dictatorial tendencies' and Malema's 'cavalier approach' in suppressing 'differences of opinion'. They pointed to 'ill-discipline and chaos owing to misguided militancy'. There was a 'lack of political programmes to attend to youth-specific challenges' and the organisation had become bogged down by 'factionalism and blackmail', while the 'politics and power of money over organisational process and principles' was killing it. The image of the naked emperor came to mind.

That document rattled Malema's cage in just the way they

had wanted it to. Fearless though he is, Malema cannot take the heat, and because he had been called to order a year earlier, he could do without more criticism. In the run-up to the vote he travelled all over the country, appealing to the youth to fall into step behind him, promising that before long they would be leading the ANC together.

Song and dance are big features of South African politics and in one of his final rallies in the north-west of the country, 60 or so young men and women rose to their feet and began to chant for Maile to become president, as they danced around the venue, parading up and down in front of Malema.

He pleaded with them to stop so that he could address them and when there was eventually a modicum of decorum that befitted his forum, he began to holler into the microphone.

'We will never impose ourselves on you, but the fact of the matter is there's a sitting leadership and that leadership must be respected and once you undermine the sitting leadership, the matter will be acted [upon] without fear, without favour,' he bellowed in their direction. 'Discipline is not negotiated.'

If you are thinking back to Malema's baiting of Zuma and the disrespect he was able to hurl at the sitting leadership of the ANC without a second thought, then you are probably using your head. But that's Malema. A rebel inured with hypocrisy.

Maile withdrew his challenge right at the very end but not before he had forced Malema to realise that his grip over the League had weakened. He took him right up to the wire, with Malema eventually offering a power-sharing deal so that he could hold on to the top job. It was only when they were all assembled inside the conference hall where the vote would take place that Maile withdrew from the race. Malema was re-elected for a second term, unopposed.

Malema delivered a closing address to that conference that sent a shiver throughout the country. He started out on his second term in as vicious a tone as he had started his first term three years earlier with his 'kill for Zuma' utterances. But Zuma was in the firing line this time.

As he bared his soul in what was in parts an unusually personal speech, he once again aired his grievances about the disciplinary hearing. He talked about the suggestion that had been made to send him to Cuba or China for a year for political training. Like the parents who can no longer control the troublesome teenager, they wanted to ship him off, as far away as possible, in the hope that someone else could do what they could not. Once out of sight, he would be well and truly forgotten. But he had defied them now by securing a second term.

'You subscribe to the policy of "kill them young and destroy their future". The youth of the ANC have spoken. We defeated you. We will never appoint and elect factionalist leaders,' he said, that last reference to Zuma.

Malema then delved into his back catalogue of political messages and gave his audience a strong shot of revolutionary talk. He called for everything he had pushed for in his first three years: nationalisation of the country's assets; a radical redistribution of the land, without compensation if needs be; and an ANC led by younger cadres; and, above all, control of the ANC.

He summed it all up in the peroration:

'Comrades, there must never be a meeting of the ANC if young people don't constitute 50 per cent-plus [of those present] if we want to change this ANC. And by the way, we are not going to win the ANC over through speaking here at Gallagher [conference centre]. We must go to the ground. We are going to war, comrades, a war for radical policy shift.'

That was June 2011. The next big event on the political calendar was the ANC conference 18 months later when his nemesis would run for a second term. Between those two dates were scattered a number of other big dates, but Malema's main focus was on destroying Zuma's future.

Of course Zuma was well aware of that and, never feeling entirely confident in his presidential shoes, he knew he would have to remove Malema, who was by far his biggest critic. Malema gave him his opportunity six or so weeks later when he called for regime change in Botswana, arguing that Ian Khama's 'imperialistic' government was a threat to the African continent and that he, Malema, was going to establish a 'command team' that would bring the change he desired.

A fortnight later the ANC disciplined him for a second time and paved the way for a hearing. Certainly, Malema's comments warranted some kind of tough action from the top, but this one would also work in Zuma's favour.

Malema was eventually expelled from the party in April the following year. He was first handed a five-year suspension in November, which he appealed. The appeals team upheld the guilty verdict the following January, but granted Malema leave to argue for a lighter sentence. Malema's behaviour was going downhill rapidly at that time and instead of lessening the five-year sentence, the disciplinary team expelled him altogether a month later. He appealed that decision as well but it was upheld, and on 24 April the anti-hero was told to exit the building.

All told it had taken eight months to reach that verdict. By most reckonings, it was unnecessarily long and drawn-out, but by dealing with it in this way, the ANC had also averted a potentially ugly crisis. On the first day of the hearing that August, riots broke out in downtown Johannesburg when hundreds of youth marched on the ANC headquarters where he was being tried, demanding that the charges be dropped. A policeman and five journalists were injured when the protestors turned violent and the city centre came to a complete halt. Surely mindful of the militancy that Malema had ramped up during his tenure, and the murmurings of a South African-styled Arab Spring before too long, the ANC thought twice. The hearings then dragged out over a number of weeks and the verdict wasn't handed down until November, and it took another five months to settle the matter, by which time the tensions had subsided. Not even the decision to expel him when it was eventually announced had any shock factor. It was a discreet and tactful move on the ANC's part.

Zuma was by then unashamed about his dislike for Malema and warned how tough life was going to be for him on the 'outside', while he conceded in private that one of his biggest regrets as president was not acting against the rebel sooner. The support that Malema once enjoyed from the ANC's executive was no longer visible and the erstwhile friendly heavyweights, the likes of Winnie Madikizela-Mandela, Tokyo Sexwale, Fikile Mbalula and a few more of their ilk vanished like breath off a razor blade around that time, in public at least. Even some of his own Youth League were beginning to round on him, openly debating his successor.

Malema was sunk but still he refused to withdraw. He wanted to hear what the rank and file had to say, and he began to lobby the party's branches.

When Mbeki fired Zuma all those years earlier, he turned to the hundreds of thousands of men and women who make up the backbone of the ANC and it was they who returned him to grace and later elevated him to the position of president. Though Malema was a more junior candidate than Zuma and a far more divisive member of the party, he began to remind his listeners that when times were tough and Zuma was the outside runner, bogged down by corruption charges and rape scandals, he had backed him to the hilt, but that Zuma dropped him like a lead balloon as soon as he had fulfilled his role.

'They used me. I was used like a condom,' was one of his favourite lines.

Of course it was a tempered version of the truth, but Malema was playing the underdog, which is never a bad move. He was also banking on the massive growth in party membership since the last conference at the end of 2007, from 620,000 to just over one million when the centenary was marked at the beginning of 2012. Rapid growth such as this in a party that cannot count on solid leadership and doesn't adhere to political education was ideal for Malema's pursuit. Many of the new members were young, perhaps vulnerable, and maybe even open to his sway. He began to check them out.

Playing the political field was not the real challenge; he had been there and done that and knew what was possible within the ANC. It was the state's prosecuting arms that worried him most and until such time as they slapped those charges on him, he really had no idea what lay ahead for him.

All that he had going for him in the South African winter of 2012 was age. He was 31, and a comeback could not be ruled out at any stage, even after a few years behind bars in a worst case scenario. The next chapter of Malema's life is 'to be continued'.

Many, if not most, African countries dallied only very briefly with the Westminster model of government post-liberation and it never did take long until the new democracies gravitated towards authoritarian states headed by the likes of Muammar Gaddafi, Idi Amin, Robert Mugabe, Charles Taylor, Laurent Kabila and all those others.

However, the collapse can be attributed in the main to the hasty manner in which the Western model was imposed. The wave of African nationalism that was ripping through the continent in the mid-1950s coincided with the Cold War and it was the cause of huge concern among the colonial powers who feared their subjects may resort to communism in order to gain independence.

British Prime Minister Harold Macmillan's famous 'wind of change' speech, which he delivered in the Cape Town parliament in 1960, carried that sentiment.

> Whether we like it or not, this growth of national consciousness is a political fact ... and our national policies must take account of it ... If we cannot do so we may imperil the precarious balance between the East and West on which the peace of the world depends.

Without giving them a chance to take root, democracies were rapidly planted all over Africa within the space of a few years. In 1960 alone, 17 countries won independence on the back of this rush. However, there was nothing on which to model their new democracies as colonisation had set the worst example of governance. The failure of Africa was therefore inevitable.

South Africa, the last to be liberated and the most sophisticated in economic terms, has always been hailed as the continent's last big hope of democracy, though the reluctant approach of the 'new' ANC to democratic rule may well shatter that notion.

14

So that's Malema: Now this is the future

Nobody could make the sensitive nostril shrivel quite like Julius Malema could, and for four or so years many South Africans looked upon him as if they were gaping at a bald atrocity. The fear he provoked turned to general delight when he was eventually thrown out of the ANC. But he defied all attempts to lay him to rest and with adamantine nerve continued to play his hand on the fringes of the party.

One of Malema's parting shots from the ANC during a well-attended and televised rally was to upbraid Zuma by calling him a dictator and telling him that he was killing the democracy with his intolerant style of rule. There had always been a palpable fear of South Africa falling into a dictatorship under Malema himself, though I never believed that would happen, for the same reasons I don't envisage it happening under the ANC either, with or without Malema in its ranks or even Zuma at the top. The prospect of a dictatorship is inconceivable today in a country so inextricably linked to the rest of the world. What I do foresee, however, and I believe is already happening, is South Africa inching towards a 'managed democracy', again, with or without young, revolutionary Malema. Zuma and his peers have been gradually paving the path for such a political set-up ever since they came to power in 2007.

The term 'managed democracy' is an oxymoron as the very nature of democratic rule is a people-centred form of governance.

It dates back to the fifth century BC when it was introduced by the Greeks, who originally coined the term *demokratia*, or 'rule of the people'. It is not perfect nor is it all wise and has had varying degrees of successes since the days of the Greeks, but to try to manage a democracy is to strip it of its core meaning and value.

A 'managed democracy' is one that is democratic on paper and for all its intended purposes, but in practice it is characterised by enhanced levels of autocracy and despotism. Indonesia practised a 'managed' or 'guided democracy' in the late 1950s. Modern-day Russia is also a 'managed democracy', as is Cambodia. A good number of African states are better described as 'managed democracies'.

In a talk he gave a few years ago, Nikolay Petrov of the Carnegie Moscow Center described a 'managed democracy' as one with a strong presidency but with weak institutions; state control of the media; control over elections; visible short-term effectiveness and long-term inefficiency. The end result is an unstable stability.

Petrov went on to argue that under a managed democracy, the system is highly dysfunctional and has poor information flows. The people are led by an iron-fisted and heavy-handed state and have little choice but to fall into line behind the powers that be.

'Smart guys make bad decisions but nobody has the big picture,' Petrov argued. 'Obedience is the first measure of performance and that creates perverse incentives. For example, a regional governor has an incentive to obey the centre, but no incentive to make his region succeed.'

While business may boom in the private sector, corruption across the board becomes rife. The judiciary is co-opted. The electoral system weakens. Protests are nipped in the bud from very early on. A political elite emerges, shouldered by a private elite that is hand-plucked from society. But both elites are underpinned by shaky foundations and cannot endure.

'Like a mule, a managed democracy is an unnatural hybrid incapable of reproducing itself,' Petrov argued.

South Africa doesn't entirely fit Petrov's description. The country still holds free and fair elections, unlike many other countries on the continent, while the Independent Electoral Commission is one of the most respected bodies in the country. In the run-up to each election, either local or national, there is always talk of how votes are bought for slim wads of cash, even as little as a bag of mealie meal, though that ought not to come as a surprise. The average shack dweller who does not know where the next meal is coming from will not think twice about exchanging their vote for a food parcel. And while there have been some incidents of political violence, some of it extreme and fatal, by and large the South African elections are held in a free, fair and democratic way.

Not so for the judiciary, parts of which have already fallen prey to political pressures, with some appointees caving in with little or no shame. It has been a slow but consistent onslaught on the part of the ANC for quite a number of years and the high-profile corruption case that Zuma was facing is a good example. A fortnight ahead of the general elections that brought him to power in 2009, the party-friendly acting head of the National Prosecuting Authority, Mokatedi Mphse, dropped the 783 criminal charges against the president-in-waiting in a political stitch-up that rocked South Africa. James Myburgh, a political journalist with a sound understanding of law, was wary of some of Mpshe's defence and 'properly curious' about how heavily he had leaned on foreign legal precedent. So he did a cleverly manipulated internet search on Mpshe's lengthy statement. A week later, Myburgh ran a story about how Mpshe had based his reasoning so heavily on a 2002 Hong Kong ruling (which he had not cited), that it raised the distinct possibility of plagiarism if not questionable judgement as well, because the Hong Kong ruling was later overturned on appeal. Despite

Myburgh's findings, Mpshe's ruling stood, Zuma became South Africa's new president on the back of the ANC majority in the election a week after that and Mpshe was appointed as a judge at one of the country's high courts. Myburgh, incidentally, won an investigative journalism award for exposing Mpshe's 'decision for the political fix that it was'[1].

If Mpshe's ruling was ever to be challenged (which it eventually was by the opposition Democratic Alliance), the case would end up with the Supreme Court of Appeal or the Constitutional Court. So a few days before he was sworn in as state president, Zuma talked of a desire to review the powers of the Constitutional Court. He said he felt uncomfortable about its supreme authority and the way its judges behave 'almost like God'. It became a recurring theme throughout his presidency until he eventually got the review he wanted, which is now underway and looking at the entire judiciary, not just the Constitutional Court. Shortly after that, Zuma began to float the idea of a review of the constitution itself.

It was also Zuma who plucked controversial judge Mogoeng Mogoeng from relative obscurity and named him the country's chief justice and head of the Constitutional Court in 2011. This came despite serious opposition from the legal fraternity, not only because of Mogoeng's previous leniency towards the accused in rape cases (in an earlier case where a husband was accused by his wife of rape, Mogoeng ruled: 'This is a man whose wife joined him in bed, clad in panties and a nightdress . . . The appellant must have been sexually aroused . . . The desire to make love to his wife must have overwhelmed him, hence his somewhat violent behaviour'), and his insensitivity towards homosexuals, but because he simply did not have the intellectual depth to lead the bench. Mogoeng dismissed their criticism saying that 'God wants me to take it'.

Though freedom of expression is another healthy feature of the South African democracy, Zuma's government has been attempting to kill it by pushing through a punitive secrecy bill. This has no public interest safeguards and would therefore make the government answerable only to the government, and land journalists in jail for up to 25 years for publishing classified information or even some of the corruption scandals mentioned earlier.

While the debate around the bill was at its peak, a journalist was jailed for exposing corruption on the part of the head of police, who was later found guilty by the Public Protector for precisely what the journalist accused him of. At the public broadcaster, the head of news was suspended for giving Julius Malema too much airtime. At one of the independent TV stations, a well-known political journalist was offered a lucrative financial package by one of the most notoriously corrupt and ambitious members of Zuma's cabinet if she would guarantee him positive coverage in return. The awful pity was that she didn't have the nerve to expose the minister in question.

With the media in a frenzy, Zuma then turned to the security and intelligence forces and appointed his old friend Siyabonga Cwele as the minister of state security, which controls the intelligence agencies. Cwele's wife was under investigation at the time for drug trafficking, a small matter which Zuma overlooked. When she was later convicted, Cwele claimed he had been unaware of what his wife was up to. What did that say about the safety of the country if he didn't know what was going on under his own roof?

Another loyalist appointment by Zuma was that of Menzi Simelane as the head of the National Prosecuting Authority, despite an earlier judgment against him while he was deputy justice minister that he was neither fit nor proper to hold public office. In the dying weeks of 2011, the courts forced Zuma to remove Simelane, who was placed on temporary suspension and replaced a few days later by an even more controversial candidate, Nomgcobo Jiba, whose record is as tainted as her predecessor's.

This is Zuma's classic style of rule: he surrounds himself with individuals who are either guilty or compromised in some way and by giving them back their power, he buys their loyalty. Most of the appointments are within the police force, the intelligence department or other security structures.

One of the most worrying appointments of all was Richard Mdluli as the head of the police crime intelligence unit in 2009, which later turned into a political scandal that badly damaged the Zuma presidency. Two years later, the special crimes unit that is known as The Hawks, and which sits within the NPA, issued a warrant for Mdluli's arrest for the 1999 murder of Oupa Ramokgibe, the new husband of Mdluli's former girlfriend. He was also accused of looting funds from the secret slush fund in the unit he now headed, utilising safe houses and cars for private use, and appointing 23 members of his family and friends – including his new wife, a former wife, his daughter, his son and three in-laws – as intelligence agents and cyberspooks within his unit. Some of the money siphoned from the fund was used to purchase fifteen cars for family use, which included a top model BMW, Jeep, Mercedes, Lexus and Audi. There was detail about the fifteen trips he took with his family at the state's expense and the plush addresses in Johannesburg and Cape Town that were used as temporary homes. Mdluli was forced to step down late in 2011 while the investigation got underway.

Yet in February of the New Year, the fraud, murder and corruption charges against Mdluli were dropped by Jiba's office in favour of an inquest being launched, and Mdluli was allowed to return to work.

The media continued to expose more and more detail about the fraud case, the bank account into which the fund money was channelled, as well as the recipients of the loot. They then exposed the reasons behind Jiba's shock decision and traced them all the way up to Zuma's cabinet, but the presidency remained largely silent on the scandal.

Then Ramokgibe's family spoke out about the ceiling of fear that had capped their lives ever since 1999. They live in the black township of Vosloorus, about 20 kilometres south-west of Johannesburg, where the murder took place. The family reported it at the time to the local police station, where Mdluli was the station commander, but it was going nowhere, despite his mother's inquiries. Ramokgibe's sister was then raped, and his mother received an anonymous call saying her other daughter would be next if she didn't back off. The young woman fled and has been under the witness protection programme ever since.

And still the South African government didn't budge, ignoring the public outcry in the hope that it would just go away.

In an attempt to make sense of him, Mdluli has been likened to J. Edgar Hoover, the founder director of the FBI who was more famed for his covert surveillance of America's elite than he was for fighting crime. Over the course of his 48 years at the helm of the US bureau, he gathered such sensitive and titillating details about the lives of the 8 presidents that he served under, it ensured him a job for life. The secrets contained between the covers of Hoover's private files were the lethal weapons that he used to harass and destroy a number of careers. He was still in the job when he died at the age of 77 in 1972, though he bequeathed a polarised legacy.

Mdluli had similar staying powers to Hoover. He joined the apartheid police force in 1979 when it was run by the ruthless Jimmy Kruger, the former minister of justice and police better known as the Himmler of apartheid. And yet Mdluli survived the suspicion and stigma attached to serving in that era and went on to become the deputy head of police in the province of Gauteng, covering Johannesburg and Pretoria, the economic and political hubs of the country.

He held that position when Zuma was accused by an HIV-positive family acquaintance of raping her towards the end of

2005, just months after Zuma had been fired by Mbeki. She reported the assault to the police and the two investigating officers who were assigned to the case reported directly to Mdluli. When the trial began the following year, the men appeared on behalf of the state but their evidence was inadmissible as one contradicted the other. The scene of the crime was also disputed by them.

Zuma maintained his innocence and insisted the sex was consensual, though he admitted it was unprotected sex (when he was questioned about the risk that posed, he said he had a shower afterwards to wash the risk away). Though the victim insisted she was raped, the judge ruled in Zuma's favour as the state had been unable to prove their case beyond reasonable doubt.

It has also been suggested that Mdluli played a key role in getting Zuma off the hook on the corruption charges. Police insiders believe, too, that he has been building up intelligence about a lot of Zuma's cabinet members. What truth there is in any of this may never be known, but what is clear is that Mdluli was being shielded by someone very senior.

He made a Lazarus-like comeback to the unit and within a few days announced his plans to overhaul it and incorporate the VIP protection unit into his team. Because the VIP unit provides the security detail for top government officials, including ministers, deputy ministers, provincial premiers and provincial ministers, senior judges and other senior civil servants, the crime intelligence chief could now monitor Zuma's top employees (among whom are his fiercest opponents) every hour of every day.

Around the same time, six of Zuma's bodyguards were promoted to the top ranks of the police force, while another bodyguard, KG 'Bhoyi' Ngcobo, was appointed to the position of chief police spy.

With all his men in place and with Mdluli back in his job,

the president had effectively established a powerful war room, a sober measure of the man's deep paranoia and insecure mind seven months out from the ANC conference.

The 70-year-old Zuma, who was an ANC spy during the apartheid era, is not alone in this; at least half of his cabinet are behind him in his ascendency and support his restructuring of the security services into a malign, political force whose power is rooted firmly in Zuma's influence.

Left unchecked, the ANC will transform South Africa into the kind of police state that Russia has become under Vladimir Putin. In the Soviet era, Putin had been a long-standing member of the KGB and resigned only days before the collapse of the Soviet Union in 1991. Seven years later, Boris Yeltsin appointed him as head of the Federal Security Service, or FSB, the main successor of the KGB. When Putin succeeded Yeltsin two years later, he filled the organisation with old friends, loyalists, KGB agents, and expanded their powers and their authority and grew the FSB into an elite, untouchable structure that helped him fight off his opponents to maintain his two-term presidency. They also supported his subsequent reincarnations as prime minister and his recent return as president. One book title aptly refers to the FSB as *The New Nobility*.

Putin also staffed the Kremlin with loyalists and ensured he had the right men and women in all of the key positions across the state and its various structures and throughout the corporate world, creating an elite and powerful band of officials commonly referred to as the *siloviki*, which loosely translates to 'power guys'. The *siloviki* control government, the private sector, public entities and civil society. In effect, they run Russia and their thinking is the same throughout. They are extreme nationalists and very anti-Western in their outlook. Despite the fact that they were drawn from the Soviet era, they do not believe in communism. They were, after all, the men who began to rise as communism began to fall, but what they have taken from that communist era is a fierce need to control Russia. They are powerful where it matters to have clout, and with their power has come the belief that no law or person is bigger than them in terms of achieving their mission.

A similar band of elites exists in South Africa called the cadres, products of the ANC's cadre-deployment system, which systematically appoints its key members to all the arms of government, semi-state bodies, law enforcement agencies, the judiciary and the corporate sector. Although it operates like an employment agency, the deployment scheme is designed 'to give black people operational exposure', in the words of the party secretary-general Gwede Mantashe.

Despite the similarities between South Africa and Russia, Zuma's desire is not to emulate Russia but China. Under President Zuma's watch, the ANC has forged close ties with the Asian giant, the country to which the ruling party now looks for guidance. In the past couple of years, dozens of the ANC's members have been sent to China to attend the communist party's political school and plans are now being rolled out in South Africa to build a similar institute in the city of Mangaung, where the party was founded 100 years ago.

However, as the ANC looks east it is not towards a system of communism or socialism it is looking, but at state corporatism, the system of governance and style of rule that the Chinese adopted during the reform era and which helped define its transition from a totalitarian to an authoritarian state over the past few decades.

An institutional mechanism employed by a state to regulate society, rather than an ideology within a political system, state corporatism has been associated with some of the most repressive regimes in the world and is widely regarded as the least palatable 'ism' of them all.

In the Chinese context, it helped the Asian communist nation make a fiercely controlled shift out of its dark ages towards a slightly more liberated state of affairs. In the South African context, however, and moving along the same spectrum, albeit from the opposite end, state corporatism is facilitating a gradual shutdown of the democratic space that was created in 1994.

South Africa is still a democracy in name and constitution. In practice, however, it is beginning to take on another form that can be hard to define, and state or authoritarian corporatism often helps to clarify some of the new grey areas.

Corporatism is a centuries-old concept that started out as a philosophy or agenda to organise society and its individuals into major groups or bodies, or *corpora*. Enormously broad in definition, almost to the point of defying it, corporatism therefore took on various forms down the centuries, across the political spectrum and in a multitude of contexts.

In its more extreme form, corporatism became the hallmark of regimes such as Benito Mussolini's in Italy. By the middle of the twentieth century, authoritarian corporatist states were emerging in Asia, in countries such as Japan, South Korea and Taiwan as they began to embark on intensive development and growth strategies.

By the latter half of the century, state and authoritarian corporatism had begun to give way to a more benign liberal or societal corporatism, which encouraged tripartite relations between government, the business sector and labour. It was this marked shift to societal corporatism that began to lay the foundation for social pacts in various European and Scandinavian countries in the 1970s.

Towards the end of the apartheid regime, South Africa was ripe for liberal corporatism, and it was from a tripartite union of voices and power groups that the National Economic Development and Labour Council (NEDLAC) was eventually formed in 1994, building on the promise of a consensus democracy.

Eighteen years on little is left of that people-centred outlook. The current ANC is leading in a heavy-handed manner. As

Malema talks up his nationalisation plans, the government is focusing on the existing state-owned entities (SOEs) to pave the way for greater intervention in the economy. Plans are afoot to cap wages and bonuses in the private sector which would place a heavy hand on the free market economy. The ANC's deployment of its cadres across all sectors of society is becoming more aggressive as the battle for control of the top positions in semi-state bodies, large private sector firms, judicial seats and various boards becomes apparent for what it really is: a form of state corporatism.

The tensions that have been brewing between the ANC and the union federation COSATU these past few years drive home this very point. A couple of years ago, when the union group found itself unable to tolerate the excesses of the 'new' ANC and hosted a meeting of civic groups to try to breathe life back into civil society, it was telling the ruling party that it was now able to conduct its business without it. The ANC was quick to respond with Mantashe calling COSATU 'oppositionist'. He went on to 'caution that any action like the one of leading a charge for the formation of, and for the mobilisation of, a mass civic movement outside of the alliance partners and the ANC might indeed be interpreted as initial steps for regime change in South Africa'.

How much more control the ruling party intends to exert over South African life is not yet apparent; nor is it clear to what extent it could succeed, if at all, in copying the Chinese model of governance, as the two countries are markedly different.

Unlike South Africa, the millennia-old Chinese state is strong, intact and, in its current stage, likely to sustain itself for some decades to come. It has developed into an important political and economic power that rests on a powerful centralised structure, the product of careful planning by the Chinese Communist Party (CCP).

A core component of modern-day Chinese planning was aggressive acceleration of capitalist development at the behest, ironically, of the communists. The high economic growth registered in the 1990s was driven by the private sector and the CCP was forced to openly admit that it needed a capitalist class to grow its economy. But rather than compete with or curb the new economic elite, most of whom were products of the CCP anyway, in 2002 it formally invited them into its political structures, though they had been informally welcomed long before that. It was a strategic move that allowed the party to exert control over the business class and the economy, rather than have the capitalists control political reform, while the country continued to benefit from their economic interventions.

Today, China's money makers exist in parallel with the CCP, if not within it, and though they have fuelled the socio-economic disparities that now define the country, they are an accepted and necessary class in the so-called communist nation.

That was the strength of the Communist Party: its capacity for reinvention without losing sight of itself in the process. Yet the CCP is a highly elite structure. Though it is the largest political party in the world, it has an estimated 75 million members plucked out of a population of more than 1.3 billion people; or, to put it differently, though the vast majority of Chinese people swear allegiance (openly at least) to the party, little more than 5 per cent are card-bearing members.

By a similar reckoning of numbers, the ANC is also small in size relative to the overall population, with its 1 million members accounting for approximately 2 per cent of all South Africans. However, unlike the ANC, the CCP is very selective about who it calls one of its own. Membership is often by invitation only and as a structure, the CCP is quite secretive.

Despite its elite nature, the influence of the CCP across Chinese society is immense, due largely to the deployment of cadres in all walks of life who entrench the ideology and identity of the party as successfully as they helped roll out capitalism.

A party representative sits on the board of every company

and they are also found within government departments and ministries, in addition to the appointed public servants. They oversee the judiciary, are active in media houses, prominent in trade unions and generally present across all sectors. Though the ANC does likewise, China's deployed cadres are not only loyal party members but highly skilled and educated men and women fit for the task at hand.

Equally pervasive is the very secretive Central Party School, which grooms future leaders, provides a think tank for decision making in the party and has become an institute of interest to political parties from all over the world, not only the ANC.

With the exception of some environment-linked NGOs, which the Chinese government allows to operate with relative freedom, by and large China's form of governance today is an ideal example of state corporatism. It is made possible by a very strong state, in the case of China underpinned by a very strong party.

The 'new' ANC is now looking to the Chinese model as it advances towards the next stage of the so-called NDR in South Africa, when it will harness control over the economy and society. However, the biggest stumbling block in achieving this aim is most likely to be party itself.

Unlike the CCP, the ANC at 100 is weak and fractured. Though it is one of the strongest political brands internationally and is widely regarded as one of the more successful modern liberation movements (thanks to the collapse of the globally hated project of apartheid in 1994, for which it alone cannot take the credit), at home the ANC has become a house of political in-fighting: ugly succession battles, opposing ideologies and a lack of the kind of discipline upon which the success of the CCP is built.

Since the current leadership came to power, the need to instil discipline in the ANC has become a regular talking point, but with little, as yet, to show for it. Malema is usually the case in point, though he is selectively singled out. It is little wonder

Malema flouts party protocol when Zuma rules in the manner he does. And whereas the CCP grooms its future leaders and nurtures their rise through the ranks, the modern ANC pulls itself apart over the very issue of who will lead next. It is likely that the CCP already knows who will lead it twenty years from now, yet no one knows who will emerge from the ANC leadership race at the end of this year, not least because Zuma has forbidden his party members from debating the matter until two months before the election takes place. Based on current trends, the winning team will surely be representative of powerful interests in the ANC and consequently unfit for the purpose of running South Africa.

Even so, the party can still count on a large degree of political autonomy for quite some time to come, something that the corporatist model requires. The general elections in 2014, when the country will mark twenty years of independence, are likely to give the ANC another comfortable majority. It might not be as large as the 65 per cent recorded in the previous elections, or earlier vote counts, but for as long as there is no viable alternative in South African politics, the ANC can count on that bulk of black votes that are still emotionally tied to it.

What the ANC is lacking, though, is the backing of a state that is strong enough to enforce a corporatist system. The South African state has many fault lines, perhaps naturally so in Achille Mbembe's view, who defines it as a 'hybrid colossus' that encompasses the authoritarianism of the apartheid era, fragments of the new democratic culture and some of the cronyism of the bantustan.

When it is broken down into its constituent parts – the legislature, the judiciary and the executive – the judiciary is without doubt the strongest of the three arms, though its independence is being steadily eroded. The legislature, or parliament, is even less strong and is weakened by the country's political system of proportional representation, which hinders parliament's ability to hold the executive to account. With the ANC resting on close to a two-thirds majority of the vote, their share of seats in parliament is allocated accordingly, therefore they effectively run the legislature.

The executive is by far the weakest spoke of the state and shows an inability and lack of capacity to deliver on what it promises and to perform in the manner it should, the core measure of any state. It is this very weakness that forced the term 'service delivery protests' into the South African lexicon in 2004.

Though a large number of key institutions – such as the electricity provider Eskom, television and radio outlets, a sizeable chunk of the rail and harbour system and the Industrial Development Corporation, for example – remain under state control, the efficiency with which they are run is highly questionable. This is not helped by the high turnover of civil servants, which Hein Marais puts at 32 per cent nationally, which weakens the public service and state performance.

The state's grip over the economy is also weak, given its international make-up and the strong financial sector for which South Africa is renowned. The fact that so many of the large corporations are still controlled by whites does little to nurture solid state–capital relations.

However, political scientist Stephen Friedman believes the South African state is a lot stronger than we often give it credit for. 'If one applies the usual criteria – that a strong state is one that is able to exercise authority – then I would say it is pretty strong,' he says.

He gives the example of the South African Revenue Service (SARS), one of the biggest success stories since 1994 in the formal economy at least, and one of the best revenue collectors in the world. However, Marais defines the revenue collector 'as a highly centralised, top-down institute of compulsion' that operates in 'an authoritarian fashion and wields formidable punitive powers', perhaps not surprising given that it was 'rehabilitated with a [former] Leninist at the helm', he says, in reference to former SARS chief Pravin Gordhan.[2] But then again, it is hard to imagine a less authoritarian revenue collector being able to fulfil its mandate. The inability to collect taxes was, after all, one of the factors that led to the collapse of Greece.

Friedman also argues that the fact that more than 15 million people receive their social grants on time each week or each month is not the work of a magic wand. There may be glitches in the system, but it is one that works. That two of the country's three top metros – Cape Town and Durban – function successfully is not bad going either, he argues, or the fact that people living in the rural areas can now access nearby offices to get their identity cards, for example, a marked improvement on recent times when distance from urban life often meant the difference between being in the system and being outside it.

Other pockets of state excellence include the ability to carry out free and fair elections, as well as the successful management of the macro economy and monetary policy. Though when we consider the two main challenges facing the country today – job creation and security – the bigger picture begins to look dysfunctional. If the institutions designed to tackle these two challenges performed at an acceptable level, and if sufficient vision, ambition and innovative thinking were in place, the country would not be beset with high crime and high unemployment.

It is not beyond the South African state to address these deficiencies, but for as long as it continues to appoint politically connected rather than technically able people to key positions, it will continue to underperform and fail to reach its goals.

In China, when a party appointee underperforms he or she is not only removed from the position, but his or her political career is terminated, yet South Africa is laden with examples of cadres ousted from various offices for some or other reason, only to be rewarded by reinstatement elsewhere or posted to one of the country's overseas embassies.

What will happen when the ANC wakes up to the fact that it is not China and does not have the political or strategic strength to do as China does? Its followers will be the first to protest against unfulfilled promises and it is likely that authoritarian tendencies will begin to emerge as the frustrations of failure become apparent.

It is at this point that the extreme nationalists are likely to emerge from this 'new' ANC. Nationalism requires an enemy and without one in sight, the ANC will have to create one. Writing more than half a century ago, Frantz Fanon warned of the pitfalls of African nationalism post-liberation, when the people become the enemy that feeds the rhetoric of nationalism.

Fifty years ago it led to dictatorships across the continent but, as argued above, that is unlikely in today's South Africa. Given the fault lines across the state, the corporatist model is likely to fail as well. What will most likely emerge instead is a 'managed democracy', driven by Malema, or any of the 'older Malemas', within the ANC. For the most part, they are one and the same.

Those who harboured concerns about the country's future believed it was Malema who was blowing out their brief candle of hope, but the flame will continue to fade without him.

The vision is there. The *siloviki* are already in place. The elite have been identified. And that unnatural hybrid that Petrov talked of will surely come to pass.

15

It's complicated

Looking back, it is almost as if Julius Malema appeared out of nowhere around the middle of 2008. One day he wasn't there and the next day, there he was, ploughing the socio-political landscape like an unguided missile, with little or no let-up ever since.

It marked an extraordinary turn of events. For years, the world had admired the iconic stature of Nelson Mandela, the peaceful and noble product of a bitter, 40-year struggle to put an end to the racial injustices that had endured for centuries. Then along came the scrofulous Malema, the creation of the fresh democracy, the face of the ANC after 100 years of struggle politics and the germ of the revolution the country was about to host. South Africa had a new problem on its hands.

Malema was an oddity who crossed several social boundaries in a country defined by separations. Though he belonged to the new political elite, it was with tremendous ease that he mingled among the underprivileged, appealing to them with his promises of a socialist future while he stuffed his trouser pockets with ill-gotten gains. Officially, he was a representative of the ANC's youth yet he was leading his party seniors by the nose, eclipsing the Zuma presidency in what had begun to look like an extraordinary political coup, until they finally forced him out. But as I said earlier, I don't think we have seen the back of Malema yet. He still has totemic value out on the streets.

Those who were against him also feared him but they were blind to any real understanding of who he was or what he stood for, as if they were viewing him through the narrow aperture that Chimamanda Ngozi Adichie talks of in her single stories. Malema represented too much for a single shot, though that's not to say that a wider angle would have made him look any better. It would just unpack the phenomenon that he had become.

His rise to prominence came at a time when South Africa was knee-deep in its transition, struggling to forge a national identity among a multitude of people drawn from the various cultural and social groups, with each one trying to make sense of the other, each one a product of his and her own past, tangled and tempered with the socio-economic conditions of today. Though the period post-1994 had been largely peaceful, society's deep wounds were not healing, and then along came Malema and he began to put words to the national discomfort but in treacherous and menacing tones.

He appeared at a time when many South Africans were beginning to settle into the new South Africa, while others were beginning to rise up at the prospect of being left behind. He lives in a country that is underpinned by a sophisticated first world economy yet is bogged down by the harsh realities of the third world and ruled by a party that is struggling with its own transition.

It's complicated. Very, very complicated. Not Malema, but the environment and the period he inhabits. To repeat the words of Antonio Gramsci from the earlier pages of this book: 'The old is dying, and the new cannot be born; in this interregnum there arises a great diversity of morbid symptoms.' Malema is not the morbid symptom, *per se*, though he epitomises it. As a product of poverty, politics, power and a racial past of which he refuses to let go, the likes of Malema should come as no surprise in a society that is not only still divided along racial lines but is sitting on a lethal mix of unfulfilled promises from the transition, gross inequality in socio-economic terms, and a weak ANC that rules with a majority vote.

South Africa's leaders made the very grave mistake of not giving sufficient thought to what might become of a society that is weighed down by gruesome poverty and yet produces more than 5,500 US-dollar millionaires a year, as it did in 2005, according to Hein Marais in his excellent account of the country's political economy, *South Africa Pushed to the Limit*. According to other data he extrapolated four years later, the year Zuma became state president, the country's top bankers were drawing the kind of salaries that would have taken the average assistant manager in the service sector 520 years to earn. Today the country has the biggest number of top-end car dealerships outside the developed world and yet 40 per cent of the workforce is earning the minimum wage of about US$10 a day. The inequality is simply staggering and it has nurtured anger among South Africans that Malema is now feeding off, but as he exploits their wounds he is tapping into his own resentments and the hang-ups he harbours from the past.

Malema is not alone. When Sarah Malema described her grandson's upbringing, she talked of a young boy reared in morbid misery and poverty; and as she did, she told the story of most South African youth then and now. She told the story of survival, one that is not confined to South Africa.

'It's about eating or being eaten,' says anthropologist Rehana Vally. 'It's about beating or being beaten. It's about survival. It's human.'

As Malema grew up, entered his teens and then matured into manhood, that sense of survival stayed with him, because in him is a fighter who will not give up. There are few like him with such a 'fuck you' attitude to life – largely white life – and each time he opens his mouth, he taps into the psycho-social features of many South Africans.

'People really desperately want to show a finger to all the

white symbols and all that comes with them. And Malema does it on their behalf,' says author Max du Preez. 'And they sit there and they enjoy it in their hearts. Here's a young man, son of a domestic worker, comes from a poor township, and he goes on national television and says "fuck you" to white people. They want to say it. But they can't. And they love him because he does. And he got that.'

What Malema also gets is the anger that is etched deep into the South African psyche. He gets the negrophobia and the self-hatred because they are psychological features that he too harbours.

The self-hatred comes from knowing you are 'hated, despised, detested, not by the neighbour across the street . . . but by an entire race,' as Frantz Fanon described it in his writings of more than half a century ago when he was explaining the South African phenomenon in *Black Skin, White Masks*.[1] That must have been an overwhelmingly powerful feeling on the part of those whites who forced themselves to despise all blacks in the way in which they did, not because they had committed some awful crime or atrocity, but simply because they were black, even though the so-called natives outnumbered them by about 5:1. At the time that Fanon was writing, in 1952, South Africa was 'a boiler into which 13 million blacks were clubbed and penned in by two-and-a-half million whites . . . in a racist structure'.[2] Not all of those whites would have harboured such illogical racism, but those who did, and they were the vast majority, strongly believed that each individual black was unworthy, insubordinate, wicked and living on the wrong side of life. They held those views so strongly that they legislated against the so-called native. And they sustained that hatred for decades.

As powerful as those feelings must have been, they would have been no match for the feelings of anger, shame and humiliation they instilled in each black individual, a humiliation that stemmed from the superiority complex which whites conferred upon themselves, which in itself is a necessary ritual in the crude act of racism, as necessary as the feeling of inferiority which blacks were and sometimes still are forced to inculcate and accept.

'And it has never occurred to a single black to consider himself superior to a member of the white minority,' Fanon argued in the 1950s.[3]

Why didn't they? Perhaps because a life lived in humiliation often weakens a person and can force him or her to doubt and even hate him- or herself. And those who hate themselves tend to be very angry and insecure individuals. That anger will always have to find an outlet, which Malema initially found in white South African society, and he would regularly rail against what he calls their 'white tendencies'. When he gave up on the whites, it was to turn on the ANC, railing against the party leadership and what he regarded as Zuma's dictatorial tendencies. When that eventually softens, there will for sure be someone or something else, and I have no doubt that the whites will feature again before too long.

'I'm not racist,' he says in defence. 'When I talk about "white tendencies" I am talking about anything that seeks to maintain white supremacy. That is what I cannot support.'

I understand what Malema means when he talks about 'white tendencies'. As if it were etched into their DNA, there is still a sizeable number of white South Africans carting around that superiority complex that belongs to another time, and when they exercise it, it reminds him that once he was inferior.

On this one, he is not alone. Consider that earlier quip of his about Helen Zille as 'The Madam'. The reason that resonated for so many black South Africans is that it's what so many of them still feel when they are subjected to white superiority, like the black maid in servitude to the white madam. Those feelings run very, very deep.

Though it is not Malema but his mother and his grandmother and her mother before her who were born and bred in a country that was defined by racism. Malema was born thirteen years before apartheid came to an end and he grew up in the swing of the transition, at a time when opportunities existed for blacks like never before. When he turned eighteen, he had the right to vote, unlike his elders before him. The party he chose to be affiliated with was no longer outlawed. He grew up in an era that was defined by democracy and he could have been anything or done anything he might have wanted to with his life, but he chose to allow a life-size chip to develop on his shoulder and nurtured an angry outlook on life.

His anger was cultivated in the society that bred him, a society that is grounded in victimisation and is still deeply fractured and segregated with no common or shared identity in any lasting or meaningful sense. South Africa showed the world just how angry it could be in the winter of 2008 when more than 60 people were brutally killed in a ghastly slaughter of so-called xenophobia. During that awful period, a Mozambican man was set ablaze by a group of South Africans in broad daylight on a street in one of Johannesburg's townships, an image that was transmitted around the world by international TV crews within hours. Yet two years later the country threw its arms open to the world in a spectacular display of xenophilia, when it staged a hugely successful and enjoyable World Cup. But the morning after Spain held up the winner's gold trophy, scenes of xenophobia were recorded on the outskirts of Cape Town, and tensions erupted elsewhere around the country as black Africans became victims all over again of black South African anger.

How can a society produce such extreme behaviour in so short a period of time? Or is xenophobia perhaps a mistaken term for something more awful at play in South African society? Is negrophobia, rather than xenophobia, not a more apt term to describe the hatred that is often unleashed on fellow black Africans by black South Africans?

Negrophobia is not the monopoly of blacks, Achille Mbembe points out.

'If we think of negrophobia as the fear and hatred of other black Africans, then all South Africans share those feelings, black and white. And there is an "entanglement" of colours in South Africa, which is what gives Malema's person a different hue. He is the product of the dark undercurrents of South African history, across the colour lines and beyond them. There is no black history in South Africa that doesn't involve whiteness. The history is an entanglement of colour lines,' Mbembe says.

His reasoning follows this thread: 'Like negrophobia, racism is not the monopoly of whites, just as self-hatred is not the monopoly of blacks. Whites hate themselves for not having been able to establish a dominion like Canada, New Zealand or Australia. They consider themselves failures in relation to those other historical contexts.'

Blacks hate themselves because for centuries they were unable to withstand white oppression.

The same logic applies to racism, 'which is premised fundamentally on some unresolved conflict with oneself and is then projected onto some other who is stigmatised, especially when you have the power to do so,' Mbembe adds.

Malema has exhibited as much of this kind of behaviour as many white men have before him. The verbal abuse he hurled at the journalist who gave him some lip during a press conference at the ANC headquarters, what Malema later referred to as 'my own house', was a case in point. There have been many more examples of the resentment he nurtures, not least his constant taunting of white people and what he refers to as their 'white tendencies'.

He is an enunciation of the entanglement of black and white in South African life, but also a vehicle for the resentment that is felt towards the perceived cosmetic agreement that brought apartheid to an end. That the current order was not established by a classic revolution galls the likes of Malema.

'I wasn't around during the negotiations, but I'm here now . . . We are leading now. We are running this country,' he told me once: words that are repeated elsewhere in this book but which speak volumes about Malema's outlook on life.

It is this 'fighting' kind of language that, in Mbembe's view, fuels a kind of 'lumpen radicalism' with which Malema has come to be associated and which is 'nurtured by illiteracy, poverty and a very short-sighted radicalism'.

What did little to quell that radicalism were the failures of the 1995 Truth and Reconciliation Commission (TRC), which was set up to try to help South African society disentangle the knots in its make-up and start to weave a new social life. It was an attempt to bring people back to life, back from 'the narrow gate of the sepulchre where centuries of racism had forced them to reside', as Mbembe once put it.

But as Gillian Slovo, the daughter of the late and respected communist leader Joe Slovo, pointed out a few years, the TRC was born out of a compromise, from an agreement between the ANC and the National Party, that none of the members of the apartheid regime, nor those who acted on its behalf, would be brought to book. Though the ANC did not want to cede the blanket amnesty that the National Party sought, it allowed for individual amnesties based on disclosure of crimes in the public court of the TRC. And in that regard, the TRC failed to bring the kinds of justice it promised.

'This was the nature of South Africa's agreement: the transfer of power without a previous settling of historic rights and wrongs,' Gillian Slovo argued. 'Out of a need to end bloodshed and to find a way forward, came political transformation of power without social transformation. As my father often used to put it: the day after the first democratic election South Africa would still be the same country as it had been the day before.'

That compromise was based on the belief that peace was more important than justice. Therefore sacrifice would replace reconciliation and the legacy of the transition, for many people, would amount to little more than a changing of the political guard, or as Malema saw it while still a child, the raising of the right flag.

The legacy of that compromise is multi-layered and it eventually drew out a band of political entrepreneurs, Malema among them, who now feed off the economically disenfranchised in order to create a place for themselves in the sun. It also put a firm lid on the anger that had been nurtured through white oppression. Mandela was leading by example when he transcended the pain and suffering of his own walk to freedom and tens of millions of South Africans were expected to follow in his footsteps and do as he was doing. It was a short-sighted dream that petered out when the lid began to slowly rise with the mounting tension that continued to bubble beneath it. The anger didn't dissipate: it simply continued to simmer until it eventually began to throw up hotheads like Malema.

By not facing up to racism, racism inadvertently became a legacy of the struggle rather than something the struggle had fought to put an end to, and in that way it encouraged a sense of victimhood, the other scourge that underwrites South African history and present-day society.

Victimhood started centuries ago when the Africans fell victim to the Boers, the Dutch settlers, in the 1600s. The Boers, following the Xhosas, later fell victim to the British after the Anglo-Boer War. The Africans then became victims of both the Boers and the British, before and after apartheid in 1948. History turned the tables 46 years later when Afrikaners and British South Africans perceived themselves as the new victims after the first democratic elections returned a black government. Today's society, with all its other faults, has produced a large crop of Africans who feel they are victims of their own people, victims of the victims, because they have yet to find a place in the new dispensation. And consequently, the new South Africa has created a body of victims who shuffle around in an increasingly fragile society weighed down by the ghosts of its past.

How does a society begin to lay so many ghosts to rest? The respected social activist, commentator and businesswoman Mamphela Ramphele tells a good tale in *Laying Ghosts to Rest* about the ghosts that haunted her childhood in the 1950s and how she tried to deal with them.

When Ramphele was growing up in the village of Kranspoort at the foot of the Soutpansberg Mountains in Limpopo, she developed a deep fear of darkness. That was long before electricity reached South Africa's villages and darkness permeated her life. What sparked her fear were not the dark nights themselves but the ghosts that legend had led her to believe were haunting Kranspoort. They petrified Ramphele. And there was only one person who could help her tame the ghosts, an old man by the name of Uncle Paulos.

'Uncle Paulos confronted each ghost by name. He would plead with the ghost to make peace with whatever unfinished business was troubling it, and find rest . . . What Uncle Paulos did in each instance was to acknowledge the ghost by calling its name. This acknowledgement opened a channel of communication between the living and those in the afterlife. Unfinished business was acknowledged and peace was made.'[4]

But South Africa chose to turn its back on its unfinished business by refusing to face up to its past and name the ghosts that would haunt it into the future.

'Think back to Joe Slovo's words,' says Vally. 'South Africa a day later would still be the same South Africa as the day before. And for millions of South Africans today, this is still the old South Africa. They are not participating in the new South Africa.'

They are out on the margins, where they resided for 40 years of apartheid and the centuries that went before it. Time eventually played its hand and the society that has emerged is laden with the legacy of the past: angry; self-hating; racially divided and racist; negrophobic; obscenely rich in some parts and desperately poor in others; often bleak and yet tragically hopeful; a mean and cruel place and yet very, very often a society with a big heart. I don't think I have ever come across people who want to make their country work as much as the vast majority of South Africans do. But then again, I don't think I have ever lived in a society as wounded as this society is.

At the height of the violence in the late 1980s and 1990s, necklacing became a common form of mob justice in the townships for anyone found collaborating with the apartheid forces, a brutal kind of torture that was endorsed by Winnie Madikizela-Mandlea. Rubber tyres would be filled with petrol, placed around the victim's chest and then set alight, and the vigilantes would watch for the twenty or so minutes it would take the victim to die before them in a grisly heap. It is one of the most brutal legacies of that era and one of the worst forms of self-hate, inflicting the most horrific form of pain and violence imaginable on a person who looks just like you. As recently as 2011, six incidents of necklacing were reported in one small town in the Eastern Cape when a community took action against a group of local youth who had broken into an elderly woman's house, stolen her TV and stabbed her lodger to death when he tried to defend her.

The high crime rate is another manifestation of it. The annual murder rate dropped in the last few years, but it is still somewhere in the region of 18,000 or so each year, the kind of figures that are found in war zones. In the current unrest in Syria, 12,000 people were killed in the 12-month period through to April of 2012, two-thirds the annual murder rate in South Africa.

The rape of women is an even greater scourge, with Interpol stating that South Africa has the highest recorded rate in the world, while local statistics suggest that a young South African woman has a greater chance of being raped than she has of learning to read. 'Jackrolling' is the fun term that young black teenagers use for gang rape. But it's not new. In the run-up to the first democratic elections, seven children under the age of fourteen were being raped every day of the week in the township of Soweto.

'The brutality is everywhere,' says Vally. 'But that brutality also gave rise to Malema.'

'Think about it,' she continues. 'What does it mean to be poor? What does it mean to survive when you are poor? You have to be brutal to get your morsel of food.'

Malema did what he had to when he was younger until he eventually pulled himself up by his socks, and various other means as it now transpires, to get to where he is today, with no attempt on my part to justify his means to wealth.

In crude terms, he became one of the new black men who has landed, politically and financially, the former enhancing the latter, feeding his sense of power, and as he looks around him, he sees poverty staring him in the face, and in it he sees his opportunity.

He sees the 15 or so million South Africans who are living on handouts from the state through one form of grant or another, people whom the state is on the one hand helping, but on the other hand telling, 'You are not able to participate in this new South Africa, in this new economy.' In this new South Africa, if one is rich, one can consume. If one is poor, one simply cannot participate. Hence they are excluded and the frightening fact is that more than half of all South Africans are now on the outside looking in. That's 25 or more million people. It's a staggering figure.

It is also an indirect admission on the part of government that it has failed to deliver on social justice. Mandela delivered the peace, but the social justice, the real justice, has yet to transpire, the kind of justice that will allow people to live in well-built homes that have electricity and running water; and to access a decent health system and an education that will train them to take part in the market economy and live a life of dignity. All of that is still lacking.

It is a feature of South African life that existed long before Malema came onto our radars. It has its roots in the early days of the transition, when the ANC-led government hinged the enormous task of the transition on the Reconstruction and Development Programme (RDP), a national framework for social development that was initially defined by the country's trade unions, but later appropriated by the Tripartite Alliance that was about to govern the country and with the blessing of Mandela, the country's first president, the RDP became the blueprint for transformation.

Despite the best intentions that inspired it, the plan was deeply flawed. It conceptualised the state as the sole arbiter of the transition, of the RDP, and in so doing it all but suffocated the voice of civil society. This in turn made people bystanders in their own lives, as Jay Naidoo, the minister with responsibility for the RDP, would later admit.

'What followed was a decade of state-led development,' he says, during which the political space also narrowed to such an extent that factionalism set in across the ANC and fear began to permeate society.

People became disaffected, not only because they were feeling excluded but also because they were being left behind. It began to dawn on them that if they were born in a shack in the new South Africa, the chances were that they would depart to their graves from one as well.

They were the damned, the masses, a large underclass of society whose lives were marked by extreme poverty, and their ranks had swelled by the time Malema came to prominence in 2008 and took them under his wing.

By then the poor had taken to staging 'service delivery protests' to try to make themselves heard and had Malema been listening, what would have echoed were their shrill cries appealing for someone to pull them out of the miserable hole of black African life and integrate them into the mainstream of the new South Africa.

The first of these 'service delivery protests' was staged in 2004 in the small township of Intabazwe on the outskirts of Harrismith in the Free State and it rocked the country for the week or so that the fires flared. It was a new phenomenon for which no one had a name – neither the protesters who staged the protest, the reporters who reported on it nor the commentators who tried to make sense of it initially knew what to call it. The locals were trying to say that they had reached the end of their tethers over the slow provision of basic services, such as water, roads and electricity, and had taken to pounding the tarmac. And so it was that the term 'service delivery protest' entered the South African lexicon.

In the following 6 years, through to October 2010, at least 315 of these kinds of protests were recorded in different hot-spots across South Africa, and yet with the exception of one or two protests that get out of hand, by and large these street riots rarely manage to capture the public imagination any longer, even though they carry the voices of millions of South Africans who reside in pathetic states of deprivation, a message that government ought not to ignore. Today, 'service delivery protests' have become a euphemism for serious social unrest. Many are now of the opinion that an 'Arab Spring'-like event is not too far off, and though that may well be true, it would be horrific if it were to happen, considering the seething anger that is bubbling inside most South Africans.

The irony is that the vast majority of the protesters are ANC voters who have faithfully returned the ruling party to power thrice since 1994, and there is nothing to suggest that they won't do so again in the general elections of 2014, in the perpetual hope of that better life that was initially promised to them.

One in every four South Africans is now living on state handouts. Of the country's youth it is estimated that one in two is jobless. More than 6 million people are living with the killer disease of HIV/AIDS. The mortality rate for children is worsening. And while school enrolment figures are improving, the number of teenagers completing Grade 12 at age 17 or 18 is teetering around the 25 per cent mark. Crime continues to burden society with annual murder rates now five times the global average. The waiting list for a state house is so long that it is expected to take more than ten years to clear it. Between 2005 and 2006, when Malema was rising through his party's ranks, the poorest 20 per cent of South Africa's population lived off 1.4 per cent of available income. During that same period, 49 per cent of African households were earning less than R20,000 a year, according to Marais' statistics.

These statistics have been trotted out numerous times before, but they are worth repeating for the sole purpose of hammering home a fundamental point: it is these social and economic indicators that partly helped to breathe political life into Julius Malema and as he interpreted these statistics, he saw a powerful calling card on which he could begin to trade: the voiceless, the excluded, the angered, the furious.

Malema was cunning in his approach. He began to ask, 'Why are you poor?' And he formulated their answers for them. 'You are poor because too many white people are rich.' Indirectly he is telling them, 'You are only good for your vote. And when you cast it, you get your grant in return.' But he could never say that because it is his own ANC that is ruling the state, the party that gave his platform legitimacy.

'Those who are on social grants are pushed further out on to the margins so that they are no longer the masters of their own destinies,' says Vally. 'And Malema knows that. And as he walks them by the hand, he is becoming the master of their destiny instead.

'It has echoes of *Mein Kampf* to it all,' she adds. 'Germany of that era was exactly about economics. Poor Germans were told that the only reason they were poor was because Jewish people were controlling the economy.'

So when Malema came to prominence, he immediately began to talk the language of the disaffected, those who make up the largest and most important constituency in the country. He was already thinking of life after the Youth League. He knew it would be constituency politics that would determine his future in the way it had decided Mbeki's downfall and Zuma's rise a few years earlier. He knew it would be pointless for him to pin his ambitions on the youth vote alone, so he turned to the tens of millions who comprise South Africa's so-called masses and presented himself as one of them, as a hapless victim of a dark era.

Of course he wasn't one of them. Malema's ship had come in many years earlier and he has not known a day of economic hardship ever since, but that did not stop him from talking up a compelling political line in favour of the disenchanted tens of millions all around him, riding on waves of discontent that have helped carry him into the world of the over-privileged.

Malema began to choose his talking points carefully, finding his strongest form of expression in the failings of the promises his own party had made in 1994. He spotted the failures, crafted the solutions and promoted them on the back of the support of millions who began to walk alongside him. He is most closely associated with the controversial debate around nationalisation of the country's mines, through which he plans to claw back ownership of the subsoil mineral assets that are valued at around US$3 trillion. Had wealth in South Africa been more evenly distributed, or had the economy been more transformed as the ANC-led government had promised, Malema would have found it difficult to broach the issue of state ownership of the mines.

But the failure to do so gave him the kind of ammunition that only a hardened populist would put to good use.

The government's aim was to have 25 per cent of the economy in black hands by 2017, but with statistics showing that the bulk of the economy has still not shifted, or that the targets are unlikely to be met, and that white minority ownership of the country's mineral resources is increasing rather than decreasing, a situation was created that was crying out for an overhaul, one which Malema chose to address with his radical call for nationalisation.

He did not address the debt burden this would create, the run it would put on foreign investment (given that the bulk of the mines are foreign owned), or how state involvement in the mines would kill the competitive edge that exists in the private sector. Instead, he based his argument on a populist line and gave it an emotional and ideological appeal in favour of the poor. He was talking directly to them, wrapping them up in the sly notion that the only means to get out of poverty would be to share out the wealth by wrenching it from the hands of the whites. To a largely uneducated and desperate class, this appealed hugely, and they gave him their rounded support in return, though he has yet to win his campaign within the party, where it will matter most.

Malema took the same tack with the protracted issue of land reform, which has lagged shamefully under consecutive ANC-led governments and became another lobbying favourite for him. Like any other country on the African continent, land reform is one of the most critical projects for a government to get right when its people were so wrongfully dispossessed, as black South Africans were.

In 1994, the ANC-led government set itself the target to return 30 per cent of the land to the people within a 20-year period. Fifteen years later, the government was forced to flag the fact that, with only 6 per cent of the land restored by 2009, it was another target would not be met. Again, Malema seized the opportunity his own party had handed him and promised full redistribution of the land 'in our lifetime', and without financial compensation.

Later he took the issue of land reform further when he called for the land to be taken back by force. In neighbouring Zimbabwe it is called a 'land grab', but in South Africa, in Malema's view, it is called 'expropriation with compensation determined by the state'. And if the seller doesn't like the offered price, 'then we take the land and give you nothing', he warned to loud applause in townships and backwaters all over the country. He had assembled the white community into his firing line for the umpteenth time.

Many continue to insist it is racism on his part, but I don't believe it is. It's race-based. There is a difference, one that lies in the fact that Malema is exploiting the problem that race and racism have never been fully addressed in his country so he has decided to exploit the racial context instead, just as he exploits the unsolved problems that continue to weigh on the state. However, suggesting that he is not racist and is instead trading off race-based politics is no less an offence and would have the same dire and hateful consequence.

Had it not been Malema who shone the light on the fault lines in this country and all of the social ills I have just described, someone else would have, and the problems would have continued to fester until that person eventually came along.

The awful pity is that it was Malema who took it upon himself to do the job. From what we now know about his business life, the way he cut himself into various money-making schemes, and the manner in which he ran the Youth League, Malema is the wrong man to claim the title of commander-in-chief of the poor or the voiceless.

Had he been a more genuine sort, he could have made such a difference in South Africa.

What is also regrettable about the Malema saga is that it could have been prevented had some solid leadership existed within the ANC to guide the party and South Africa in the direction it ought to be headed.

Mandela was an extraordinary leader, and he had the ability to bring everyone with him at one of the most challenging and difficult times when the country could so easily have slipped into a civil war. The ten years of the Mbeki era that followed were markedly different. The Afro-Saxon Mbeki was an aloof character, and his mistake was to distance himself from his party and his people. While he had some good leadership qualities, there was an authoritarian streak to him that eventually brought him down.

Zuma, on the other hand, appears unfit to govern the country and has too few redeeming qualities, if any at all. He is uninterested in anything but himself, power, his four wives, his twenty-plus children and their new business empire.

When Malema was eventually expelled from the party, many were of the view that Zuma was finally beginning to behave like a president by standing up to the troublesome youth, though that is a view that is mistaken. Zuma simply could not handle Malema and chose to get rid of him instead. The leadership vacuum therefore still exists within the ANC and Malema, or others like him, can only be expected to make gains on it at some time in the future by throwing up hasty solutions to the complex problems with which the state is struggling to deal.

'And that's the danger,' says Vally. 'There will come a time when people will stop depending on the state and try and access the wealth and the land themselves. And who will they turn to? Malema.'

That's what makes Malema what he is: a dangerous player with an uncanny ability to read the socio-economic conditions around him; a man with a past that can empathise with real hardship; a man who has been at the receiving end of race-based politics; and despite the legal challenges he faces, a man with a fairly solid political power base among the masses, though like a heartless charmer he is taking advantage of their innocence.

It is a mix of the past and the present, of the psycho-social and the structural in a particular blend at a given time, that gave rise to Julius Malema, but it was his arrogance that eventually got the better of him.

His arrogance will not save him from the charges of corruption that he now faces but it is all too possible that the 'managed democracy' we are beginning to inhabit will get him off the hook. Should that happen, South Africa can expect an even more emboldened Malema than they have seen before, a man who will pull out all the stops to get his hands on the ANC. Should he succeed, we can expect to hear more interpretation of history, more of the events of 1949, more of the militancy and that revolution he still wants to happen.

To repeat the words of Karl Marx in *The Eighteenth Brumaire*: 'Men make their own history, but they do not make it as they please . . . The tradition of all dead generations weighs like a nightmare on the brains of the living. And just as they seem to be occupied with revolutionizing themselves and things, creating something that did not exist before, precisely in such epochs of revolutionary crisis they anxiously conjure up the spirits of the past to their service, borrowing from them names, battle slogans, and costumes in order to present this new scene in world history in time-honored disguise and borrowed language.'

But as Marx also noted in that text: 'Hegel remarks somewhere that all great world-historic facts and personages appear, so to speak, twice. He forgot to add: the first time as tragedy, the second time as farce.'[5]

In an exhibition he staged halfway through 2011, the renowned artist Beezy Bailey depicted the iconic stature of Nelson Mandela through his inimitable pop art. In one installation he cast the old man in a large, open expanse. But instead of one Mandela there were several men walking through that landscape, each one cast in a different colour, as if he personified a rainbow.

Bailey called it Rainbow Notion, then lent the name to the entire exhibition 'because the idea of the nation is struggling', he said when I saw him around that time, 'so the idea of the notion seemed more fitting'.

I asked him what imagery he would use if he were to depict Julius Malema at that stage in his political life, or what visuals come to mind when Bailey thinks of the then Youth League leader.

'A threshold,' he responded after only a couple of seconds of thought.

'I see him at a threshold,' he continued. 'On a cusp. He's in a beautiful garden. That garden is South Africa. It's full of beauty. But some of the fruits are poisonous. There's a slip in the path. And he can go down the dark side or the light side. He will use stuff from the dark side to get into power. But after that, we don't know. We're just watching. We're all on that threshold with him. And at the same time, he is that threshold.'

'So what about the rainbow notion?' I asked.

'Well, that's precisely it,' Bailey answered. 'Here is the old man cast in the rainbow across the country. The whole world is captured by the beauty and the utopia of it all. But it's not really working.

'And then I look at the young man, Malema. And I see the threshold. And he is the man who can make it a nation or just a notion.'

A year later, and not long after Malema had been expelled, I went back to hear what Bailey had to say. The idea of Malema as the threshold still stood for him. And it was all a notion rather than a nation, still.

What about the rainbow, the term used by Archbishop Emeritus Desmond Tutu to describe the multi-coloured people as they began to walk towards nationhood in 1994?

'That's the problem,' says Bailey. 'When I think of the treasure at the end of the rainbow, I know that by the time we get there, these guys will probably have already stolen it on us . . .'

To be continued . . .

Acknowledgements

There were a couple of dozen people and more in Polokwane who helped me to tell this story but for all the obvious reasons they cannot be named, but it is safe to say that without them, this book would have been incomplete. My thanks to all of them and to the following people who helped in a number of ways: Joe Matthews, Tom Lodge, Peter Limb, Rehana Vally, Barbara and Terry Bell, Thabo Makunyane, Rayne Stroebel, Sisonke Msimang, Stefaans Brummer, Craig McKune, Rian Malan, Moeletsi Mbeki, Redi Tlhabi and Heidi Holland. A special thank you to Achille Mbembe, my structural editor. To IDASA for the office space it provided, and the Association of Non-Fiction Authors of South Africa for its technical back-up. To the team at Picador Africa and, in particular, their publisher, Andrea Nattrass, for the support she gave that so often went beyond the bounds of duty. And a very special thank you to my sister, Edel.

But my biggest thanks go to Julius Malema himself, who took me into his confidence and into his world in allowing me to relay his unauthorised biography. Though he may not like some of what is contained between these covers, I hope he will agree that, overall, this is a fair portrayal of who he is.

Appendix 1

100 years of ANC struggle politics

1909   The South Africa Act is passed which strips blacks of their rights.

1910   The Union of South Africa is formed.

1912   The South African Native National Congress is founded in response to the 1909 Act as a nationwide movement that will lobby for civil rights. It is started in the city of Bloemfontein on 8 January, with John Dube as its first president.

1913   The Native Land Act allocates 7 per cent of land to the black majority in newly created black reservations. They can only enter white areas if they are working for a white person. It prompted ANC founder Sol Plaatje to write the following historical line: 'Awaking on Friday morning, 20 June 1913, the South African native found himself not actually a slave, but a pariah in the land of his birth'.

1918   Rolihlahla Dalibhunga Nelson Mandela is born on 18 July in the small village of Mvezo in the Transkei province, what is known today as the Eastern Cape.

1923   The SANNC is renamed the African National Congress.

1944   The ANC Youth League is founded by, among others, Mandela, Oliver Tambo, Walter Sisulu.

1946   African miners paid twelve times less than their white counterparts.

During apartheid

1948   The white South African electorate vote for the National Party on the back of their project of apartheid, or apartness, a short-hand for racial segregation.

1949   The ANCYL's Programme of Action is endorsed by the ANC, paving the way for a decade of civil protests in the new struggle against apartheid.

1950/1   Regime introduces a number of acts that set the tone for the apartheid era and prompts the ANC to respond. The Suppression of Communism Act outlaws the Communist Party of South Africa, while the Population Registration Act categorises people into whites, blacks or coloureds and the Group Areas Act determines to which suburbs each group is restricted. Marriages of mixed race are outlawed in order to maintain racial purity. The Group Areas Act determines which suburbs each racial group can inhabit and the hated 'pass books' are introduced to record the movements of blacks. Meanwhile the Bantu Homelands Act comes into effect and defines black reservations as bantustans and legally classifies them as independent nations. Ten bantusans appear on the South African map as a result of the act that also strips blacks of their South African citizenship as they must now apply to enter the white-only areas but are granted passes if employed by whites.

1952   The ANC responds to the acts with the Defiance Campaign, a movement of mass non-violent resistance to the various pieces of apartheid legislation.

1953   Preservation of Separate Amenities Act demarcates 'whites only' public areas, such as public benches, beaches and parks. The Bantu Education Act introduces an inferior standard of education for blacks and denies them permission to attend universities.

1955   The Freedom Charter is drafted with contributions from black communities all over the country and lays out the demands for a free South Africa in which 'the people shall govern'. It would survive the apartheid era as a revolutionary programme for ANC members.

1956   One hundred and fifty-six activists, among them a great number of ANC members, are arrested for treason and the Treason Trial begins. It drags on until 1961 by which time only 30 of the accused are still facing trial, among them are Mandela, Sisulu, Ahmed Kathrada and Joe Slovo. All 30 are acquitted.

1959   The Pan Africanist Congress (PAC) is formed by a group of defectors from the ANC who believe the liberation movement is not sufficiently Africanist and condemns its collaboration with Indian and coloured activists and white communists.

1960   Sixty-nine people are gunned down in the township of Sharpeville when hundreds defy the regime by refusing to carry their pass books.

The government declares a state of emergency.

The ANC is outlawed along with all other black political parties.

Oliver Tambo leaves the country with the first round of ANC exiles and in the years that followed the exiles would concentrate in camps in Tanzania, Zambia, Angola, Uganda, as well as Europe and the former Soviet Union.

The then President Albert Luthuli becomes the first African to win the Nobel Peace Prize.

1961   The ANC takes up arms and forms its own military wing called Umkhonto we Sizwe, or Spear of the Nation, more commonly known as the MK.

Over the next 18 months, the MK carries out more than 200 acts of sabotage.

The regime responds by legislating the death penalty as punishment for sabotage and allows the police to detain activists for up to 90 days without trial.

1963   The core leadership of the MK is arrested at its hideout farm in Rivonia on the outskirts of Johannesburg, charged with 221 acts of sabotage and faces the death penalty.

1964   Though they escape execution, Mandela is sentenced to life imprisonment on Robben Island along with Sisulu and eight others when the now famous two-year Rivonia Trial comes to an end. The impact on the movement within South Africa is drastic.

1969   The ANC conference in Morogoro agrees to open up membership to whites, but the executive and the leadership must remain black African.

1976   Black school students in Soweto protest against Afrikaans – the official language of the regime – as the mandatory medium of instructions in schools, sparking a wave of protests all over the country in which more than 500 teenagers are killed in the space of 8 months in what became known as the Soweto uprising.

Thousands of youth go into exile in Tanzania and elsewhere on the continent.

1977   The United Nations Security Council responds with Resolution 418 which imposed an arms embargo, which the regime quickly began to circumvent.

1981   Julius Malema is born on 3 March.

1982   The 'Release Mandela' campaign is launched in South Africa and abroad, sparking what would become critical international awareness around the ANC's struggle against apartheid.

1984   Archbishop Desmond Tutu is awarded the Nobel Peace Prize

1986   A state of emergency is declared on the eve of the tenth anniversary of the Soweto uprising as the anti-apartheid movement grows throughout the country. The crackdown is more draconian than previous emergencies and introduces curfews, bans TV crews from filming political arrest, and prohibits meetings and gatherings, both public and private. The international community has begun to impose economic sanctions on the country which begin to hurt more than the previous arms embargo.

Winnie Madikizela-Mandela, who had been placed under house arrest for several years, steps up the fight against apartheid and endorses the 'necklacing' of all traitors. The ANC denounces the move.

1987   Mandela begins secret negotiations with the regime leaders from prison, a top-secret move that only became public years later.

1989   The Rivonia Trialists are released, but Mandela is kept in confinement in a prison on the outskirts of Cape Town.

F.W. de Klerk replaces P.W. Botha as president and repeals the Forced Separation Act.

Unbanned

1990   Thirty-year ban on ANC lifted and exiles begin to return home.

Mandela walks free after 27 years in prison.

The government and ANC sign an agreement to end the armed struggle.

1991   De Klerk repeals the remaining apartheid acts and international sanctions are lifted.

ANC holds its 48th national conference, its first on home soil.

Mandela is elected president of the party, taking over from Oliver Tambo who led the party since 1969 and from exile.

CODESA begins, a forum for formal party-to-party talks to negotiate an end to apartheid.

1992/3   Violence erupts in townships all over the country between members of the black-led IFP and the ANC.

1993   Hugely popular communist leader Chris Hani is assassinated sparking concerns of a civil war. Mandela goes on national television and appeals for calm. His appearance signals an imminent shift in power.

Mandela and de Klerk are jointly awarded the Nobel Peace Prize.

Tambo dies from stroke complications and doesn't live to see the end of the struggle he dedicated his life to.

In government

1994   More than 19 million South Africans queue to exercise their new right to vote on 27 April and elect the ANC to lead them.

Mandela is sworn in as the country's first black president on 10 May and promises that 'Never, never and never again shall it be that this beautiful land will again experience the oppression of one by another'.

Thabo Mbeki is sworn in as his deputy.

The Government of National Unity is formed.

South Africa joins the United Nations and returns to the Commonwealth.

1996   The Truth and Reconciliation Commission begins, chaired by Archbishop Desmond Tutu, to hear the human rights abuses committed by both sides during apartheid.

1996   Parliament adopts the new constitution.

Government of National Unity ends when National Party

withdraws, leaving ANC as the ruling party.

1997   Mbeki succeeds Mandela as ANC president and Jacob Zuma
is elected as his deputy.

1999   Mandela steps down as state president after a single five-year
term.

He is succeeded by Mbeki as the head of the government.
Zuma becomes deputy president.

The multi-million rand arms deal is sealed which will
later be exposed as one of the biggest cases of corruption in
the new South Africa.

Six million South Africans are HIV-positive, representing
about 15 per cent of the population at the time.

Mbeki begins his era of AIDS denialism, arguing that the
HIV virus doesn't cause AIDS and rejects anti-retroviral
drugs on the grounds that they are toxic.

2003   Veteran leader Walter Sisulu dies at the age of 91.

Winnie Madikizela-Mandela is found guilty of 43 counts
of fraud and 25 of theft and sentenced to 5 years in prison.
The bulk of her convictions would be overturned a year
later on appeal, though she would be left with a three-year
suspended sentence.

2004   Mbeki is re-elected as state president, with Zuma as his
deputy on the back of 70 per cent of the vote, the ANC's
best performance in a general election yet since 1994.

On the eve of his 85th birthday, Mandela announces his
retirement from public life, telling the world 'Don't call me,
I'll call you.'

2005   Mbeki fires Zuma from the presidency as allegations of
corruption emerge.

The ANC membership rejects Mbeki's move and vows to
return Zuma to power.

Zuma is charged with corruption.

A month later Zuma is accused of raping a family friend,
who was also HIV-positive.

2006   Zuma is acquitted of rape and his corruption case collapses
– though it would later be reinstated.

ANC Chief Whip in Parliament Tony Yengeni is convicted
of fraud in relation to the arms deal and sentenced to four
years, but only serves five months.

2007   Mbeki loses the party leadership to Zuma.

Corruption charges against Zuma re-instated less than two weeks after his victory.

2008   Zuma marries his fourth wife.

Malema becomes president of the ANCYL.

Sixty-two Africans are killed in horrific scenes of xenophobia, though among them were 22 South Africans.

Police chief Jackie Selebie is charged with corruption and suspended while the case unfolds.

Harvard researchers claim 300,000 deaths were caused by Mbeki's AIDS denialism.

Mbeki is sacked as state president and eleven of his cabinet resign in solidarity. Kgalema Motlanthe is sworn in as caretaker.

The Congress of the People is formed by pro-Mbeki ANC seniors who defect from Zuma's ANC.

2009   The acting head of the National Prosecuting Authority drops the 783 charges of corruption, fraud and racketeering against Zuma a fortnight ahead of the general election.

ANC wins third consecutive general election with 65.9 per cent of the vote.

Zuma becomes the new president of South Africa.

Government refuses to grant the Dalai Lama a visitor's visa.

Malema makes his first call for nationalisation of the country's mines and invokes a line from the 1955 Freedom Charter that 'South Africa belongs to all who live in it'.

2010   Zuma marries his fifth wife, but three weeks later admits he fathered a 'love child' with the daughter of soccer guru Irvin Khosa – the first scandal to rock his presidency.

2011   ANC government denies Dalai Lama a visa for a second time.

Parliament votes in favour of the punitive secrecy bill.

Former police chief Jackie Selebie is sentenced to fifteen years for corruption.

Meanwhile the new police chief Bheki Celi is suspended while corruption charges are investigated, and a cabinet minister is placed on suspended leave for defrauding the public purse.

2012   On 8 January, the ANC celebrates 100 years of struggle
         politics, against a backdrop of infighting, factionalism and
         political scandal.

         Zuma marries his sixth wife.

         Government starts a fresh investigation into the 1999
         arms deal.

         On 24 April, Malema is expelled from the ANCYL and
         the ANC.

Appendix 2

Questions put to Julius Malema

As I mentioned earlier in the book, when I concluded my investigations into Malema's businesses and financial dealings, I put the allegations to him in writing so that he could have fair say. The most significant of these questions are shown below:

1. On 14 October 2009, when I shadowed you for a week and which provided the basis for two newspaper articles that subsequently appeared in the *Sunday Independent*, I asked you what was helping to foot your lifestyle. You said that you had no other income other than your ANC Youth League salary. Your words were, 'No, this is it.' It would later emerge that you were also earning an income from SGL (see below).

1a. Why did you deny that extra income when I posed that question in October 2009?

1b. Have you ever declared your extra income to your employers, the ANC (ANC Youth League)?

2. What have been your sources of income over the past 10 years (be it in the form of salary, gifts, donation, loans)?

3. Your colleague and friend Pule Mabe told me that together, you and him, 'did tenders', 'small tenders', many years ago. That information was offered voluntarily by Pule during an interview I did with him in 2011, at your request, when I wanted to know about the early tenders you dabbled in. He told me that you and he won the following:

   – A public tender to provide branded plastic bottles for Lepelle Water in Limpopo. Please confirm the amount you earned from this tender. Please confirm how this tender was won.

- A public tender to supply uniforms at your old high school, Mohlakaneng (which you had also confirmed to me). Please confirm the amount you earned from this tender. Please confirm how this tender was won.
- A public tender to supply uniforms at a school in Dendron. Please confirm the amount you earned from this tender. Please confirm how this tender was won.
- A public tender to organise the inauguration of a mayor in the Waterberg district of Limpopo (which you also confirmed to me). Please confirm the amount you earned from this tender. Please confirm how this tender was won.

4.   How much did you earn from the public tenders you won through the South African Rail Commuter Corporation (SARCC)? Please confirm how this tender was won.

5.   You have been officially linked to the following legal entities in a business capacity:
   - SGL Engineering Projects
   - SGL Engineering Projects CC
   - Segwalo Consultancy Engineers
   - Segwalo
   - 101 Jun Jus
   - Ever Roaring
   - Blue Nightingale
   - Ngape Mining Investments
   - (You have separately told me you are involved in On-Point)

   Please detail the income you have earned from them since they were legally established, including the source of each income and, if they resulted from tenders, whether you brokered the tenders or took any action to influence the award of the tender in favour of the entity concerned.

6.   You told me on two occasions you are involved in On-Point (something the media recently reported on). What is your shareholding in that company? If it is not a shareholding, in what way are you financially involved in On-Point?

7.   You are also linked to another legal entity – the Ratanang

Family Trust – of which you are both a donor and a trustee on behalf of your son Ratanang Ramohlale – and which you established on 25 October 2007 (the name of the Trust hangs on a plaque outside the church you donated to the people of Seshego). Has the Ratanang Family Trust earned any income since 2007, by way of properties or other assets attached to it or monies lodged into its accounts?

8.   I understand that in 2004 a meeting took place at the Ster Park home of Matome Sathekge of Bakgaloka Building Construction and among those present were yourself and the two directors of SGL. Please explain the outcome of that meeting and how it linked you to SGL.

8a.   Did you ever help or ensure that SGL won tenders from 2004 through to the present day (even though SGL now operates as On-Point)?

8b.   If so, did you receive any financial reward for doing that?

8c.   If so, how much did you receive in terms of a commission for each tender you may have helped SGL win?

8d.   If you were paid such a commission, how was that money paid out to you (e.g. cash, cheque, etc.)?

9.   In 2006 your company Blue Nightingale became a 3 per cent shareholder in a venture that won a lucrative waste management public tender. The media subsequently reported that you were paid out for the equivalent of what your shareholding might have earned over the duration of the tender. However, I understand that that payout, in 2006, which was in excess of the amount listed by the media reports, was not a payout of the value of your shareholding but instead a loan.

9a.   Can you confirm that this is true?

9b.   If so, can you confirm the exact amount of that loan?

9c.   Have you repaid that existing loan, in full? If so, when?

9d.   It has also been explained to me that you requested that loan so as to build your mother a house (see below). Please confirm whether or not this is true.

9e.   I also understand that you remained as a shareholder of the firm until the waste management tender expired last year. Can you confirm if this is true?

9f.   If you remained a shareholder throughout this period, what was the total income you earned from this public tender?

10.   My understanding is that Blue Nightingale was a shareholder in a business arrangement with Beta Projects and Beta Projects Consortium. Can you confirm the amount of the shareholding?

10a.   If so, please explain the nature of the arrangement and the public tenders it involved.

10b.   If so, please also explain the amount of money such an arrangement earned for Blue Nightingale.

11.   What public tenders did Ever Roaring win that would have linked the company to Vuna Health Care?

12.   You once stated – around the end of 2009/early 2010 – that your net salary as ANC Youth League president was slightly in excess of R40,000. Yet at that time you were paying R18,000 each month in rent on your Sandown property at Silvela Road – prior to you purchasing it. When you took on the lease of that house, the agreement was R18,000 per month, plus a deposit equivalent to two months' rent. You paid the entire amount – one year's rent plus two months' deposit – up front, in a couple of bulk payments. Was this made possible by the extra income earned in addition to your ANC Youth League salary?

13.   You have been reported as saying in the press that you live on donations and handouts *(Mail & Guardian* article), which may partly explain the perception of wealth that has been created around you.

13a.   Who are your main donors?

13b.   If you are not prepared to divulge the names of such individuals to me, can I ask why not, given your political profile in South Africa today?

13c.   Do your donors expect anything in return for the money and/ or gifts they give you?

13d.   If so, what do they expect in return?

14.   Have any of the businessmen who have donated money and/or gifts to you or who have paid for certain aspects of your life – as mentioned above – ever been linked to SGL (or any of its sister companies) or On-Point in any way?

14a. If said businessmen are not associated with SGL (or any of its sister companies) or On-Point today, have they been associated with those entities at any time in the past?

15. Has Martin Kingston ever donated any gifts or money to you?

15a. Did Martin Kingston give you money towards the down-payment of your residence at 25 Silvela Road in Sandown?

15b. If he did not give you money towards the down-payment of the house, did he give you money around the time that you purchased 25 Silvela Road in Sandown?

16. Are you linked to any loan account in any company or business entity that is currently operating in South Africa?

16a. Is the Ratanang Family Trust linked to any company or business entity that is currently operating in South Africa?

Properties

You have purchased a number of properties in the past few years, among them the following:

- A site at Ster Park in August 2006 for R222,000
- A house at 23 Mopane Street in Flora Park in May 2007 for R1 million (with a bond that has since been cleared)
- A house at 25 Silvela Road, Sandown, in August 2009 for R3.6 million, which has since been razed to the ground and is undergoing a reconstruction
- A farm in Palmietfontein in June 2010 for R900,000
- A house in Faranani Estate, also in June 2010, for R1.36 million

1. What was the source of extra income and/or money that was available to you to purchase such properties?

2. When you purchased the site at Ster Park it was from Matane Edwin Mphahlele. He had purchased it directly from the municipality for a price of R222,300 in August 2006. When it was eventually transferred to his name, it was immediately then transferred to your name for the same amount of R222,300.

2a. How do you explain the fact that Mphahlele sold the site to you for the same price as he bought it, even though it was on prime land and he could have made a substantial profit on it?

2b.   The transfer documents bear consecutive numbers – T44230/2007 (Mphahlele) and T44231/2007. Why was this so?

2c.   The property was sold for R680,000 six months later, through a property agent. How much did you actually receive for the site after the property agent's cut was deducted? My understanding is that it is significantly less than what appeared on the deeds records.

3.   You then bought Mopani Street and took a bond out on that house. You carried out extensive renovations on house and property, including the erection of high walls around the house; the installation of a swimming pool; the erection of a lapa; new windows. How much did these renovations cost and who paid for them? If it was you, please explain the source of that income, as my understanding is that at that time your only official source was your Youth League salary as provincial secretary.

4.   Do you have any financial interests in Gwama Properties?

Income tax

1.   Have you accurately declared all of your income that is taxable and that which is non-taxable?

2.   Have all of the legal entities with which you have been associated (as listed in 5 above) fully declared their income to SARS and paid all outstanding and liable dues?

3.   Some of the cars you have driven in the past, or which have been driven by your security men on your behalf, have not belonged to you but to other people known to you. Have you declared the cars as so-called 'perks' for tax purposes?

4.   Based on the media scrutiny around your alleged lavish lifestyle, would you consider subjecting yourself to an independent audit, carried out by an independent audit firm of your choice, which would carry out an audit on your instruction and work towards giving you a clean due diligence report?

5.   Would you grant me permission to confirm with SARS that your returns are in order and up to date?

Appendix 3

Malema and his money

Julius Malema's business dealings became a matter of public interest during his first term as ANCYL president. His conspicuous wealth contradicted his pro-poor politics and begged the obvious questions: where did he get it?

Late 1990s   Malema wins his first public tender while in his late teens to provide school uniforms for his own high school.

2000/2001   He and his former political and business partner Pule Mabe win a public tender to provide labelling for plastic bottles at a public water board in Malema's home province, Limpopo.

He and his former political and business partner Pule Mabe win a public tender to provide labelling for plastic bottles at a public water board in Malema's home province, Limpopo.

The pair win a second public tender, again in Malema's home province, to lay on entertainment for the inaugural ceremony of a local mayor. Malema's profit share was R30,000.

2002/2003   Malema is awarded a public tender by Mabe, who by then works for the state-owned railway company. He refuses to disclose the amount.

2004   He begins to work as a 'consultant' for a budding engineering firm in Polokwane called SGL, allegedly securing a 10 per cent cut in each contract he swings their way from the local and provincial government.

At Blue Nightingale Trading 61, another company he starts with some of his family members, he wins a 3 per cent share in a R200 million waste management contract, with payouts lasting until 2010.

Financial records show that Blue Nightingale held a

10 per cent stake in Beta Consortium providing multi-million rand public cleaning services in Limpopo.

As the provincial youth league secretary, earning in the region of R20,000 per month, he purchases a brand new Audi A3.

2005 Malema starts a company called Ever Roaring Investments with other political peers in Polokwane. One of the public deals they are cut in to is a multi-million rand health contract to provide medical supplies across Limpopo, which earns them a small but steady payout over a number of years.

2006 Malema buys a plot of residential land in the most exclusive suburb of Polokwane from the local municipality for R222,000, though the purchase is initially disguised through a frontman. Malema sells the site five months later for R680,000.

He contracts a new house for his mother, which is built in the rear garden of his grandmother's home, though she died suddenly before the narrow two-storey house was finished.

He becomes a director of Ngape Mining Investments, but public records suggest he resigned soon after, though his shareholding, current or past, is not known.

2007 He purchases a house in a Polokwane suburb for just under R1 million and pumps a further R500,000 into it in renovations. It is the first home he owns in his name.

He starts a company 101 Jun-Jus but little is known about its dealings.

On the eve of the ANC national conference that brought Zuma to power, Malema opens a discreet trust, which he names the Ratanang Family Trust, and through which he begins to channel some of his money. It is officially registered at the deeds offices in May of the following year.

An SGL insider claims 2007 and 2008 were record-breaking years for the consulting firm, thanks to the public contracts Malema facilitated (he denies this).

2008 He purchases his first Mercedes.

2009 Malema purchases a second house in the upmarket

Johannesburg suburb of Sandown for R3.6 million, a year after he moves to the city to begin his presidency of the ANCYL.

He is appointed a director of SGL, but later insists the directorship was registered without his knowledge.

He trades in his Mercedes for a new and superior model.

On-Point, which is part-owned by Malema through his trust, wins a multi-million rand contract at the Department of Roads and Transport and through which the company secures further public tenders.

The Ratanang Family Trust donates a church to the people of Seshego, in honour of his late mother Florah.

2010   Lesiba Gwangwa, a founder director of SGL, starts a company called Gwama Properties, in which Malema holds an undisclosed share through the Ratanang Family Trust.

Malema purchases a farm on the outskirts of Polokwane for R900,000.

He adds his grandmother, Sarah, as a named trustee on the Ratanang Family Trust.

The Public Protector is called upon to investigate Malema's links to SGL but finds that he did not appear to unduly influence the contracts that were awarded to the company during his directorship.

Malema purchases a two-storey in an exclusive housing estate in Polokwane for R1.4 million. His son, Ratanang, and Maropeng Ramohlale, the mother of the child, inhabit the house. The house is purchased through Gwama Properties.

Malema buys an Audi A5 for Ramohlale.

2011   Gwama Properties purchase another Polokwane home that the company uses as a guest house for security staff as well as staff of On-Point and SGL.

Malema razes his Sandown home to the ground and plans are revealed for the R8.5 million home he is building in its place. He rents a house nearby when the construction gets underway.

He changes his car for a Mercedes S600 V12.

Malema demolishes his grandmother's house in Seshego and constructs a two-storey house in its place for her.

Local newspaper *City Press* exposes the Ratanang Family Trust as a 'slush fund' with evidence of a Polokwane businessman who has paid R200,000 into the trust in return for Malema ensuring he wins a public contract.

Gwama Properties adds a R4 million farm to its portfolio.

The Public Protector re-opens her investigation into SGL and On-Point.

The special crimes unit The Hawks launches a similar investigation.

The National Treasury unearths evidence of gross abuse of public funds in three of Limpopo's provincial departments – the Department of Roads and Transport, the Department of Education and the Department of Health – and commissions accounting firm PwC to forensically investigate all three (A R314 million tender awarded by Health to a string of companies, one of which is owned by Malema's younger cousin Tshepo, falls under the investigation, as does On-Point's dealings with Transport.)

2012   Malema calls a halt to construction of his new Sandown home, as the state-led investigations appear to tighten their net.

SARS launches an inquiry into nineteen companies in one way or another linked to Malema.

Malema is expelled from the ANC.

Notes

Chapter 2: The man with nine lives

1. Gramsci's use of the 'two frames' is outlined in in Zygmunt Bauman, *44 Letters from the Liquid Modern World* retrieved at http://archive.truthout.org/interregnum57851

Chapter 6: (Re)writing history

1. Dubow, Saul, *The African National Congress*, p.3.
2. Walshe, Peter, *The Rise of African Nationalism in South Africa*, p.35.
3. Meli, Francis, *South Africa Belongs to Us*, p.38.
4. Of what is written about the early years of the ANC, I have focused on the following: Peter Walshe's *The Rise of African Nationalism in South Africa* (1970), which stands out as an excellent account of that era, as does Saul Dubow's *The African National Congress* (2000) and Tom Lodge's *Black Politics in South Africa since 1945* (1983), particularly his take on what led to the formation of the ANCYL. There is also the 1988 work of Wellington Madolwana, a member of the ANC's NEC as well as the central committee of the SACP and one-time editor of the ANC's monthly magazine *Sechaba*. He was better known in the ranks by his pen name Francis Meli (the pseudonym standing for Marx, Engels, Lenin Institute). Oddly, Meli, as the biographer of the ANC, was exposed as a spy before his death in 1990. In 1987, Morgan Norval wrote *Inside the ANC: The Evolution of a Terrorist Organization*, the title of which speaks to the contents of the book. There is also Brian Willan's 1997 title on Sol Plaatje, *Sol Plaatje: Selected Writing* and Brian Bunting's 1975 biography of Moses Kotane, *Moses Kotane, South African Revolutionary*. The most recent addition to the record of history is Peter Limb's *The ANC's Early Years* (2010).

5. Walshe, p.36.
6. Ibid., p.40.
7. Dubow, p.7.
8. Walshe, p.44. One morgen = 0.008567 square kilometres. However, it is important to note that the South African morgen is different in size to morgens in other Dutch colonies where it was used at the time, or in Germany and other parts of northern Europe today.
9. Willan, Brian, *Sol Plaatje*, p.186.
10. Norval, Morgan, *Inside the ANC*, p.8.
11. Meli, p.66.
12. Walshe, p.258.
13. Lodge, Tom, *Black Politics in South Africa Since 1945*, p.25.
14. Norval, p.8.
15. Bunting, Brian, *Moses Kotane, South African Revolutionary*, p.34.
16. Norval, p.33.
17. Ibid., p.32.
18. Ibid., p.33.
19. Walshe, p.254.
20. Ibid.
21. Meli, p.88.
22. Walshe, p.258.
23. Meli, p.88.
24. Mandela, Nelson, *Long Walk to Freedom*, p.113.
25. Lodge, p.25.
26. Ibid., p.21.
27. Mandela, p.112.
28. Ibid., p.112.

Chapter 7: The shock troopers come in

1. Callinicos, Luli, *Oliver Tambo*, pp.159–60.
2. Mandela, Nelson, *Long Walk to Freedom*, p.110.
3. Ibid., p.111.
4. Lodge, Tom, *Black Politics in South Africa Since 1945*, p.21.
5. Mandela, p.113.
6. Lodge, p.25.
7. Baai, Sandi, *O.R. Tambo*, p.99.
8. Lodge, p.25.
9. Ibid.

10. Mandela, p.113.
11. Walshe, Peter, *The Rise of African Nationalism in South Africa*, p.352.
12. Mandela, p.123.
13. Ibid., p.124.
14. Walshe, p.357.
15. Bunting, Brian, *Moses Kotane, South African Revolutionary*, p.144.
16. Mandela, p.131.
17. Lodge, p.27.
18. Walshe, pp.355–61.
19. Lodge, pp.29–30.

Chapter 8: From underground to above ground
1. Meli, Francis, *South Africa Belongs to Us*, p.165.
2. Ibid., p. 167.
3. Lodge, Tom, *Black Politics in South Africa Since 1945*, p.301.

Chapter 9
1. Bakhtin, Mikhail Mikhailovich, *Rabelais and his World*, p.7.

Chapter 14
1. Myburgh, James, 'Did Mpshe plagiarise a Hong Kong judge?'
2. Marais, Hein, *South Africa Pushed to the Limit*, p.350.

Chapter 15: It's complicated
1. Fanon, Frantz, *Black Skin, White Masks*, p.89.
2. Ibid., p.64.
3. Ibid., p.68.
4. Ramphele, Mamphela, *Laying Ghosts to Rest*, pp.7–9.
5. Marx, Karl, *The Eighteenth Brumaire of Louis Bonaparte*, p.122.

Select bibliography

Baai, Sandi. *O.R. Tambo: Teacher, Lawyer and Freedom Fighter* (Skotaville, 2006).

Bakhtin, Mikhail Mikhailovich. *Rabelais and his World*. Trans. by Helene Iswolsky (Indiana University Press, 1984).

Bunting, Brian. *Moses Kotane, South African Revolutionary: A Political Biography* (Inkululeko, 1975).

Callinicos, Luli. *Oliver Tambo: Beyond the Engeli Mountains* (David Philip, 2004).

Dubow, Saul. *The African National Congress* (Jonathan Ball, 2000).

Fanon, Frantz. *Black Skin, White Masks*. Trans. by Charles Lam Markmann (Pluto Press, 1986).

Limb, Peter. *The ANC's Early Years: Nation, Class and Place in South Africa Before 1940* (Unisa Press, 2010).

Lodge, Tom. *Black Politics in South Africa Since 1945* (Ravan, 1983).

Mandela, Nelson. *Long Walk to Freedom* (Abacus, 2002).

———. Quoting Walter Sisulu in the *Leaders* DVD series (produced and edited by Afravision).

Marais, Hein. *South Africa Pushed to the Limit: The Political Economy of Change* (UCT Press, 2011).

Marx, Karl. *The Eighteenth Brumaire of Louis Bonaparte*. First published in the first issue of *Die Revolution*, 1852, New York. Online version: Marxists Internet Archive (www.marxists.org).

Meli, Francis (Wellington Madolwana). *South Africa Belongs To Us: A History of the ANC* (Zimbabwe Publishing House, 1988).

Myburgh, James. 'Did Mpshe plagiarise a Hong Kong judge?', in *Troublemakers: The Best of South Africa's Investigative Journalism*. Edited by Anton Harber and Margaret Renn (Jacana Media, 2010).

Norval, Morgan. *Inside the ANC: The Evolution of a Terrorist Organization* (Selous Foundation, 1990).

Ramphele, Mamphela. *Laying Ghosts to Rest: Dilemmas of the Transformation in South Africa* (Tafelberg, 2008).

Unger, Jonathan and Anita Chan. 'China, Corporatism and the East Asian Model', *Australian Journal of Chinese Affairs* 33 (1995).

Walshe, Peter. *The Rise of African Nationalism in South Africa* (Donker, 1987).

Wiardia, Howard. *Corporatism and Comparative Politics: The Other Great Ism* (M.E. Sharpe, 1996).

Willan, Brian. *Sol Plaatje: Selected Writings* (Wits University Press, 1997).

Interviews conducted by the author

Beezy Bailey; Terry Bell; Max du Preez; Stephen Friedman; John Githongo; Ronnie Kasrils; Jeff Legodi; Tom Lodge; Pule Mabe; Siviko Mabunda; Winnie Madikizela-Mandela; Lebogang Maile; the late Henry Makgothi; Thabo Makunyane; Julius Malema; Maropeng Malema; Sarah Malema; Tshepo Malema; Frank Maponya; Lawrence Mapoulo; Matlala Maremane; Lehlogonolo Masoga; David Masondo; Cassel Mathale; the late Joe Matthews; Fikile Mbalula; Achille Mbembe; Andrew Mlangeni; Moshoeshoe Monare; Kenny Morolong; Clifford Motsepe; Sydney Mufamadi; Thomas Namathe; Patti Nkobe; Aziz Pahad; Freddie Ramaphakela; Sam Rampedi; Daisy Sebate; Jackie Selebi; Gillian Slovo; Vuyiswa Tulelo; Rehana Vally.

A further 27 people were interviewed for this book, but because of the fear and loathing referred to in its pages, they asked not to be named.